Managing the Literacy Curriculum

The transition period from primary to secondary school is a critical one for children. Many teachers are concerned that it is during these years that children stop reading, and want to know what can be done to help pupils develop competence in using literacy across the whole curriculum. In this book, the authors challenge conventional models and theories of how children develop this competence, basing their writing on findings from a five-year research programme in the Centre for Literacy Studies at the School of Education, University of Bristol.

Evidence from collaborative work with schools is presented to show how teachers can 'audit' the curriculum, the conceptual maps teachers hold, and how schools can design more effective learning environments for literacy. Using ideas drawn from Vygotsky and other socio-cultural accounts, a new framework is presented in straightforward but compelling terms.

Managing the Literacy Curriculum identifies crucial aspects of teachers' knowledge of learning processes, discusses the critical role of the teacher in establishing a literate community, and offers clear classroom strategies for using literacy as a tool for learning. Issues examined and put into perspective include 'falling standards', controversies over reading methods, and 'back to basics'.

Representing the cutting edge of literacy in context, this publication challenges current thinking and sets a new course for raising the quality of teaching and learning in schools. It will be useful to teachers across the primary and secondary age range, teacher trainers, advisers and researchers in the field.

All three authors are based at the University of Bristol. **Alec Webster** is Director of the Centre for Literacy Studies, **Michael Beveridge** is Dean of Social Sciences and Professor of Education, and **Malcolm Reed** is Lecturer in the School of Education, and a former Head of English in a secondary school.

Managing the Literacy Curriculum

How schools can become communities of
readers and writers

Alec Webster, Michael Beveridge
and Malcolm Reed

London and New York

First published 1996
by Routledge
11 New Fetter Lane, London EC4P 4EE

Simultaneously published in the USA and Canada
by Routledge
29 West 35th Street, New York, NY 10001

Typeset in Times by Solidus (Bristol) Limited
Printed and bound in Great Britain by
Biddles Ltd, Guildford and King's Lynn

British Library Cataloguing in Publication Data
A catalogue record for this book is available from the British
Library

Library of Congress Cataloging in Publication Data
A catalogue record for this book has been requested

ISBN 0-415-11294-X (hbk)
ISBN 0-415-11295-8 (pbk)

'Words are clues to the things people believe to be important.'

Frank Smith, 1992

Contents

Figures

Tables

Appendices

Acknowledgements

A work of this kind, undertaken over several years and involving many schools, reflects the efforts and insights of a great number of individuals and it is impossible to acknowledge them all.

The central figures in the book, those teachers who tolerated our presence in their classrooms and subjected themselves to public scrutiny, deserve the highest acclaim. We are indebted to the staff of the Withywood cluster of primary and secondary schools, in particular, and this research stands as a testament to the professionalism of the teachers involved.

Dr Albert Osborn of the Research Support Unit in the School of Education of the University of Bristol provided valuable help with the statistical analyses. Anne Mallitte gave unstintingly of her time in preparing the disk and manuscript. We are also grateful for the help and advice of Dr Geoffrey Moss in relation to 'scaffolding' and the learning process.

Introduction

... the difference between good and bad reading teachers is usually not to do with their allegiance to some particular method, but to do with their relationships with children and their sensitivity in matching what they do to each individual child's learning needs.

Bullock Report, DES, 1975

This is a book which offers an important challenge to all teachers in primary and secondary schools. It focuses on critical experiences, particularly at times of transition between phases of schooling, when the demands made on children's literacy change fundamentally, and during which children establish lifetime patterns of reading or non-reading. It is a challenge which concerns the meaning and centrality of literacy within the curriculum, and the role of the school in creating a community which promotes literacy as a vital element of all learning.

Over the last five years the authors have been working with teachers in a range of schools, developing methods of describing and enhancing aspects of the learning environment where reading and writing are used. This work was initiated at a time when vigorous debate over reading standards came once more into the public eye, and when arguments over methods were aired. For example, 'real books' and 'apprenticeship' have been contrasted with 'reading schemes' and 'phonics' in an argument which frequently polarizes around the issue of whether less structured approaches to teaching are responsible for an apparent fall in reading standards.

In our view these arguments over methods and standards are sterile and unproductive. They fuel a popular, but misinformed criticism of schools which politicians conveniently endorse, that teachers are failing in their responsibilities to teach basic skills to children because of 'trendy' ideas. At the same time, attention is distracted from some crucial issues to do with what children are expected to know about literacy as they move through the school system, the nature and complexity of the demands made by different subject areas, and who should take responsibility for literacy within the curriculum.

CONTEXTS FOR LEARNING

The evidence drawn together in this book is based on the view, supported by the experience of the authors, that classroom practice is far too complex to claim a causal link between standards and methods. There are so many influences which affect children's engagement with literacy, such as time spent reading, home influence, the way classrooms are managed and resourced, that to look for single factor explanations of relative differences in achievement is seriously misguided.

Instead, what we set out to do was to provide a much finer-grained account of how literacy is used functionally within real classrooms. In fact, we anticipated a rich variety of methods and resources in use within the same class groups, with certain pupils engaged in literacy-related tasks much more effectively and for much longer than others. Furthermore, from our own experience as and with teachers, we would never expect that everything which happens in classrooms is geared towards effective learning. Much of what transpires is concerned with establishing or maintaining order, discipline and cooperation. Our major concern has been to identify those aspects of teaching and learning contexts which lead to strong or weak environments for pupils acquiring literacy, and which teachers can modify for themselves.

An important consideration of our research has been to examine differences in the views of teachers working in primary or secondary contexts. Are teachers clear about the demands which schooling will make on pupils at different Key Stages and is this reflected in their work? Are there mismatches between primary and secondary teachers with regard to what pupils are expected to know and do? Our studies have attempted to map the range of teaching strategies in classroom contexts where literacy is used, together with the range of literacy functions which children require in order to cope with the curriculum across subject boundaries. Rather than focusing only on methods, or children who fail, this work has continued to analyse something of the nature, quality, depth, frequency and purpose of children's encounters with print which make up schooled literacy.

Importantly, our approach considers the teaching and learning of literacy in terms of teacher, school and inter-school processes. In this way literacy is also seen as an 'ecology' constructed in the social system of classrooms within and between schools (Barton, 1994). We see little point in discussing literacy issues outside of the systems which nurture them.

RESPONSIBILITIES OF THE SCHOOL

We shall be arguing that it is the school's own particular responsibility to prepare children to meet the demands of the curriculum by embedding literacy-for-learning within all subject domains. As schools receive less professional support from LEAs, with the diminishing role and scale of advisory services, support teams and educational psychology services, it is important that schools begin to manage these issues for themselves. It is also important that communication between the primary and secondary sectors is sustained and improved by the schools themselves. In order to get started, schools require a well-signposted route in relation to literacy, which will no doubt become one of the yardsticks by which schools are judged as they enter the 'market economy'.

The book offers a critique of current approaches to the defining and teaching of literacy in schools. Despite the time which has elapsed since the publication of the Bullock (DES, 1975) and Kingman Reports (DES, 1988), both of which made many recommendations about literacy across the whole curriculum, few schools have a plan of action where literacy is concerned. When reading and writing difficulties arise these are most often perceived retrospectively, as a failure of individual children to acquire the right skills at an earlier time, and thus outside the remit of current teachers. Inescapably, for those who follow our line of argument, all teachers must have an agenda for literacy in their classrooms, whilst schools themselves must develop clear policies and identify where, in the curriculum, literacy belongs.

LITERACY WITHIN THE CURRICULUM

In this book we present data and arguments which contradict the view that literacy should be considered as a set of taught skills which must be acquired before or outside the curriculum. Such a view implies that literacy is somehow only a vehicle or medium for more serious subject study, a requirement or precondition, rather than the outcome of learning. The central question for all teachers, whatever their subject specialism, is the relationship between the growth in children's understanding and what is required of children within each learning context, what we refer to as their 'critical practice'.

The very nature of literacy is constituted in the wide variety of forms and functions literacy serves in different learning contexts. Put more directly, literacy *is* the curriculum. Ways in which pupils come to know and use reading and writing are determined by the examples, requirements and processes of different subject areas, as well as contexts outside of school. This view of literacy has enormous implications for schools in relation to teachers' perceptions, who should take responsibility for enhancing learning, approaches to assessment, the appraisal of children's literacy difficulties and how intervention could be shaped towards modifying the learning environment, rather than the child.

CREATING A COMMUNITY FOR LITERACY

Understanding this relationship between what children learn and the quality of the learning process requires new models and new methods. In this book we present a practical framework for analysing adult–child encounters using written language, based on observations made in real classrooms. This model has been used to help teachers evaluate their own work, enhance pupils' experiences and provide richer, more focused environments for learning.

In order to achieve a consistent, 'whole-school' approach to literacy, the book takes teachers through a process of enquiry. The starting point is a re-examination of what literacy means in the classroom context, and of the nature of the tasks that pupils undertake. Drawing on our research and in-service work with teachers, steps are suggested which enable school staff, including managers, to keep in touch with how literacy is currently perceived by teachers and effectively used within different classroom contexts. Finally, we suggest how individual teachers might work towards a cohesive policy and management framework, tailored to the needs and circumstances of the school.

If schools are concerned to become more literate communities, teachers need to be aware of the strategies which are most effective in bringing literacy alive for children. Managers need to support staff in sustaining a momentum for tackling things differently. The notion which we hold of the 'learning school' is one characterized by responsivity, flexibility, an interest in how children progress, an openness to look critically at how things are done, and an honesty to draw from its own experience. The ideas in this book should help all teachers to raise appropriate questions and find the focal points for good classroom practice.

1 Rethinking the meaning of literacy

Everything should be made as simple as possible, but not simpler.

Albert Einstein

No-one seriously questions the need for all children to become literate. In most modern, schooled societies, children are surrounded by examples of written language and literate ways of thinking from birth. Most children enter school at four or five with considerable awareness of the significance of literacy for coping with everyday life. Children are usually orientated to explore what print can do, to realize its power.

Children of all ages come to the classroom with a richness of experience of story and song, and will have shared something of their family's myriad of mundane reasons for using print, such as paying bills, filling in coupons, choosing items from catalogues and writing shopping lists. However, the differences between children in terms of their various experiences of family literacy, their dialogues around stories, access to books, libraries and other print-related resources, are more important to the teacher as indicators of differences in experience and opportunity, than as indicators of ability.

The question of how to develop every child's emergent understanding of the purposes and practices of storymaking and other forms of writing and representation, is a central one for education, especially in the early years. Schools introduce children to very specific ways of using print, and in so doing, stimulate new ways of thinking and provblem-solving. In the course of this book we shall be arguing that a key challenge for all teachers concerns how to provide and sustain learning experiences and teaching contexts which enable all children to share the power of literacy, its scope and application.

If pupils spend far more time than previously, particularly when not at school, engaged with other forms of media to which print is secondary, such as video games and films, teachers have to find ways of utilizing these interests, making links and demonstrating the powerful functions and limitations of different media forms in ways which inform and elaborate pupils' choices. If literacy *per se* is to become an 'amplifier of human capabilities', as Pumfrey (1990) suggests, then the school's particular role is to find the most effective opportunities for all children to be so 'enlarged'.

Debates about literacy have a tendency to be conducted at a high level of generality around a number of common themes. These often include the notion that children read and write less well now than in the recent past. This is the 'standards are falling' complaint. There is also an influential 'progressive' view that many children have been impeded and alienated by the 'meaningless' ways in which reading and writing have been taught. This is often contrasted with an opposing belief that literacy has suffered because of the abandonment of 'traditional' classroom methods. A further, perhaps less dominant, theme concerns the changing demands on children's literacy in an increasingly technological society.

The arguments which centre around these themes are important, if only because they are part of an educational and political climate through which any new approaches, including our own, will be interpreted.

EVIDENCE OF FALLING STANDARDS

We begin by examining the evidence concerning falling standards of literacy and how schools might interpret it. Evidence of falling standards has to take account of differences in bench marks, as well as the motives of those presenting the data. Even so, important questions are raised for teachers and for children, in relation to where the problem is located and who should take responsibility for it. One of the arguments which we shall put forward concerning the fall in standards complaint, is that evidence is collected and presented to answer questions which are least likely to inform what teachers do in the classroom. Put bluntly, the wrong questions are being addressed in a debate which is staged frequently without, or in contradiction of, informed perspectives or clear research (Reed et al., 1995).

A number of studies in the last twenty-five years have highlighted an apparent decline in reading achievements across particular age groups, such as the NFER study *The Trend of Reading Standards* (Start and Wells, 1972). Closely following this publication, a committee of inquiry was set up under the chairmanship of Sir Alan Bullock. Its brief was to consider all aspects of the teaching of English in schools, including reading, writing, spelling and oracy. The Bullock enquiry encountered difficulties in finding an acceptable definition of literacy upon which everyone agreed, an issue to which we shall be returning in due course. It also had problems interpreting results from different tests carried out in different areas to arrive at an estimate of national trends. Notwithstanding these serious question marks over the status of the evidence available, the 'Bullock Report' did allege a general decline in reading performance from the age of seven years onwards, relative to children in the same age groups in previous decades.

Bullock ascribed the causes of reading failure to factors in the child's home background ('where conversation is limited and books unknown', DES, 1975, para 18.5); to children's 'limited natural abilities'; to the displacement of reading by watching television; and to badly trained teachers and poorly organized remedial teaching. 'The Bullock Report' suggested that 'literacy is a corporate responsibility' in which every teacher shares. It made 333 specific recommendations to schools, many of which were accepted at the time, but few acted upon. Our own research gives a clear indication that, despite the 'Bullock Report's' call for 'language across the curriculum', literacy currently seems to belong nowhere, certainly not in the whole-school policies envisaged.

Perhaps the most important source of information about standards of pupil achievement, drawn on for example, in the 'Three Wise Men' Report on primary schools (Alexander et al., 1992) is the data collected by the Assessment of Performance Unit. From 1975 onwards the APU began to devise methods of monitoring the attainments of school children and to identify the incidence of underachievement. The APU undertook five annual surveys between 1978 and 1984, which involved some 2 per cent of 10-year-olds nationally in English, maths and science testing, whilst a second phase of testing in English took place in 1988. In fact, the APU data showed that on the measures devised for testing reading and writing, national standards appeared to have shifted very little overall in this age group.

Evidence of a decline in reading standards amongst 7-year-olds was at the heart of the controversy which arose when the results of tests administered in the 1980s by nine anonymous Local Education Authorities were published by Turner (1990). In his view, changes in methods of teaching reading account for pupil failure in recent years. He argues the traditional case, that reading is not a natural activity, but a set of gradually acquired component skills which must be taught. Consequently, declining standards can be blamed on teachers moving away from more traditional, skill-based approaches involving reading schemes and 'phonics', in favour of informal 'apprenticeship' models and the use of 'real books'.

As we shall illustrate later, the most important problem with this view is that, if one actually studies real classrooms with real children and teachers, an exclusive reliance on new, more fashionable methods and an absence of traditional approaches is not characteristic. The real problem with the teaching of literacy lies in aspects of its management and organization, not simply its method.

In support of this view is the recent report drawn up by HMI entitled *The Teaching and Learning of Reading in Primary Schools 1991* (DES, 1992). From the visits made to 120 schools, HMI surmised that general standards of teaching and learning of reading have either improved or remained the same, certainly not declined. The HMI report did point out some worrying inconsistencies in the way pupils were taught and between the achievements of pupils in broadly similar schools. HMI also highlighted many of the factors which appear to contribute to high pupil progress. These include clear policies on literacy and effective leadership by the head teacher, managing the work to match pupil needs, classroom organization factors, use of resources and the skills of the teacher.

HMI suggests that the great majority of teachers use a variety of approaches to teach reading, including 'real books', 'phonics', and reading schemes. In other words, HMI proposes that 'within-school' factors, such as class management, account for much of the difference between high and low achieving pupils. Over-reliance on one method of teaching to the exclusion of others is neither significant nor typical.

Perhaps this HMI view is not a surprising one. Since HMI is directed to evaluate the quality of educational provision, it is likely that our attention will be drawn to the difference good teaching makes, in contrast to the damage wider social inequalities may wreak. However, teachers who sustain high-quality opportunities with a variety of well-chosen and carefully managed methods of teaching do bring about considerable achievements for pupils, particularly in areas of social deprivation.

Other evidence on reading standards is more equivocal. In the autumn of 1990 the government commissioned a survey of the evidence on reading standards of 7-year-olds held by LEAs. This survey, carried out by the National Foundation for Educational Research, considered information from ninety-five LEAs out of a total of 116 in England and Wales. In only twenty-six of the LEA returns was it possible to make a judgement about changes in standards. In three instances no change was indicated, one showed no consistent pattern at all, whilst three other LEAs reported a rise. Of the nineteen where a decline could be interpreted, this mainly occurred in the 1980s and often was offset by a more recent rise. The NFER report concluded that it was impossible to make an accurate judgement from these data regarding the national trends in reading standards for 7-year-olds.

More recently, results from the first administration of National Curriculum assessments in 1991 show that 61 per cent of Year 2 pupils attained level 2 in English, with 17 per cent at level 3. Since this was the first run of National Curriculum assessments, with teachers new to the procedures, many local variations in resources and training, and the possibility of wide discrepancies in how statements of attainment are interpreted, it is difficult to draw any firm conclusions from these results.

Had the current English Orders remained in place long enough for data from further cohorts of children to be considered against these initial baselines, it might have been possible to make comparisons. The new Statutory Orders for English which change the level requirements, particularly at the entry level of KS1, mean that any data gained from 1996 onwards will not be directly comparable with the data collected so far.

Of course, one consequence of implementing the National Curriculum, particularly in English, is an inescapable pressure on schools to follow the content of the programmes of study, whatever principles are compromised in the process. As the English Orders continue to dictate rather than describe effective practice, there is a danger that literacy will be considered as a basic, isolable subject on the curriculum, taken care of by English specialists.

LITERACY HEALTH WARNINGS

How should teachers respond to this range of data and what is its significance? We suggest a number of health warnings should be appended to any particular interpretation of literacy figures, drawing attention to unproven assumptions and speculative conclusions.

What all of this evidence of attempts to standardize a measure of literacy illustrates, is the difficulty of arriving at a valid national picture. It is particularly important to remember that, despite the widespread use of tests in schools, these differ in scope, content and focus, and are carried out at different points in time on different age groups and samples. Such test data cannot easily be summarized. We are left with no cumulative picture of the direction in which standards may be moving, or if they are moving at all. If, like most European railways, reading tests followed a standard gauge, then we might be able to assess performance by different rolling stock over the same track. Given that the gauge is actually as variable as those of toy trains in High Street shops, the resulting measurements do not lead to useful comparisons.

Furthermore, existing large-scale survey data provide no explanation for any differences observed. Links which have been intimated between changes in reading standards and the adoption of new teaching methods by schools are based on assumption, not evidence.

Inevitably, individuals with political ends in view will select the research evidence which suits their immediate purpose, hoping that others will not query the basis of their argument. This way of discussing the issues suggests that educators are ill-advised to enter the political debate on falling standards. Nevertheless we would emphasize that:

1   There is no consistent evidence of a general decline in reading standards;
2   General descriptions of teaching methods have not been shown to account for any differences in children's reading test performance;
3   Teachers will not find strategies for more effective teaching of literacy in simplistic philosophies like 'back to basics'.

There is one important question which remains. Independently of whether standards are rising or falling, we need to know better how to prepare all pupils to cope with increasing demands on literacy as they move through the school system and encounter a world in which they will have to compete for work. This issue cannot be dealt with retrospectively by looking back at children's failure to achieve. We must pose this question prospectively, breaking the current discourse on standards with an equally common-sense assertion that quality of education starts from now and progresses for each and every pupil. How schools can begin to address more effective literacy teaching for the future is the substance of the chapters which follow in this book.

However, we should emphasize that we are not, as this book makes clear, complacent about the development and use of literacy by pupils. Our view is that in the midst of heated arguments about falling standards, important issues about educational process in relation to literacy are being ignored.

MODELS OF READING AND WRITING

Over the last fifty years, models of reading or writing processes have fallen in and out of favour. They are usually adopted because they reflect the particular concerns of people with influence at the time. They, in turn, are influenced by the political climate, research culture and prevailing educational values. Some models of reading and writing concentrate on the perceptual/ cognitive acts – what might be going on when a person is actually scanning and encoding the printed word, identifying and defining letters, words or larger units and sequences of text. Other models are concerned with some of the consequences for individuals of learning to read and write – how this may change problem-solving, reasoning, the organization of information, and conceptual growth.

It is sometimes forgotten in the desire for certainty that our models of reading or writing are based on incomplete knowledge. Of course, even complete knowledge would still be expressed in terms of models, analogies, theories or rules. However, in the case of reading or writing, the available models rely on very limited data. It is also tempting to believe that models of

---

a) ... it is the total pattern or schema or gestalt of the word that young pupil and mature reader alike first observe – mature readers, of course, may take in two or three word wholes in a perceptual span or unit.

Schonell, 1945, p. 13

b) Reading, then is a process of transfer. We have, as it were, to recognise (on British Railways, for instance) that the sound of a whistle has a visual alternative – the waving of a green flag: by both of these the train guard may say to the engine driver 'proceed'.

Wilkinson, 1971, p. l98

c) We make predictions about what we are about to read in order to comprehend, and we make hypotheses about what a particular word or passage is likely to be in order to learn.

Smith, 1978, p. 98

d) Access to print, demonstrations of written language use, and opportunities to use written language represent a continuum ... where the meanings of literacy and literate acts are cooperatively explored within an interactive environment ... in which children can construct, realistically, images of themselves as genuine users of written language.

Wray et al, 1989, p. 72

Figure 1.1 Examples of different models of reading since 1945[1]

reading – the mental processes involved as individuals exercise their literate skills – can be turned into, or reduced to, programmes and stages for the teaching of literacy.[2]

However, as we shall see, modelling the cognitive processes involved in skilled reading or writing is not the same as modelling how children learn to become literate. We wish to stress that, in our view, children's learning proceeds in relation to the opportunities and practices in which literacy is engaged.

In some circumstances, models can help us to understand more and to reveal underlying principles at work. However, there is a danger that issues may be vastly over-simplified and our understanding misdirected. In this book we propose that existing models of literacy have not been very helpful as far as informing and enhancing teaching and learning processes. This is not surprising, since the models evolved have been encouraged by the political climate to focus on rapid, quantitative measurements of normal readers or readers with disabilities.

However, the decade or more during which children learn to read at home and in school, encompasses a vast array of potential and actual encounters with literacy. All of these encounters could be incorporated in a more complete model of the literacy acquisition process. In fact, the processes of identifying, categorizing and studying these experiences has already begun where they can be seen specifically in psycho-linguistic terms, such as in the early developmental stages (Bryant and Bradley, 1985; Goswami and Bryant, 1990).

Some of what happens in early literacy development is essentially the re-encoding of aspects of language into the relevant rules of the printed word, for example, through grapheme–phoneme (sign–sound) correspondences. And, perhaps not surprisingly, performance on relevant language tasks predicts success in this aspect of the reading acquisition process (Goswami and Bryant, 1990). However, school requires that literacy becomes a tool for thought. It is this process, which inevitably involves identifying factors in teaching and learning contexts, which is the focus of this book. How, if at all, does this happen in school? How do teachers understand the strategic role of literacy and how can we develop and test descriptions of practice which help them to do so?

STANDARD MODELS OF LITERACY

Standard models of literacy have usually been categorized according to whether they focus on features of the text, or alternatively, on features brought to the text by the reader or writer, in the form of language and experience. The term 'bottom-up' has been used to refer to those approaches which are concerned with identifying the significant units on the page which readers attend to and analyse, in order to decode the message. Text-based analyses, by definition, are highly focused and exclude many factors and influences which most teachers consider important to reading. In fairness, these models derive from the experimental work of researchers whose concern lies not with teaching, but with describing the nature of the perception, analysis, storage and retrieval of linguistic information.

In contrast, 'top-down' models suggest that reading is guided by decisions which draw on the structure of stories and other text genres, and general knowledge of the world. Top-down models should be, in principle, closely aligned with the theme of this book in that they tend not to isolate literacy from other aspects of the child's learning. However, it is one thing for a theory to be consistent with good practice and another to express clearly the nature of the connections and its practical applications. All these theories specify reading and writing, not as special activities, but as natural extensions of the possibilities of language. Also, such 'whole language' theories postulate that reading should be acquired like spoken language, by immature users being surrounded by more mature users, who support the young child's active and emerging mastery of the system. An appropriate way of referring to this is as a form of 'apprenticeship', a term popularized in the writing of Waterland (1988).

Reading as a natural language activity

The view that reading and writing are natural extensions of children's language use, drawing heavily on what children know about language and have experienced in the world, is one which most teachers are in accord with. In the 1970s, Goodman made famous the dictum that 'reading is a psycholinguistic guessing game' (Goodman, 1972). At the heart of Goodman's theorizing is the belief that reading, like spoken language, draws on the natural capacity of children to make sense of any language system to which they are exposed. Children approach reading expecting to find particular things and, as naturally curious problem-solvers, make hypotheses about the written word from their existing knowledge of the properties of spoken language. The reader is said to bring meaning to print, rather than derive meaning from it.

Goodman drew attention to the miscues (the deviations from the specific wording of the text being read) that children make when reading, revealing something of the active processes of reconstruction which go on in the reader's mind as use is made of sentence context, pictures and knowledge of stories to search for meaning. According to Goodman, readers who make mistakes are not guessing at random. Proficient readers have developed their sampling and prediction procedures to the point where they use the least number of clues necessary, given the redundancy of information available. The reading process goes awry because the poor reader is less proficient in sampling the text and putting forward hypotheses that accurately predict the unfolding of meaning.

In fact, the strength of the reader is indicated by whether miscues preserve the sense of a sentence, whether errors are self-corrected, and whether any substitutions made are of an appropriate grammatical class to fit the syntax given. Goodman talks of a continuous cycle of prediction, sampling the text for cues, confirming and disconfirming, as the child asks questions of print which are actively checked out and give rise to new questions. In his view, fluent readers have learned to make 'guesses that are right the first time' (Goodman, 1967, p. 127).

Top-down theorists such as Goodman believe that fluent readers are much more sensitive than poor readers to the information provided by the context, and that this facilitates ongoing word recognition. This view prompted Smith (1973), another well-known proponent of top-down models, to argue that reading is not primarily a visual process. In other words, the meaning derived by the reader arises from the brain behind the eye, as the reader utilizes only as much information in the text as is required for understanding. On this basis, Smith argued vehemently against the use of structured approaches in teaching reading, such as phonics, since these distract children and fragment a process that must remain 'whole'. He believed that fluent reading is too rapid for letter-by-letter decoding, whilst the spelling-to-sound correspondences of English are too inconsistent to be anything other than confusing to learners. In Smith's opinion, 'Learning to read is not a matter of mastering rules' (Smith, 1973, p. 184) and teachers can only proceed by supporting children in the business of reading for meaning.

These approaches to literacy have had a powerful impact on certain areas of some teachers' practice, although as we shall see later, teachers have not generally endorsed all that these theorists have said. Rather than emphasizing rules for decoding print, many teachers are convinced of the value of exposing children to stimulating and interesting texts, stressing enjoyment and meaning-making in both reading and writing. Assisting children through apprenticeship is often perceived as part of a holistic policy to foster children's development through a language experience approach.

Problems with 'natural language' models

We can draw attention to a number of ways in which top-down models of reading are now thought to be less than fully accurate. Assumptions are made about the nature of spoken (or signed) language and problem-solving applied to reading, which need to be questioned. One of the defining features of any human language is its creative potential, its capacity to generate an infinite number of novel combinations of meaning and effect. On the other hand, the morphology of a language which describes the word forms which people use in sentences, is relatively stable. It is at the level of the word that we find the greatest predictability, whilst language itself is essentially unpredictable. This is borne out by work on speech comprehension which shows that listeners only guess at meaning and use contextual cues when the speech signal is degraded. Speech comprehension is very largely controlled by the sound signals of the spoken word and is not driven by top-down processing (Tyler and Marslen-Wilson, 1982). What theorists such as Goodman and Smith have tried to suggest reverses these priorities by claiming that good readers, in parallel with spoken language users, are more driven by context, rather than by code.

A number of studies have shown that good readers do not rely solely on hypothesis testing and prediction when reading, nor do they rely on experience or contextual cues to meaning. For fluent readers the visual processing of text is automatic and very rapid, leaving thinking space for interpreting the content of reading, relating new knowledge to old, and working through implications. It is the weaker readers with less automatic skills who direct their attention to other sources of information within the reading context. Because they have not mastered rapid decoding of text, poor readers rely more on context clues and guesswork (Beveridge and Edmundson, 1989; Webster, 1986; Webster and Wood, 1989).

Supportive evidence for direct visual access to meaning through print has also come from eye movement research, which shows that fluent readers fixate nearly all the words as they read in small windows of text, leaving no time for hypothesis-testing or prediction. The term 'immediacy theory' has been coined to refer to the direct access to meaning through brief word fixations during fluent reading (Just and Carpenter, 1985).

However, from the perspective of this book, the crucial difficulties with top-down theories are that they do not help us identify how children's reading behaviour interacts with the wide range of text forms and challenges presented through the different subject domains of the curriculum. We also need to know much more about what teachers do that makes a difference for children as they cope with print as a medium for learning.

Reading as decoding

Teachers might be forgiven for assuming that many reading researchers, especially psychologists, have a very narrow view of literacy. It is true that much experimental research has tended to focus on the different components which affect an individual's ability to recognize units at the letter or word level in isolation. Cognitive psychologists have a general interest in understanding how humans process information. The study of reading is often undertaken to test aspects of information processing, and not to throw light on the most effective ways of teaching.

For many research psychologists, the reading process works upwards from letter or sound features towards higher levels such as words and sentences. As indicated earlier, these are often referred to as bottom-up models since they characterize reading in terms of an accumulation of subskills. This research has provided a sizeable body of evidence on the developmental stages associated with word recognition and production, summarized, for example, in Pumfrey and Reason (1991).

One potential source of information is the features of letter shapes. A reader might use this awareness of the invariant configuration of letter shapes to identify the string of letters which make up individual words. The reader would then have to use this visual representation of the word to recover details about pronunciation, grammatical class and meaning, held in some sort of inner store or lexicon, and built up through teaching and experience. Most teachers are familiar with claims that dyslexic individuals may confuse letter shapes in reading, invert or reverse letters in writing, and that these problems arise from some kind of perceptual deficit. However, there is also a view that dyslexia is part of a spectrum of language-related difficulties involving motor coordination, memory and sound processing (Webster and McConnell, 1987).

Instead of taking the letter as the basic building block, some researchers have argued that the reader identifies whole word patterns. Information may come from spelling regularities, or from the length and distinctive visual character of a word. A number of experiments have attempted to establish whether subjects can more easily identify real words or isolated letters or nonsense strings. The 'word superiority effect' acknowledges that readers do, on the whole, respond to some property possessed by real words but not letters, such that the whole unit is greater than the sum of its parts.

Another line of approach is that the basic building block of reading is sound-based rather than visual, thus, dependent on the set of rules for pronouncing letters, blends and sequences which enable print to be decoded into corresponding speech sounds. Work by Frith (1985) tries to establish whether children's ability to read emerges first through recognition of words as visual wholes (or logographs), or through alphabetic strategies whereby spelling units (orthographs) are used as a basis for pronunciation.

Most theorists agree that children start out, in the logographic stage, by recognizing whole words supported by context. This explains why young children are able to read what they cannot spell. The alphabetic stage is when letter-sound knowledge develops, driven largely by the practice of spelling when writing. Finally, at the orthographic stage children read and spell by a direct route based on automatic grasp of grapheme–phoneme links, which do not require encoding or decoding. It is in this last stage that many psychologists locate the specific reading difficulties of dyslexic children.

Rhyme, alliteration and analogy

Bryant and Bradley (1985) have demonstrated a strong relationship between children's awareness of the phonological patterns in print and development in reading, with an especially strong link for rhyme. Even after controlling for factors such as social background, memory and intelligence, pre-school children's rhyming skills were good predictors of later spelling and reading achievements. They found that training children in rhyme and alliteration could improve reading, whilst weaker readers also had poorer rhyme skills than younger children reading at the same level.

For psychologists, these findings do more than highlight the importance of acquainting children with nursery rhymes and word games in infancy, they also suggest that explicit teaching of phonological skills is critical, especially for children with reading difficulties. However, it has been pointed out that factors thought to be prerequisite to literacy, such as phonological skills, may also develop through reading experience, as a consequence. Determining cause and effect in these issues is problematical (Webster and McConnell, 1987).

Goswami has moved on this work still further (Goswami and Bryant, 1990). She suggests that the link between phonological awareness and reading is through analogies. A child who is good at rhyming may realize that shared sounds between words often also means shared spelling patterns, and that words such as 'rat' and 'hat' not only rhyme, they also share an orthographic unit (or rime): '-at'. Later on, children may work out how to recognize a word which they have not seen before, through analogies with other more familiar words, such as 'head' from 'bread' or 'fright' from 'light'.

Goswami proposes that children's knowledge of both orthography and phonological links develops reciprocally as an interactive process, with the one helping the other. By applying analogies, learning complex spelling rules will help to provide a finer-grained phonological analysis, and vice versa. Goswami says it is time to stop thinking of reading development as a series of stages, since many of the processes involved are interdependent.

Interactive-compensatory model

Finally, we consider here another model of the reading process which, although giving priority to code factors in reading and writing, also attempts to include broader aspects. The interactive-compensatory model drawn up by Stanovich (1980) holds that both bottom-up and top-down processes can occur alongside each other. The reader has several sources of information: letters, sounds, words, syntax which arise upwards from the page. The reader also makes predictions which act downwards on lower levels, each of which operates independently and simultaneously, but which influence each other. So, information gained from the word or sound cues will influence expectations about meaning, whilst the reverse process will also operate.

The interactive-compensatory model differs from the top-down view in its pure form because it emphasizes the critical importance of low-level, data-driven strategies for good readers. Stanovich argues that direct, automatic access to word meanings is necessary to free up the child's thinking and comprehension capacity. When word recognition is slow, readers can compensate by drawing on other sources of information at other levels, such as hypothesis-testing or context-redundancy. But to do this the reader sacrifices thinking space.

In these terms, the crucial difference between good and poor readers is speed of word recognition, an important issue for pupils as they move into the secondary phase of schooling. Poor readers use up attentional capacity because they rely on context, prediction and higher order language skills to work out what words mean. Comprehension and thinking about text suffer as a consequence. It could be that some educators engage in practices which run contrary to the implications of this work. Good readers may be taught to rely more heavily upon context, whilst poor readers are taught low-level decoding skills, such as phonics. The former emulates the strategies of weaker readers, whilst the latter denies poor readers access to supplementary sources of information in text.

Some new reading tasks in school will be best approached by good readers using contextual information, others not. Summarizing the plot of a novel demands different strategies from drawing information out of a biology textbook. This is the issue of identifying and teaching appropriate reading processes to match the nature of the task to the mind of the pupil.

Limitation of code-based models

We said earlier that cognitive psychologists pursue an understanding of how information processing takes place, and this focus for research is unlikely to lead to identifying the most effective way of fostering literacy across the curriculum. Studies of the component skills involved in reading usually take place under controlled experimental conditions, not classrooms, often involving fluent readers completing tasks which are devoid of context. Whilst we may have a richness of data from this field of research on individual differences in reading and the mechanisms involved, questions regarding effective teaching are largely unanswered (Carr and Levy, 1990).

Cognitive research has made an important contribution to the issue of what readers do when they deal with limited samples of text. Reading cannot be understood solely on the basis of informed guess-work: what readers 'expect to see'; nor can it be understood in terms of the successive recognition of separate print units. Much of this work has fostered a view of learning to read and write as the staged acquisition of a hierarchy of target skills to be mastered outside of most subject areas of the curriculum. We strongly reject this interpretation of cognitive research. We wish to emphasize that different demands are made on pupils' retention and recall, speed and automaticity of reading, the collation of information and the drawing together of conclusions, organizational and analytical strategies, in different subject areas.

It follows that, rather than thinking of literacy as a sequence of skills to be mastered outside the curriculum, we should identify those experiences which help to form the distinct literacies of different subject areas. A proficient reader in some contexts may be relatively unproficient in others. Rather than thinking of the cognitive components of reading as skills or abilities, we should see them as processes requiring specific opportunities to become practices, which change when performed in a variety of contexts.

INDIVIDUALIZING FAILURE

What is missing from the focus on target skills is evidence of how young children learn most effectively and under which conditions adults enable children to behave more like readers and writers. Earlier we suggested that, as a teacher, the key to understanding literacy development lies in the relationship between children's critical practice in the classroom, and changes in the child's thinking through using different textual forms for a range of purposes. More effective learning for all children, including those perceived to 'fail', will only come from teachers having greater understanding of those factors in the teaching context which promote development. This book shows how we have attempted to develop such practical understandings with a group of schools.

We are particularly concerned to avoid the problem we have termed the 'individualization of failure'. This uses psychological constructs such as short-term memory, sequencing skills or reasoning capacities, to present a deficit model of why children fail. Even those more positive approaches to raising individual skills such as *Teaching to Objectives* (Solity and Bull, 1987), *Direct Instruction* (Carnine and Silbert, 1979), and *Multi-sensory Teaching* (Hickey, 1977) lead to complaints from teachers that they take no account of the logistics involved in real learning contexts and are based on a mistaken assumption that teaching can be considered as a form of applied child psychology.

Our own view, and the focal point of our enquiry, requires that researchers pay more serious attention to the contexts in which learning encounters take place. If researchers ignore the situation (whether domestic or institutional) of learning, they will continue to ask questions which are unhelpful to teachers.

To summarize, in this section we have considered some of the arguments put forward by different theorists in favour of one model of reading or another. In the main, most reading researchers until this point have detached literacy from its classroom context, focusing on component stages and skills. Others have tried to suggest that in order to become literate all pupils are required to do is to use what they already know about language and the world, and to read. We concluded that it is insufficient to identify what are felt to be skills, stages or rules in literacy development, and then turn these into a recipe for teaching.

As Goswami and Bryant (1990) have recently argued, it is time to stop thinking of literacy development as a sequential series of steps. Instead, we must examine a wide range of overlapping and interdependent processes which make up the specific literacies of specific areas of the curriculum. Most importantly, it is what the teacher does in the context of the classroom, rather than what the pupil has failed to acquire outside the curriculum, which determines effective environments for literacy.

Literacy is an issue for all teachers and for the whole curriculum. The focus of our own research also goes much further than the language difficulties experienced by a few 'special' groups of children. Schools seeking to 'raise standards' of reading and writing will, in our view, make little progress if they start by examining the extent of individual failure to acquire basic skills. To move forward requires a step which hitherto few researchers, psychologists or teachers have taken: examining how literacy is harnessed, within each school subject domain, to the practices of listening, categorizing, thinking and concept-forming, information-seeking, problem-solving, recording, analysing, communicating, reflecting and planning.

The problem is not simply that of teaching the mechanics of reading and writing, but going beyond to nurture a sense of literacy as a tool for wider enquiry and understanding. This is an issue of fundamental importance to both primary and secondary schools. It is out of the sustained challenge to use and think through the language of texts within the functional demands of each subject area, that creative and flexible teaching environments are made, and a strong literate community established for all pupils.

SCHOOL EFFECTS ON LITERACY

It may seem like an impertinence to suggest that we need more information on the way teachers, classrooms and schools make a difference to how and what children learn. They are, of course, not the only sources of differences in children's literacy development. Children arrive in both primary and secondary schools with very disparate stocks of knowledge, strategies and experience. The subtlety with which literacy interpenetrates the family lives of children, together with parental attitudes and support, exert a powerful influence on what pupils of all ages have learned about the purposes and processes of literacy as they enter school (John-Steiner et al., 1994).

In a review of the factors which have an impact on early literacy development, Raban (1991) points out that the children who make the greatest progress in reading are those who have comparatively advanced notions of the functions of reading and writing drawn from their home experience. Raban's own research should not be taken to mean that schools contribute nothing to children's learning; rather, that schools do not significantly alter the overall rank order of children established on entry.

In both primary and secondary phases, surveys have marked out those characteristics of schools associated with high standards of literacy. HMI (DES, 1991), for example, make reference to firm leadership from the head teacher, a language co-ordinator, a school reading policy and a wide variety of resources. In Raban's (1991) review mentioned earlier, high-quality book environments and reference resources are positively associated with high achievement, together with attempts to match children's needs and also challenge pupils with texts of appropriate interest and readability levels. Time spent reading and writing are also important variables. We know that when observations of individuals are made within the same classroom, some pupils spend but a few minutes a day on literacy-related activities, whilst others spend many hours of practice using and composing texts for one purpose or another. Results obtained by Allington (1984), for example, showed that some primary children read as little as sixteen words in a week, whilst other, more competent pupils read several thousand. It is because of this kind of discrepancy that the term 'Matthew effect' has been applied to educational settings which, however unwittingly, support the rich to get richer and the poor to get poorer.

Several studies have provided detailed descriptions of how time is distributed amongst a range of classroom activities, including literacy-related tasks. In the ORACLE study (Galton, Simon and Croll, 1980) of some sixty primary and middle-school classes, teaching is characterized as being 'overwhelmingly factual and managerial' with very little time devoted to problem-solving or collaborative work. Mostly children worked on their own, even when 'grouped'. The majority of their interactions with the teacher consisted of being 'talked at' rather than 'talked with', whilst conversations with other pupils were mostly unrelated to work set.

On average, less than 10 per cent of the teachers' time was spent on reading and this diminished rapidly with age, such that 10-year-olds and their teachers spent about 2 per cent (or twenty minutes per week) of curriculum time on reading. Even less time was spent on oral language work. Writing took up a greater proportion of time, but even here, activities tended to be restricted to extracting information or copying from workcards and books.

THE NATURE OF CLASSROOM TASKS

In a more recent study (although still carried out prior to the National Curriculum), Bennett et al. (1984) considered the nature of the tasks which teachers provide for primary pupils, those crucial features of classrooms which link teachers to learners. The majority of the tasks observed, particularly in language work, demanded rehearsal of familiar routines and existing concepts, a 'staple diet of little new knowledge and large amounts of practice'. Rarely did tasks involve the discovery or construction of new or different ways of perceiving problems, or the application of existing skills to new contexts.

Teachers generally had great difficulty matching tasks to pupils' attainments and achieved such a match on approximately 40 per cent of tasks. Even after specific training most teachers were unable to set tasks on the basis of children's understanding, but relied mainly on direct teaching, with little reference to how children responded.

In writing, there was an emphasis on procedural rather than conceptual processes, with a stress on the physical production and presentation of work. Typically, writing lessons were prefaced by a reiteration of the teacher's rules for spacing, use of word books, neatness. Even when an exciting stimulus had been presented, such as the discovery of a spider in the classroom, lively discussions were often followed by routine writing demands. The teacher had the children copy sentences from the blackboard as a preliminary to writing their own material on spiders. Three-quarters of writing tasks observed were geared to quantity of output or the practising of neatness, punctuation and accuracy. The majority of ideas for writing came from the repertoire of the teacher, whilst classroom interchanges were dominated by spelling requests. When teachers gave feedback to children about their work this was usually done in crisis moments on the basis of performance or output, not on how a task had been tackled in relation to an intended purpose or audience.

The most comprehensive study to date of the use of literacy within primary and secondary schools, was carried out as part of a Schools Council Project involving pupils aged ten to fifteen years (Lunzer and Gardner, 1979). The project studied pupils' capability to use reading for learning, the incidence and context of varied strategies for reading in the classroom. Observations were made in different subject areas on a range of factors, including time spent reading or writing for specific purposes. In the subject area of English, personal writing was found to be the predominant genre of written response; in other subject areas by far the greatest proportion of time was taken up by copying without reflection, or working from textbooks.

Most classroom reading occurred in bursts of less than fifteen seconds in any one minute, suggesting that such reading is discontinuous, fragmentary and uncritical. For primary children, an average 33.4 minutes of reading per day was recorded, but of this time the greatest incidence of continuous reading took place when children were reading privately to suit their own purposes, rather than to complete an assigned learning task. This changed markedly in the secondary school where classroom reading shifted to following instructions or answering questions.

The broad conclusions drawn from Lunzer and Gardner's study are that reading is not widely used in primary and secondary schools as an integral part of teaching or learning, whilst little effort is made to teach more efficient reading as pupils move through the school system. Since many of the secondary teachers in the study regarded reading in lesson-time with suspicion, the authors describe a general 'retreat from print' in secondary school. Teachers appeared to be pessimistic about the virtues of reading for learning, and since opportunities for analysis, discussion and reflection were not taken, there seemed little chance of pupils improving. These authors recommended as 'a fundamental necessity', the provision of a meaningful experience of reading for pupils in science, social studies, mathematics and English, together with real opportunities for 'partaking in a discourse which illuminates reading'.

HOW TEXTS CHANGE CHILDREN'S THINKING

Beveridge (1991) has drawn attention to the lack of explicit teaching of literacy once children have transferred into secondary education.

Furthermore, questions are raised about whether primary teachers are kept sufficiently in touch with the challenges which secondary pupils face, to prepare children adequately for using literacy across the curriculum. Beveridge argues that since the spoken discourse of secondary classrooms is largely inadequate for teaching pupils all they must know, recourse is frequently made to complementary media, such as video, textbooks, diagrams, worksheets and other visual resources. He cites the example of a science text which demands that the pupil extracts precise conceptual relationships.

> In certain parts of Australia crops grew very badly because there was no molybdenum in the soil. When the soil was sprayed with a very diluted solution of molybdenum the plants grew splendidly. Very little molybdenum was needed because too much of a trace element may have a damaging effect on plants.

In this short sample we have an example of how science texts are full of explanations of changing phenomena that emphasize time/space relations. We see language which expresses spatial (where), temporal (when), causal (because) and conditional (may) relationships, together with the introduction of technical vocabulary, indications of relative quantity and quality, and scientific explanation of events. For this kind of text it is inappropriate for pupils to impose their own personal organization upon it; reading and learning depend upon unambiguous recognition of the exact nature of the relationships and technicalities expressed. This is a good example of what Donaldson refers to as the 'language of systematic thought' (Donaldson, 1989).

As we saw earlier in this chapter, most models of the reading process look backwards to the competences which children are expected to bring to learning. We are shifting the focus of interest to the nature of the curriculum and its demands on pupils, rather than viewing literacy as a set of skills acquired outside of the learning context. We emphasize that schools introduce children to a wide range of very specific ways of using print which embody the processes and functions of different subject areas. As a consequence of learning to use these functions properly, children's powers of analysis and problem-solving are changed.

Donaldson (1989) gives a number of examples of the kind of impersonal language associated with different subject areas, particularly at secondary level. Words which pupils may have encountered in everyday settings are given very precise meanings. Terms such as 'wave', 'work' or 'power' in physics must be redefined within a scientific context. In maths, notions such as 'raising a number to its power' must be distinguished from terms encountered in humanities, such as 'the power of the law'. Donaldson suggests that the majority of children, especially those for whom reading experience has been confined to stories, will not simply 'pick up' the language of systematic thought. These new forms of language must be explicitly taught. Children's awareness of how language is structured and how it functions in different contexts, must be deliberately planned for and fostered. Donaldson suggests that teaching children the flexibility of language as a tool for thinking should begin in primary school.

The important association between the development of logical thinking and literacy, is a theme taken up by Wood (1988). He dismisses as a gross over-simplification the view that when children learn to read they are acquiring a new and *neutral* code for representing what they already do with and know about speech. Rather, children are introduced to radically new ways of thinking about language itself. Being able to write well demands the capacity to think objectively about language, to take other people's perspectives into consideration, to anticipate any likely sources of mis-understanding and take them into account in the absence of a face-to-face audience. Literacy fosters the ability to plan, to self-regulate, to edit and self-correct, to reflect on the linguistic devices of written language which achieve different emphases and effects.

Wood raises the issue of whether pupils make slow progress in literacy because they have insufficient experience of understanding why different types of writing exist, and ways in which variations in purpose are reflected in stylistic and structural devices. In other words, they do not know how to interact with text; they do not know how to become actively engaged in interpreting what they read (Webster and Wood, 1989).

There is some evidence from American research (Palincsar and Brown, 1984) that intervention techniques can help pupils to become more active interrogators of text: 12- to 13-year-olds with severe reading difficulties were taught to ask relevant questions of text, to resolve ambiguities and speculate about the author's intentions. These researchers claim high success rates in bringing comprehension levels up to age norms, although, prior to the study, the pupils' teachers had persisted in trying to establish 'word-attack' skills, rather than deal with the real problems faced by the pupils in different subject contexts.

GENRE THEORY

A number of attempts have been made to analyse the range of texts which children encounter as they move through the school system, and the demands which these texts make on pupils in order to produce and understand them. The particular discourse forms associated with different subject areas of the curriculum are known as genres. Examples of different genres include narratives, explanations, opinions, arguments and analyses. There is good reason to believe that different genres place different information-handling demands on children (Kress, 1982; Swales, 1990; Beveridge, 1991).

Both the existence of genres as potential written forms of discourse available to the writer, and explanations conveyed by teachers regarding the manner in which genres work, may encourage pupils to organize their thinking in particular ways, to select and emphasize different aspects of their knowledge and understanding in relation to a given audience and intention.

However, we are sceptical of claims that a greater *taught* awareness of generic characteristics in writing will on its own improve children's literacy (Christie, 1987; Cope and Kalantzis, 1993).

In our view, the generic characteristics of any given text, whilst being linguistically complex, are less powerful determinants of children's literacy development than social interactions around those texts, during reading or writing. Genre theory runs the risk of overemphasizing the linguistic evidence of different text types at the expense of social context factors, which written genres may reflect, but rarely construct.

The issue of how and when to introduce children to written genres, is still a vexed question for teachers and linguists, and one which our own research has deliberately not pursued to any depth. Where we do make reference to genre, this is mainly to assist our own descriptions of how texts may be organized in different subject areas of the curriculum, not as prescriptions for teaching.

FAMILY LITERACY AND PARENTAL PARTNERSHIP

In one important sense, children never approach anything in school completely afresh, without a history. The extent to which parents, family and friends, display and encourage an interest in reading and writing, is the single most important factor associated with children's progress. In relation to literacy, the attitudes, habits and experiences which pupils bring from their home and community, will determine many individuals' motivation and commitment to learning.

For these reasons, some investment has begun to be made in developing family literacy, as a means of influencing children's school progress. For example, the *Adult Literacy Basic Skills Unit*, with Department for Education (DfE) funding, has recently set up regional family literacy projects aimed at extending the uses of literacy within the day-to-day business of people's lives. The argument runs that by increasing family literacy and demonstrating the importance of reading and writing, for example, in seeking employment, more positive attitudes to literacy and the modelling of literate behaviours, will transfer to the children.

There is also a body of evidence which demonstrates that direct parental involvement in reading with their children raises achievements and improves motivation (Beveridge and Jerrams, 1981; Beveridge et al., 1987). A number of partnership initiatives have shown that by involving parents in the classroom and by demonstrating positive strategies which can be used at home, there can be gains in attitude and general communication between home and school, raised levels of enthusiasm and commitment, together with improvements in confidence, independence and the quantity of reading undertaken.

The precise form of parental involvement, from family reading group to paired reading workshop, appears to be less important for success than organizational issues which sustain momentum. Similarly, the exact nature of the resources used, from library books to reading schemes, appears to be less significant for impact on pupil progress than the strategies which adults adopt for interacting with pupils around text (Topping and Lindsay, 1992). Quite obviously, any serious attempt by a school to manage the literacy curriculum effectively must involve parents in the process. This is, of course, easy to say, but the important question is how this can be sustained.

In the wider perspective of this book, we are concerned with the nature of schooled opportunities that assist children in becoming literate. Where there are marked differences between children, for example, on entry to primary school, these may reflect (and continue to reflect throughout schooling) distinctive patterns and gaps in literacy experiences at home. When opportunities are provided for children to extend their use of literacy in classroom contexts, but these fail to be followed-up or enhanced in the intimacy of the family, the onus on the school increases; making a difference at school becomes much more difficult. Children need both family and school literacy to recognize and support each other.

THE INFLUENCE OF TELEVISION

One important claim is that children spend a great deal of their time at home watching television, playing video and computer games, and that these activities have effectively displaced reading. Television has not only ousted reading for pleasure, it is argued, but has also reduced time spent by children making things, such as models from kits, and enjoying shared activities with peers, family and friends; for example, by scripting plays, making up adventure stories, or playing boardgames.

It is certainly the case that children spend more time watching television than in pursuit of any other leisure activity. Pre-schoolers in America have been estimated to spend as much as one third of their waking hours watching television (Schiller, 1979). Watching television and playing video games cannot in themselves be considered to be wholly negative. Any potentially damaging or displacement effects are not intrinsic to the media, but grow out of ways in which the media are used. There is a case to be made that television, like other forms of media, should be considered in terms of what children do, in the contexts in which they are familiarly used:

> children's 'cognitive understandings' of television cannot be separated from the social contexts in which they are situated, or from their affective investments in the medium.
>
> Buckingham, 1994, p. 39

Greenfield (1984), in considering the impact of electronic media on children, argues that these newer media forms can be a positive force in children's lives. However, teachers do need to be aware of the influences which electronic media have on children's thinking and attention, and some of the attendant risks of passive long-term television watching.

In just the same way as print literacy introduces children to new ways of using language, which in turn stimulates new ways of thinking and problem-solving, so too television literacy has specific consequences for thinking and behaviour. In watching television programmes, children may be said to 'read' the ways in which images are constructed and narrated in the audiovisual medium, in much the same ways that they learn to interpret features which are represented in the silent and atemporal medium of print. At one level children learn to interpret editing techniques, such as the function of close-up shots, whilst at another level children learn to follow multiple sub-plots and complex formats (such as *NYPD Blue*). In these instances, children are learning about codes of representation and narrative structures which process multiple pieces of information in parallel.

What kinds of thinking are stimulated by the technology of new media, their forms and its code? The characteristic that sets television apart from print media is visual movement which attracts children's attention. However, the continuous movement and rapid pace of most television programmes, unlike print, does not allow for reflection or close analysis. Television is a medium that unfolds in real time and therefore paces the viewer. Evidence shows that heavy television viewing is associated with increased impulsivity and restlessness (Greenfield, 1984). Children who spend a great deal of time watching television are less persistent with other tasks, and may become 'passive assimilators', unused to active engagement in learning.

We have considered the part played by television and electronic media at this point because of the concerns expressed by many teachers that literacy has been displaced by, and cannot compete with the immediacy and visual power of television. So any attempt to manage the literacy curriculum has to harness the positive potential of television (Buckingham, 1992). Inevitably, the media themselves are beyond the control of schools and are here to stay. Many schools depend on television and video as a means of introducing topic material to groups, for example, in a lead lesson. Turning television from a passive to an active medium is central to exploiting its teaching potential, since the stimulus of television, though attention-holding, is not enough to ensure learning.

Greenfield (1984, p. 153) suggests that a pervasive finding of television research is the crucial factor of interacting with children during viewing to develop a more reflective approach, 'adding media to the original medium of face-to-face interaction with the teacher'.

RESEARCHING THE CLASSROOM

In the final section of this chapter we turn to what is perhaps the most important issue for the purposes of the research study we have undertaken: the nature of adult–pupil encounters in teaching and learning. In fact, there is very little empirical evidence which throws light on the quality of encounters enjoyed by teachers and pupils in relation to text, and what appears to make a difference to children's progress and understanding. Some would go so far as to say that we know very little about the quality of children's learning experiences generally (Bennett et al., 1984). As Raban (1991, p. 53) points out, 'What is needed is close observation and cataloguing of teacher behaviours across a range of classrooms in order to detect more or less successful strategies.' However, it is no easy matter to observe busy, complex teaching environments with twenty to thirty individuals and select those aspects which are significant in terms of pupil learning, in order to make systematic records and come up with practical recommendations. How do we know what children are gaining from the tasks and activities set, or even what the teacher intended? How can we probe the nature of their learning to achieve a fine-grained account of those critical features which move children on in their thinking?

Despite the abundance of advice (Desforges, 1988) on how to design more effective learning environments, these suggestions may have very little impact. This is because such advice often depends on some kind of restructured delivery of basic skill teaching to individuals, and ignores the dynamics and organization of classroom life. It has long been recognized that classrooms are social contexts in which much of the teacher's time is devoted to establishing routines, boundaries and adult control, with pupils having to discover what the teacher requires. But classroom-based research has tended to produce over-simplistic analyses and a narrow interpretation of events (Shipman, 1985).

It should also be said that no social context, including classrooms, can be described in full. This limitation is not just one of *data capture*: the difficulty of observing everything that happens. It also derives from the well-recognized point that social data, like all scientific evidence, require a theoretical frame of reference to become meaningful, and that there is a considerable array of such frameworks which apply to classroom life. For example, research into friendship or gender would assemble the data of classroom activity somewhat differently from our own interests in literacy acquisition.

Each research focus requires a theoretical model which generates principles for data organization if it is to be studied usefully and vigorously. It is often the case that no such single agreed model exists for the domains of educational research. However, good research still adopts the practice of leaving the relationship between its theoretical position and its research tools open to inspection.

ADULT–CHILD PROXIMATION

Addressing the issue of growth in children's understanding and its relationship with the nature of the teaching demands made in different subject domains, requires setting literacy in a conceptual framework which is different from other approaches. Adult–child proximation is a term we have coined to refer to those instances where adults enter into close exchanges with children where information is handed over, explanations are given, and events are interpreted. This is what we mean by mediation: helping children to contruct accounts of events in terms they understand. Adult–child proximation is examined in the nature and quality of interactions, such as conversation, or question and answer routines. Our approach stems partly from recent attempts to study teaching and learning as socially-mediated activity (Wood, 1988; Webster and Wood, 1989; Moll, 1990; Bruner, 1986).

Drawing on the work of Soviet writers, particularly that of Vygotsky, and more recently, Bakhtin, these accounts reject an atomistic or reductionist approach to learning generally, and literacy in particular, as a fragmentation of what transpires during learning, which tends to ignore the complex ways in which new information becomes meaningful (Burgess, 1993; Wertsch and Bustamante Smolka, 1993).

A core idea is that adults frequently help children to accomplish things which they could not do by themselves. Similarly, what adults assist children to achieve collaboratively, prepares children for more independent enquiry in the future. The gap between what children can do on their own and what they can achieve with the help of others more skilled than themselves, is known as the 'zone of proximal development' (Vygotsky, 1978). Through social interaction with the more mature, children are exposed to practices and examples of how others tackle problems and manage their thinking.

Effective teaching, in these terms, is much more than the transmission of information from one individual to another. Rather, successful teaching is constituted in certain styles of cooperation and negotiation. The importance of this view is that learning depends more on the teacher's dialogue with individuals and groups than on the transfer of information in the form of 'true' statements made by the teacher and remembered by the pupils.

Our focus in this book is on the teaching and learning of literacy as both a teacher, school and inter-school process. More precisely, we are concerned to study the teaching of literacy set in a system of classrooms within and between schools. Our research tools must consequently have a generality which is applicable across a range of contexts and yet must be realistic to the teachers concerned. The model we eventually put into use began its development from consideration of how to identify the dialogic approach to literacy as used in everyday teaching through mediation.

Teaching as 'mediation'

We can identify some of the key features of teaching as mediation or proximation in relation to literacy. There is an emphasis on meaning, relevance, the functional uses of literacy and the creation of classroom environments in which many different types of literacies can be explored and developed. Teachers who follow this approach will emphasize the creation of social contexts in which children actively use text to achieve specific purposes, avoiding the reduction of reading and writing to skill sequences or stages.

It is the teacher's task to work towards the pupils' mastery of their own learning. Mature thinking involves a degree of self-regulation, planning, suggesting, reminding and evaluating oneself. Through social interaction with the more mature, pupils are shaped towards more systematic organization and self-control: they achieve a critical reflection on how they went about their learning, what went well, and what could be done better. This critical reflection can operate at many levels of the reading or writing process, including low-level factors such as how letters are formed and spelling units assembled. But it is important that pupils do not lose sight of why something is being read or written, the larger purpose of using literacy as part of the demands, intentions and procedures of different subject areas.

A further issue concerns what it is that is learned or changes. Much of school learning can be characterized as recitation, where the main routines of instruction are those of illustration, explanation and information-giving. The pupils' task may be construed as that of absorbing and reciting content for assignments and examinations. Effective learning, in proximation terms, is about the pupil coming to know 'how', not 'that'. Knowing 'how' is instantiated in pupils' meaningful grasp of procedures which enable learning to be generalized from one context to another. For example, when children are taught how to manipulate abstract symbols in solving mathematical equations without understanding the concepts which underlie them, or how they can be applied in the real world, empty knowledge – procedures without meaning – is the result.

Rather than simply learning rote facts and information contained *within* the subject, pupils must acquire some of the processes, strategies and objectives which *underpin* the subject and those who practise it. At all levels, effective learning means that children are asked to behave as historians, scientists or readers, from the outset. This is more than simply arranging a set of classroom events in which subject literacy plays a role, for example, re-enacting the Battle of Hastings and writing an account. For effective learning to take place, pupils must be led to internalize some of the thought processes of a historian, such as a consideration of the provenance of available evidence.

The next point concerns how teachers can work effectively as mediators. Teachers have an overview of their subject domains and how small units of enquiry (for example, topics within a scheme of work) relate to the larger direction in which teaching is leading. Hence, teachers are in a good position to identify priorities, to mark out those subject areas which need to be covered thoroughly, and to know which processes have to be mastered.

Effective teachers help pupils make informed choices about their learning, rather than simply directing them to get on with a task. They help pupils select appropriate problems to tackle; draw attention to relevant or overlooked information; negotiate resources, materials and potential strategies. Wherever possible, pupils are asked to think of themselves as sources of information, to be creative in their own questioning and independent in their decision-making. However, this does not preclude rote practice in areas where memorization is required, such as learning to spell unusual words. Similarly, learning to play the trombone or to make a screenprint, requires work with the instrument or equipment. It is an important part of the teacher's role to explore the best ways of achieving the aims set in relation to the pupils' starting points.

Contingencies in teaching

Perhaps the best way to characterize the teacher's role is in terms of contingency. By this we mean the timing of intervention in order to assist children's performance of a task, particularly when difficulties arise. This involves gauging a pupil's (or group's) moment-to-moment understanding of a task, providing more information and help where needed, using questions to move thinking forward, allowing more initiative when pupils succeed.

Wood (1992) argues that most classroom settings are actually very *low* in intellectual challenge. He feels that most of the dialogues teachers hold with pupils do not promote reflection, analysis, enquiry, or sustain interest and motivation. Many questions asked by teachers, for example, are closed, factual questions, with known right answers. Teachers get to ask practically all the questions, whilst pupils strive to provide the right answers. Typically, teachers give pupils around one second of 'wait time' in which to formulate and produce a reply. Simply increasing wait time produces more effective classroom dialogue. Wood suggests that, rather than test questions to check what pupils know, alternative strategies include teachers giving their own thoughts and ideas to pupils, speculating, suggesting, surmising, interpreting, illustrating, listening, planning with, sharing and acknowledging what children have to say.

An important aspect of teachers' lesson management involves devising opportunities in which feedback can be given. Having tackled a task, there is an important review stage when pupils are asked to reflect on their learning, what they have gained, how they could have proceeded any differently, what to move on to next. At this evaluation stage teachers must be careful to respond to the process or strategy that a child has chosen and not simply to mark the product, quantity or output. This is an important phase of helping to make explicit the criteria by which learning is evaluated. Creating an atmosphere which highlights joint hypothesis-raising and problem-solving, also includes a conscious awareness of the language required to comment on the process of learning. This exposes some of the links between learning dialogues and the mental processes acquired by pupils.

Effective teachers recognize that not everything can be left to the pupil's initiative and that some achievements must be won through sustained, deliberate practice or study. We are not suggesting that the best teaching is informal, or indeed highly structured, since the crucial issue is whether pupils recognize the reasons for embarking on a particular learning route and where it is leading. It is a question of teachers standing with pupils in a shared enterprise, recognizing that while children enjoy solving problems, they may need help to find the right questions and the appropriate means to tackle them.

To do all this makes many demands on teachers themselves, requiring them not only to be experts in the tools, techniques and content of their subject specialisms, but also to have expertise in how children think and learn. This is why we have suggested that literacy, as both tool *and* technique, should be on every teacher's agenda and is interwoven with the whole curriculum.

This brings us to the last, but not least, element in adult–child proximation: the ability of teachers to decentre, to think about the pupils' perspectives as well as their subject, to learn from pupils' responses, to adjust their teaching reciprocally as they interact with children in the classroom. Another way of expressing this is to add to the notion of 'apprenticeship' a two-way effect: the events of learning not only influence conceptual changes in pupils, they also produce conceptual changes in the adult. Good quality dialogic literacy teaching occurs when teachers act with particular under-standings which are both fluid and responsive.

SUMMARY

We began this chapter by examining the current concerns for standards of attainment in reading and writing, whether these have fallen in recent years and whether teaching methods can be blamed for any apparent changes. Our considered advice is that teachers should be wary of test results, many of which are conflicting, none of which provide a satisfactory basis for moving forward. Importantly, these unproductive arguments about methods and standards reduce the complexity of children's literacy development to unitary, simplistic notions.

In the past, what has fuelled the debate over literacy teaching has been a number of contrasting models of the reading process, derived from quite different research traditions. We have illustrated how models have changed over time, and highlighted some of the constraints attached to analyses of literacy in terms of bottom-up, top-down or compensatory factors. None of this work has adequately addressed how literacy is acquired in real classrooms, and how children's reading behaviour interacts with the wide range of text forms and subject challenges, as children pass from primary to secondary school.

We also have scant evidence on what makes a difference to children's learning of literacy, under what conditions, and in response to what kind of teaching. Currently, there is a tendency for many teachers, particularly at secondary level, to view literacy as someone else's specialist responsibility, outside the mainstream curriculum and unimportant to most other subject teaching.

Much of the evidence we have reviewed suggests that the teaching of literacy is mostly perceived in terms of discrete steps or skills, which pupils ought to acquire by the later stages of primary school. It also appears that from infant school onwards, less and less attention is given to literacy teaching, such that by secondary school, the likelihood of pupils being given help to cope with the burgeoning literacy demands of different subject areas decreases rapidly. Indeed, there are some alarming figures which show the limited amount of time when pupils engage in literacy-related tasks, particularly for continuous reading. In writing, teachers tend to emphasize secretarial skills, neatness and volume, and writing for personal reasons rather than dealing with the written functions of tasks within subject domains.

On the whole, teachers and curriculum legislators have a tradition of neglecting literacy for learning. In the terms by which teaching was defined earlier in this section, literacy does not appear to be developed in the dialogical forms we have outlined. Given the prescriptive and content-laden philosophy that underlies the National Curriculum, which manages to leave literacy out of its broad context, teachers have been further discouraged from seeing literacy as a challenge for the whole curriculum and an integral part of every teacher's agenda.

In this chapter we have set the scene for a new framework for managing literacy in schools, which will focus on the nature of the curriculum itself and the way in which different subject areas introduce pupils to specific ways of understanding and generating text. These diverse literacies, including television literacy, have the potential for influencing how children think and behave. It is critical, in our view, to try and establish under which social-interactive conditions of teaching and learning children acquire adult approaches to problem-solving. In our view, these processes of systematic thought must be explicitly captured in classroom discourse and experience.

NOTES

1   The first two extracts are concerned with visual perception, discrimination of patterns, eye movements, transfer and 'gestalt' theory: the perception of whole units. The extract from Smith includes key constructs of prediction and hypothesis-testing, whilst Wray et al., refer to cooperative exploration and self-images of language users. The changes reflect a shift in the view of how language itself is acquired, away from perceptual, mechanical aspects of decoding, towards outcomes of interactive social experience.

2   Importantly, because we can account for the functioning of complex systems in terms of models or rules, this does not mean that the systems in question are actually being driven by, or rely on, those rules. To take an example, the motion of the planets in the solar system has been represented in terms of specific mathematical rules, but it would not be claimed that Venus or Saturn are *following* such rules. There is a crucial distinction to be made here – one which informs much of our current thinking about literacy – between 'rule-described' and 'rule-following' behaviour.

2 A framework for understanding literacy teaching and learning

> Real concepts are impossible without words, and thinking in concepts does not exist beyond verbal thinking. That is why the central moment in concept formation, and its generative cause, is a specific use of words as functional tools.
>
> Lev Vygotsky

In this chapter we consider a new and alternative way of defining literacy in relation to the teaching contexts of the curriculum, across a range of subjects and in different phases of schooling. As we began our research with teachers, we confirmed our belief that all classrooms are highly complex contexts which defy simplistic description or analysis. Isolating reading and writing from wider aspects of how learning is managed and organized, the nature of tasks set, and how time is spent, appears to us to ignore some of the most important factors. Researchers have a tendency to simplify issues: in this case we had to find a way of describing and accounting for the specifics of literacy-related activities within the bustle of everyday teaching and learning contexts in a typical school.

We can define a classroom context in terms of recurrent experiences which have discrete characteristics and boundaries. School contexts are constrained in part by organizational rituals and the need to maintain rules and behavioural norms. This implicit understanding of the behaviour teachers expect, such as appropriate ways of addressing adults in school, is picked up quickly by most pupils, and often forms part of a kind of hidden curriculum. There are similar expectations of how pupils should respond to tasks set, the relative values of neatness, quantity or original ideas in written work, which teachers also transmit, however unwittingly and unintended. All of these issues are part of the fabric of mundane teaching contexts to which pupils are regularly exposed and in which much of their learning takes place.

This, then, was the starting point of our research programme: to examine the current pattern of learning encounters where literacy forms a part and in which aspects of literacy schooling are shaped, modelled and given value. All of the schools we collaborated with had expressed an interest in determining the nature, frequency, depth, quality and purpose of literacy-related encounters in their classrooms, what we consider as a form of curriculum *audit*. The aim of the research programme was to explore with teachers the ideas they hold, their conceptual maps of literacy teaching, together with direct observation of classroom practice, as a basis for generating more effective learning environments. Given objective evidence of classroom experience to consider and debate, our assumption was that teachers themselves would find strategies for developing their work. Our researcher's role very quickly expanded to include that of facilitator, once schools had embarked on the process of change.

LITERACY AS 'INTERNAL' OR 'INTIMATE' PROCESSES

From the brief review of existing literacy research presented in Chapter one, it can be seen that most models of reading, including top-down and bottom-up research, treat aspects of literacy as essentially *internal* or intimate. By internal, we mean attempts to describe features of the textual code which an individual must master, the units of language felt to be important, or the cognitive accomplishments necessary for reading or writing. Some experimental psychologists, for example, are very much concerned with the processes of perception, analysis, storage and retrieval of information during reading, and individual differences in the development of these component processes.

Whether concerned with features of the print on the page, or what individuals bring to reading in terms of language and experience, these researchers are dealing with an essentially private world, inside the child's head. It is also important to remember that the mental processes involved during skilled reading may tell us very little about the processes which serve children as they learn to read: how cognitive systems get set up in the first place. Modelling reading is not the same as modelling learning to read.

Alternatively, other approaches which are more aligned with the concerns of reading teachers, attempt to elucidate the nature of adult–child roles in intimate encounters. Approaches such as 'Apprenticeship' (Waterland, 1988) or 'Reading Recovery' (Clay and Cazden, 1990) focus on the moves which adults make in close, intensive, reading-designated sessions with children. No doubt all of this research has added to the body of knowledge on the reading process and the strategies which can be adopted by adults in teaching key skills. As we pointed out earlier, however, much of the thinking to date has promoted a view of literacy as a structured, linear process, which interprets progress in terms of an individual's grasp of the right skills at the right time. Instruction for those pupils who fail to read is therefore seen to include more intensive programmes to practise target skills, outside of most subject areas of the curriculum.

THE 'SITE' OF LITERACY FORMATION

The theme of this book is that for most pupils as they progress through primary school, and especially on transfer to secondary school, increasing sophistication in reading and writing must come from experiences of using written language in different subject domains, within the complex social and cultural contexts of the classroom. However, when researchers have compared the amounts of time spent on a range of literacy activities in different age groups, for example, in the ORACLE study (Galton et al., 1980), time spent specifically on reading rapidly diminishes to less than a few minutes a day for Year 6 pupils. Time devoted to literacy by teachers in this age range is largely organized around individual skill training programmes for those having difficulties.

This general reduction in opportunities specifically designed for developing reading or writing within the curriculum, continues into the secondary school. Some teachers, evidence shows, are more than suspicious about the virtues of reading in lesson time (Lunzer and Gardner, 1979). For the majority of pupils as they move through school, we can question whether there are enough opportunities for developing literacy systematically and regularly, within the recurrent teaching contexts of the mainstream curriculum.

The reason for addressing literacy in this way, in terms of all the curriculum, is not simply to involve more teachers in taking responsibility for raising standards of spelling, handwriting, reading or writing, as a kind of DfE directive. The strong argument for reconceptualizing literacy as an intrinsic part of every subject, is that we begin to understand more about effective teaching and learning. We shall be arguing that the different literacies of science, contrasted with history or design technology, introduce pupils to different ways of thinking, organizing and recording. As a consequence of learning to use these separate functions, pupils' powers of analysis, conceptualization, and problem-solving are changed. We made the point in Chapter 1 that literacy is not a neutral code which exists outside of the work which pupils do across the timetable. This flexibility of written language, with its power to influence how students plan, operate and respond, must be made explicit and cultivated.

In these terms, literacy can be considered as an integral part of a set of complex learning experiences which support higher mental processes. In order to understand and improve literacy teaching we need to examine the ways in which children's reading and writing practices are set within the cultural values of real classroom contexts. Willinsky (1994) uses the term 'new literacy' to describe how some teachers have moved away from teaching reading or writing as isolated skills, towards including literacy as 'a social process in the daily landscape'.

The shift in thinking associated with this 'new literacy' is, first, that students take increasing control over the texts they use or construct. Second, that the work of the classroom recognizes the importance of using text effectively in different subject areas, starting from the students' own awareness and experience. Third, and most importantly, that the relationship between teacher and pupil is changed from that of handing over information, to working together to extend the pupils' range of meaning-gaining and meaning-making: achieving certain ends with certain materials in a given setting.

Lankshear (1993), in a book which also rejects the notion of going back to a 'golden age' of teaching basic skills, argues that literacy should not be considered as a set of abilities or techniques which are independent of the curriculum. Rather, we can only understand literacy by observing the forms which reading and writing actually take, or are made into, within particular social contexts. The views pupils have of what literacy comprises, what they see as worth doing or appropriate, are shaped by the examples, processes and requirements of all formal areas of schooling, as well as in home and leisure contexts. In other words, how teachers model uses of reading and writing in different subjects, what teachers introduce, recommend, demonstrate, emphasize, cherish or ridicule, determines the way in which pupils learn. It follows that if we want pupils to acquire a wide range of literacy forms, it is the curriculum within which their critical practice must be sited.

A FRAMEWORK OF ADULT–CHILD PROXIMATION

How, then, to design a research framework clear enough to be readily understood and interpreted, yet with the power to analyse the literacy curriculum *in situ*? If we accept that research on individuals out of context is unable to generate much of practical use to teachers in the classroom, then we must focus on teaching and learning activities in context. The units of analysis must be applicable to the situations in which literacy is shaped and realized. What we required was a way of examining teaching and learning, whilst also accommodating some of the complexities of classroom reality: the framework had to embrace a wide range of views and practices. Ideally, as well as generating descriptors which could be used to quantify aspects of the teaching process, our schema would also provide signposts for professional development, for improving teaching encounters and remaking literacy within the curriculum. Not surprisingly, such a framework was not easily come by.

As our research developed, ideas were tested out amongst teaching colleagues and in workshops held in the schools where data were to be collected. Importantly, any theory which we presented at this stage had to be user friendly, look as though it might work in practice, and make links with what teachers already knew about teaching and learning. The final version of our framework, having been ratified by teachers and incorporating their ideas, is shown in Figure 2.1.

Two continua provide the structure for the framework. The horizontal axis is concerned with the degree of initiative, engagement and active involvement of the pupil in learning. The vertical axis is concerned with the

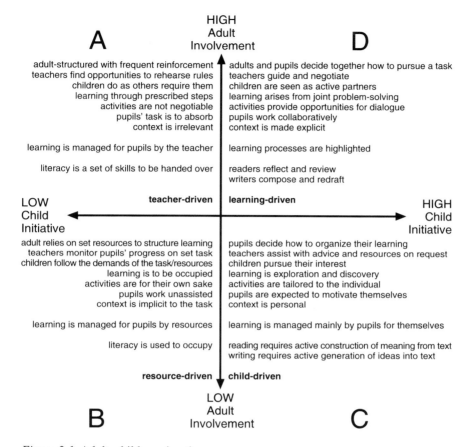

Figure 2.1 Adult–child proximation

level of management, control and mediation exercised by the teacher. Using these two continua, fundamental to all teaching contexts, we were then able to describe the nature of interactions between teacher and taught, the way exercises are set and problems tackled, the quality of questioning and the nature of assessment, how process issues are discussed or reviewed, the relative emphasis on activities such as rote drilling compared with discovery learning or free choice.

In effect, the model reflects different images of the roles of teacher and pupil which influence how the business of learning in the classroom might operate. The two continua provide a clear summary of what can be valued in any teacher's professional activity. The model also highlights different zones of interaction: above the horizontal axis is essentially the teacher's domain, characterized by high adult management and control, whilst the area below this axis characterizes the pupil's domain, where learning is mostly managed by pupils themselves or is dependent on resources.

The framework is not intended to be a precision instrument, but a way of looking, of gauging relative emphasis. We would not expect that all that transpires in a classroom could be 'measured' by our model, or that individual teachers or pupils could be located precisely within it. The intention is to identify predominant kinds of teaching and learning styles, how they overlap or emerge, and the possible consequences for pupils' experience of literacy.

Although our major concern was to develop a useful framework for description at this stage, teachers drew their own conclusions about how and why they worked in certain ways rather than others. Important to say is that we provided the framework initially without judgements attached regarding the quality or merits of the separate quadrants defined by the two axes. There are some accounts of classroom environments which suggest that, for most teachers, establishing and maintaining order and cooperation are the highest priority (see, for example, Doyle, 1986). We would expect some teachers to spend some time with some groups of pupils, in didactic mode, managing learners rather than learning. We also know, from research such as that carried out by Bennett et al. (1984), that strong emphasis is placed by many teachers on the practice of routine tasks and consolidating learning, perhaps using occupier resources or activities. At other times pupils may be encouraged to research problems for themselves with little direction, to pursue their own pathways and make their own discoveries or mistakes. Opportunities may also be designed for collaborative tasks which emphasize joint planning, partnership and the weighing of process issues.

What this amounts to is that teachers are adaptive to the conditions in which they operate and which prevail at any moment in time. Volatile teaching groups, where demanding tasks are difficult to sustain, may have to be managed by coercion and a high degree of structure and control. In order to deal with some of the business of the day, teachers may require some pupils to work unaided without requesting help. Group work and experiential learning are higher risk activities requiring more cooperation and preparation. Some tasks, such as learning to use a sewing machine, bunsen burner or lathe, demand more closely supervised practical experience than others in which rote practice may be essential, such as learning tables in mathematics or how to count in a foreign language.

What teachers do is constrained by the nature of the learning, the resources available, levels of pupil interest and cooperation, together with a myriad of other factors which impinge on the social context of the classroom. Effective learning may or may not be high on the agenda. The types of experience characterized in the four quadrants of the model enable us to describe the dynamics of a particular teaching context in terms of adult–pupil proximation and to understand how aspects of literacy are embedded within these contexts. Our use of the term quadrant is not to imply a quasi-scientific rigour, but to indicate a teacher's sense of direction, emphasis or orientation.

Quadrant A: teacher-driven

Quadrant A in the framework is characterized by high teacher management and didactic styles, rote teaching and prescription with little negotiation, where the pupil is assigned the role of passive recipient. All the teachers who have worked with the model recognize this image of the adult as a purveyor of knowledge, where pupils are viewed as empty vessels, some more receptive than others. In this domain, literacy teaching is seen as a set of skills to be handed over and drilled. Learning would typically progress through a sequence of adult-controlled steps, largely decontextualized, with relevance and meaning more apparent to the teacher than the learner. Learning is viewed as a matter of building, through direct teaching, from simple to complex, from smaller to larger skill sequences.

Practice of subskills or rules might take place outside of a subject context. Questioning is likely to be teacher controlled, of the what, who or why variety to check out factual retention. As teacher control increases, opportunities for student interaction decrease. The teacher works hard, carefully defining what pupils must do, directing them step-by-step, but leaving little to the initiative or ingenuity of the learners. Pupils are expected to master what is taught, at the time it is taught. Evidence of learning takes the form of the correct reproduction or completion of a pre-determined response. Hence, risk-taking by children is discouraged or penalized. Since correctness or compliance is valued, many children experience varying degrees of failure.

As an example of high teacher management, teaching by recitation, mentioned in Chapter 1, is a technique whereby teachers firmly pace question and answer exchanges, allowing pupils to participate in short, rapid bursts. Recitation often has three basic components: teacher initiation, pupil reply and teacher evaluation. The teacher usually nominates who should respond, directing and eliciting pre-determined 'correct' answers. The technique has its benefits when managed successfully, permitting a very ordered turn-taking with individuals in the context of a large group, encouraging high attention levels and alertness, keeping in touch, though superficially, with student understanding. It can also be used as a way of re-engaging pupils whose interest has been diverted, to the task in hand: the teacher has a sense of delivering, of being in charge.

The following exchange occurred in one of the lessons we observed, where a Year 7 group of pupils working in pairs had been asked to look through a book of poetry, highlighting aspects of poems they liked using yellow Post-it stickers. This was preparatory work for a discussion on personal preferences in poetry and the construction of a matrix from the blackboard. In the context of the lesson, the teacher's intervention at this point is not intended to elicit information but to register the fact that a pupil is 'off task' and there may be consequences:

'What have you found that you like in your poems, Shelley?'

'Miss, do we have to do this?'

'Well, you can do it now or in your own time.'

Another example of a teaching activity which would typify quadrant A is a remedial reading programme based on highly controlled exposure to sight vocabulary, or phonic rules taught separately from the context of an individual's, or someone else's writing, as a discrete exercise. A further example is provided by a teacher who, having just introduced the rule of 'full stops at the end of every sentence' to a group of infant children, realized her misjudgement of the pupils' understanding when almost all the work completed by the children subsequently, showed full stops after every word. Rule-driven teaching sometimes does impart the kind of empty knowledge – procedures without meaning – referred to earlier.

In Chapter 1 we cited some other examples of intervention approaches directed at individual instruction based on behavioural objectives, which would also fit this kind of teaching, such as 'Direct Instruction' (Carnine and Silbert, 1979) and 'Teaching to Objectives' (Solity and Bull, 1987). Assessment in quadrant A is likely to be based on the attainment of skill criteria or teaching objectives set by the teacher. Because it is high in teacher management and control, quadrant A is described as teacher-driven.

Quadrant B: resource- or occupier-driven

In contrast, quadrant B is characterized by lack of explicit theory, adult or child initiative, and a limited amount of management, direction, modelling, adult or child initiative. In this domain, literacy may be used mainly to *occupy* pupils. For example, pupils may be simply supervised in a library area without any specific reason for being there other than for those who can get on independently with their own reading.

In this quadrant, the teacher's role may be one of supervising or overseeing with little interaction, as pupils proceed through a worksheet, set resource, programme or other instructional materials. There may be few external signals, such as teacher questions or prompts, to steer pupils in the right direction, evoke responses or engage pupils, remind them of the key issues and what they are trying to achieve. Pupils are generally focused on completing individual tasks set by some remote person: a classroom version of distance-learning. Questions initiated by pupils may be discouraged. Assessment takes the form of monitoring, rather than as a basis for planning or weighing what children have learned.

A good example of this kind of teaching arose when a Year 11 Personal and Social Education (PSE) group were set an exam-type task which involved reading a photocopied newspaper article entitled 'Putting the bullies on trial', with a set of comprehension questions to complete. During the lesson the teacher made it clear that pupils must work independently and in silence.

There was no discussion of how pupils might proceed with the task, questions were not permitted, and the teacher's own inputs to the lesson were those of monitoring and marking time: 'Can we have quiet please?'; 'Ten minutes left, finish as far as you can.' Whilst the pupils were exposed to a range of resources and activities involving reading or writing, since there was no modelling or joint consideration of how to proceed, the lesson format precluded any real extension of pupils. The teacher's choice of format ('Think of this like an exam') constrained how literacy was applied. An important point, which we will return to during the course of this book, is that in terms of literacy development, the group were putting to use the existing knowledge and competence which they had brought with them into the lesson.

In a recent review of factors in the classroom context which influence learning, Weinstein (1991) discusses the extensive use of 'seatwork', which occupies as much as 70 per cent of instructional time. Seatwork is characterized by pupils copying, working through set schemes or worksheets, usually unassisted, with limited communication or direction. Pupil engagement follows a typical pattern of pupils beginning their work, attention wanes, the noise level and other activities increase, the adult intervenes, pupils return to their assignments. These cycles are repeated until there is a final spurt to complete the work within time limits. During periods of off-task behaviour, students may chatter, go to the toilet, fetch materials and equipment, sharpen pencils, or simply hover: hang around looking busy. These observations of classroom activities belong in our quadrant B.

Because it is low in teacher management, pupil initiative or engagement, quadrant B is described as resource- or occupier-driven. In this kind of experience, pupils may have contact with a wide range of written language, but there is little sense in which texts are central to *interactive* learning encounters.

Quadrant C: child-driven

Quadrant C draws on child-centred models of teaching and learning, and the view that pupils are basically the architects of their own understanding. The image of the pupil is one of a self-motivated individual or mini-scientist, whilst the teacher's role is to provide a wealth of materials to furnish a rich and stimulating environment. The pupil takes much of the initiative in determining a learning pathway, and is encouraged to pursue an interest but with little guidance, structure or management.

This quadrant is consistent with many interpretations of Piaget's work in relation to education. At the heart of Piagetian theory is the view that learning and development arise out of the child's own action and problem-solving. What sets the pace in the child's thinking is the individual's exploration, experiment and discovery. This has often been translated by teachers into the dictum that children should learn by direct, hands-on experience. Since it is the child's interaction with the physical world which provides the timing and motivation for change, any social facilitation of development only works when the child is ready to move forward. Processes of social interaction involving teachers and other adults thus have a low-key effect and are not really important in fostering development.

From our own research data, a good example of this kind of activity arose when Year 10 pupils were engaged in writing down and rehearsing episodes of a dance sequence using choreography sheets. Most of the lesson was given over to pupils generating their own dance interpretations, whilst the teacher provided resources, information or help when requested. The pupils' creative work led to a number of mini-performances which the group then judged.

Another example arose in a Year 3 group of children who were set, for the very first time, the task of researching and writing up a topic of their own personal choice. There was some discussion of possible topics, such as 'Foxes', 'My Family' or 'Spacecraft'. The children were provided with a folder, but very little else in the way of guidance or assistance. These were very much the children's own projects, to be carried out and presented as individuals decided for themselves. No doubt, parental assistance and domestic resources play a large part in bringing this kind of enquiry to a successful fruition.

Quadrant C defines literacy in terms of immersion of pupils in books as sources of enjoyment and information, and in self-motivated written investigation. There may be an assumption, for younger children, that they will read when ready and need to be surrounded by a richness of stories and print. For older pupils, there may be an assumption that the wider range of textual forms and written genres is acquired spontaneously from exposure and induction, without explicit teaching.

In this quadrant, questioning may be largely under pupil control, with opportunities taken to raise the issues which concern them. Assessment is concerned almost exclusively with the qualities of the child's unique production or performance. Because it is low in teacher management or collaboration, this quadrant is described as child-driven.

Quadrant D: learning-driven

Finally, quadrant D ascribes active roles to both teachers and pupils in a learning partnership. The emphasis is on learning which is facilitated, but not controlled, by the adult. Learning is viewed as a complex process, more than just the sum of a number of small sub-skills. In fact, the smaller units of a task are seen as more readily acquired within the context of a meaningful whole. Essential to effective learning are opportunities to take risks and make mistakes in collaboration with partners who contribute different perspectives and understandings: learning is a social enterprise which draws on the immediate resources of participants.

Different ways of pursuing an enquiry may be devised and reviewed, as children examine the consequences of alternative problem-solving procedures, not just the correctness, quality or quantity of their output. Learners are not seen as isolated individuals who succeed or fail by their own efforts. Teaching and learning are treated as social and communicative processes, whereby knowledge is shared and constructed in particular cultural settings, such as the school. We could go so far as to argue that culturally specific institutions, like schools, have a major influence on how people interact with each other, and how artefacts, tools and resources may be used, such as textbooks, computers, libraries or listening centres.

In quadrant D, literacy takes the form of a dialogue in the making. Pupils collaborate with adults and other partners to construct writing or interrogate a text, draw inferences, analyse or evaluate their own and other people's written material. Attention is drawn to different ways of telling, turning text to certain forms and functions, for given audiences. Tasks are contextualized in the sense that teachers share meaning and purpose with pupils in defined settings. Questions are often process-orientated or speculative, of the 'what if?' or 'how?' variety. Assessment is reflective and formative, reviewing how tasks were tackled and identifying key issues for next teaching steps.

Because it is concerned with adult sensitivity to the needs of pupils, how learning takes place and the requirements of the task, quadrant D is described as learning-driven.

SOCIO-CONSTRUCTIVISM

The kind of experiences we have described in quadrant D draw on attempts to consider development in terms of adult–child proximation, or socially-constructed activity. In Chapter 1 we made reference to the socio-constructivism of Wood (1988), Vygotsky (1978) and Bruner (1986), where many of these ideas are articulated, and which rejects a simplistic, skill-based account of learning generally, and literacy in particular. One problem with many of the ideas which stem from the socio-cultural perspective, is that of applying them to large group classroom contexts, where factors which have nothing to do with learning *per se*, often determine the teachers' priorities, and where teachers have to engage groups of learners, not just individuals.

The essence of social-constructivist theory is contained in three concepts: 'scaffolding', the 'zone of proximal development' and 'appropriation'. It is these concepts which underlie quadrant D and our perceptions of literacy development within this domain. Scaffolding provides a metaphor for the quality of teacher intervention in learning, and it means more than just help to accomplish a task. Scaffolding begins with the teacher marking out with pupils a specific line of enquiry, recruiting participants, designing activities tailored to the needs and experience of a group. The teacher is aiming at some new level of independent competence on the pupils' part and supports their activities or problem-solving, without taking over. This may be achieved through dialogue in which the adult elicits information or responses from pupils which leads them along a particular line of thinking. The teacher may draw attention to key issues or points of information, reminding pupils about the task in hand, giving prompts and shortcuts, making suggestions and identifying some of the steps which may need to be taken to pursue an enquiry (Norman, 1992).

In Chapter 1 we introduced the term 'contingency', which is a fundamental quality of good scaffolding. Contingent adults pace the amount of help given to pupils on the basis of their moment-to-moment understanding, holding back when enough of the task has been grasped to allow room for initiative, intervening when pupils are veering off course, maintaining interest, purpose and momentum. Scaffolding has been described as taking steps to reduce the degrees of freedom in carrying out a task, so that pupils experience success by constraining a problem to smaller specifics, without losing sight of the whole. This restructuring or remaking of tasks with pupils includes helping to plan and use available time effectively, highlighting possible pitfalls, weighing the significance of any findings with pupils, addressing how the task was tackled and what might be carried forward to next time, giving insights into how the adult might manage the problem (Wood, Bruner and Ross, 1976).

The second concept – the 'zone of proximal development (ZPD)' – refers to the gap between what children can do on their own, and what they can achieve with the assistance of others more practised than themselves. In these terms, successful teaching is pitched just ahead of current achievements. Pupils who can accomplish tasks set without adult assistance or scaffolding are therefore unlikely to be working in their ZPD. As we have seen, many tasks which pupils are set in school are repetitious, demanding rehearsal of familiar routines and existing concepts. They may in fact be designed to occupy pupils rather than challenge them, when adult assistance is in short supply. Such pupils are more justly described as working in the 'zone of previous development'.

To move on in their thinking, children require experiences which confront existing understanding and ways of proceeding. To do this effectively in large group settings places enormous demands on teachers and requires an extension of the concept of the ZPD to include a collective or group zone of proximal development. Such experience is pivotal, in the sense that once having grasped something new, there can be no turning back. It is in precisely this sense that we have referred earlier to children's *critical* practice in the classroom. Dialogic interaction, for social-constructivists, provides the support children require in order to grasp new concepts.

The third concept of 'appropriation' will be less familiar to teachers. It is a term which is used to describe how children pick up, or appropriate, the ideas and opinions of others who share their social and cultural contexts. Children appropriate their families' attitudes towards books, their patterns of literacy use, and bring these into school. What they do in school has a social history often rooted in domesticity, and this, we have argued, is one of the compelling reasons for parental involvement schemes in reading.

Appropriation also refers to the reciprocity of teaching and learning. By this we mean the ability of teachers to think about the pupils' perspectives as well as their own, to learn from the way in which pupils respond and the ideas they present, to adjust their teaching reciprocally as they interact with pupils in the classroom. In Chapter 1 we suggested that the notion of apprenticeship in teaching has such a two-way component: the events of learning not only move children on in their thinking, they also influence teachers in what they understand and do next.

The following example, taken from our own research data, illustrates the kind of experience which characterizes the socio-constructivism described in quadrant D. A Year 6 mixed ability group were working on fractions in a maths lesson. This began with the maths teacher demonstrating how to distribute 30 sweets amongst 6 pupils, as an illustration of how to solve the problem 1/5 of 30 = ? The teacher's time in the rest of the lesson, devoted to using a range of resources to work through problems involving fractions, was spent collaborating with pupils, prompting, reminding, suggesting alternative strategies for going about a task, offering short cuts ('Save all that counting on your fingers'), giving feedback, breaking processes down into manageable chunks, and reframing problems ('1/10 of 20 – look at it this way – if I've got 20, how many groups of 10 are there?').

The teacher managed to work contingently at both individual and group level, through a combination of knowing her subject and making on the spot judgements about what her pupils were learning, whilst modifying tasks accordingly. The teacher gauged pupils' progress, understanding and need for help, by frequent visiting and through exploratory talk.

These different images of teaching and learning, represented in Figure 2.1, generate different constructions of what literacy is, and how it can be brought alive. We said that, at the outset, the framework was presented to teachers without value-judgements attached. We did not suggest that the best teaching is formal, laissez-faire or collaborative. Most teachers recognize that when left to their own devices, some pupils achieve very little and that some achievements can only be won through persistent, deliberate practice and effort. Teachers generally adapt what they do to meet the multiple demands on their time.

Having devised the research framework, it was important to check out what teachers made of it, and to orientate them to the principles of adult involvement and child initiative. Importantly, we needed to know whether this way of looking at teaching and learning – denoting certain kinds of emphasis and approach – made sense of their own classroom realities. It was at this point that teachers' strong preferences, as well as some major differences, began to emerge.

TEACHERS' CONCEPTUAL MAPS

The research framework was designed to encompass the variety and complexity of teachers' work in the classroom, to reflect both the sophistication and practical realism in what teachers do. However, around the time we commenced our research partnership with schools, heated debate about 'falling standards' of reading and the efficacy of different methods of teaching, had begun to take up space in the popular press. In a number of very recent official documents, these points about the neglect of conventional methods and teachers' lack of sound principles for what they currently do, have been reiterated.

The Department for Education's view is made clear in the discussion document written by Alexander et al. (1992), which considered aspects of the work of primary schools. Whilst acknowledging serious inadequacies in the available data, the authors persist with the claim that progressive and informal methods have had a profound effect on the quality of teaching and have brought about serious downward trends in learning. In the Alexander review, teachers are accused of adopting practices which lack 'any serious educational rationale' and of neglecting traditional classroom and skill-based teaching in discrete subjects, in favour of low-level challenges, through, for example, informal topic work. During the consultations held over the National Curriculum Orders for English, the DfE continued to press for a narrowing of the curriculum focused on grammar, correct English and basic skills. The case was built around the argument that 'teachers do not possess a conceptual map of reading development' (DfE, 1993, para 6.7).

The DfE's central message to schools was summed up recently in a speech made by the Chief Inspector of Schools, Chris Woodhead, where he questioned the 'prevailing ideologies' of child-centred teaching and discovery learning:

> What, too often, we have is an emotional commitment to beliefs about the purposes and conduct of education which militates against any genuinely searching educational debate. A commitment, for example, to the belief that education must be relevant to the immediate needs and interests of children; that the teaching of knowledge must be less important than the development of core skills; that the adjective 'didactic' must necessarily have pejorative connotations.
>
> Chris Woodhead, January 1995, annual lecture by HMCI

What concerns us more than anything about the treatment of these issues by politicians and the press, is the persistent polarization of teaching into opposing and highly simplified positions. We saw other examples of this in Chapter 1 when we considered the polemics of the standards are falling debate. Assumptions are made about the prevailing beliefs of teachers and their commitment to certain ways of working, without any supportive evidence. Critics would prefer teaching, particularly the teaching of reading, to be simple to define and therefore simple to deliver.

Despite the extended and heated debate about classroom methods and the teaching of reading, real evidence of teachers' understanding, attitudes or beliefs about their work, particularly in relation to literacy, is lacking. No data have been collected to support the view that teachers have shifted their teaching styles, cling to 'child-centred' approaches, or have swept away much that was tried and tested over the years. Furthermore, no effort has been made to substantiate the claim that teachers fail to reflect on what they do and have elected to use ineffective methods, because of a mainly emotional commitment.

One of our first tasks was to research whether teachers possessed a full and organized understanding of how children acquire literacy and what teaching should aim to achieve at different stages of schooling. Are teachers clear about how to design effective learning environments, and which resources or methods to adopt in order to foster different aspects of literacy? Do teachers now eschew formal skill teaching and are there inconsistencies in approach? Are primary teachers clear about the demands which the secondary curriculum will make and is this reflected in their work? Are there mismatches between primary and secondary teachers with regard to what pupils are expected to know and do? Answers to these questions would enable us to confirm or refute the 'official' view that teachers lack a conceptual map of literacy.

Explorations of teachers' conceptual maps must also be considered alongside observations of what teachers do in the classroom. We need to know what teachers believe in and what they value, how they conceptualize their work. But we also need to know how these intentions are translated into classroom practice and what obstacles or constraints are encountered which prevent these aspirations from materializing. In the context of our research programme, answers to these questions would help us respond productively to the often reported claim that teachers already know how to teach ten times better than they ever can (Brown, 1968).

LITERACY QUESTIONNAIRE

The framework of adult–child proximation, shown in Figure 2.1, was used as the basis for constructing a fixed item questionnaire. Working with teachers, and drawing on the National Curriculum Statutory Orders and Programmes of Study, we identified a number of aspects of literacy considered to be important. These included features at the code level (alphabet, letter sounds, phonic blends); vocabulary (developing vocabulary, establishing sight words); reading (assessment and diagnosis, selecting books, classroom environment); writing (spelling, handwriting, presentation, purpose); and a range of curriculum issues (teacher constructs, ownership, design, children who fail, supporting learning).

The four quadrants were used to generate statements about each of these

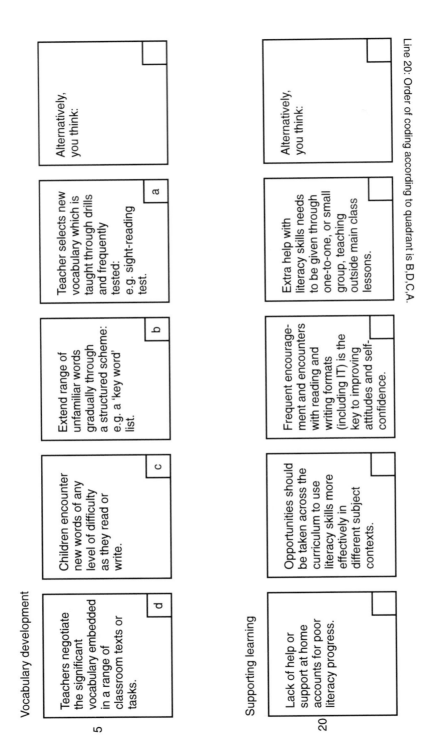

Line 20: Order of coding according to quadrant is B,D,C,A.

Vocabulary development

Alternatively, you think:	Teacher selects new vocabulary which is taught through drills and frequently tested: e.g. a sight-reading test.	Extend range of unfamiliar words gradually through a structured scheme: e.g. a 'key word' list.	Children encounter new words of any level of difficulty as they read or write.

a · b · c · d

Teachers negotiate the significant vocabulary embedded in a range of classroom texts or tasks.

5

Supporting learning

Alternatively, you think:

Extra help with literacy skills needs to be given through one-to-one, or small group, teaching outside main class lessons.

Frequent encouragement and encounters with reading and writing formats (including IT) is the key to improving attitudes and self-confidence.

Opportunities should be taken across the curriculum to use literacy skills more effectively in different subject contexts.

Lack of help or support at home accounts for poor literacy progress.

20

Figure 2.2 Extracts from literacy questionnaire

aspects of literacy. Eighty statements in four sets, corresponding to each of the four quadrants, were set out in a fixed item format (see Appendix 1 for full questionnaire). Teachers would be asked to identify one of four statements for each questionnaire item, which they felt most corresponded to their own views. At the point when they were given the questionnaire to complete, the underlying four-quadrant framework was not revealed to the respondents.

We give here some examples to show how the questionnaire works and what it highlights. Quadrant A of the framework reflects didactic teaching, rote or decontextualized learning and high teacher management. This quadrant was used to generate statements such as 'Presentation skills are best practised as a specific exercise, e.g. cursive writing within tramlines'. Quadrant B represents minimal adult or child initiative, lack of modelling, and resource-driven or non-interactive learning. This quadrant was used to generate statements such as 'The alphabet should be gradually absorbed without direct teaching'. Quadrant C depends on an image of the child as self-motivated to explore books, whilst the adult's role is to supply resources and materials. This quadrant reflects child-centred or discovery learning. It was used to generate statements such as: 'The teacher's task is to immerse children in a wide range of written forms and genres'. Lastly, quadrant D is characterized by collaborative partnership approaches where literacy is developed within an active dialogue involving both adult and child, emphasizing purpose, process and contingency. This quadrant was used to generate statements such as 'Spelling strategies are discussed as an integral part of the composing, editing and publication process'.

The full questionnaire attempts to expose how teachers view different aspects of literacy teaching and learning, what they value, and how they would tackle a particular issue in the classroom. We had to be sure, before using the questionnaire, that the research framework was sufficiently clear cut and robust, that teachers agreed the basis on which it was constructed, including the relationship between the quadrants and the questionnaire statements which they generated.

In a pilot study, twenty teachers were asked to work in pairs during an in-service session, to re-allocate the eighty questionnaire statements to the quadrants which produced them. Using a statistical procedure devised by Fleiss (1971) for measuring agreement among many raters, a figure of $p = 0.87$ was calculated, which incorporated a correction factor for the extent of agreement by chance alone. This can be interpreted as approaching 90 per cent agreement amongst the twenty teachers that statements in the questionnaire fitted the model proposed. Given this reasonable coherence of the questions in the context of the framework, we were confident to give the finalized questionnaire to a larger number of different teachers.

ANALYSING THE QUESTIONNAIRE DATA

The data we report here were collected in the southwest of England from a sample of primary and secondary schools in urban and rural environments, including schools serving inner city, multi-ethnic communities and a wide range of housing types. Since we were interested in any differences between primary and secondary teachers, questionnaire data were analysed from fifty Year 6 primary teachers (from fifty primary schools) and fifty Year 7 secondary teachers, including English, science and humanities subject specialists (from five secondary schools). (See also Webster et al., in press.)

As can be seen in Table 2.1, the sample surveyed showed a high degree of consistency. It should be remembered that, at the time of completing the questionnaire, the nature of the underlying model was not revealed, whilst the questionnaire items were scrambled to prevent teachers responding in stereotypic fashion. Even so, the largest share of questionnaire responses was allocated to quadrant D by all teachers. This reveals a clear tendency to stress the importance of teaching literacy through approaches which involve collaboration, negotiation and active learning partnerships, with an emphasis on process issues, relevance, purpose and meaning. Around 50 per cent of overall responses from both primary and secondary teachers identified quadrant D.

The remaining 50 per cent of responses, while emphasizing child-centred factors (quadrant C), also suggested use of more prescriptive, rule-based approaches (quadrant A) together with resource-based learning (quadrant B). For example, 42 per cent of primary teachers said they would use graded reading schemes; 66 per cent felt that time should be given to practising letter shapes and handwriting; 62 per cent noted children's enjoyment of activities based around rhyming or spelling patterns without a context. However, 82 per cent of primary teachers said they would not attempt to correct or rehearse spelling outside of the process of children composing, editing and presenting a piece of writing for a specific audience.

Table 2.1 Mean literacy questionnaire responses (out of 20) in four quadrants for primary and secondary teachers

	A	B	C	D
Primary	1.7	3.8	4.6	9.9
Secondary	2.1	4.2	4.2	9.5

Differences between primary and secondary teachers

The data also revealed interesting differences between primary and secondary teachers in a number of areas. Primary teachers are more likely than

Table 2.2 Differences between primary and secondary teachers in aspects of literacy

	Chi Square	Degrees of freedom	Probability
Selection of graded reading materials	8.0	3	<0.001
Teaching of spelling	11.1	3	<0.02
Practising of handwriting	13.2	3	<0.01
Rhyming and spelling activities	8.6	3	<0.05
Literacy as integral to all teaching	8.5	3	<0.05

secondary teachers to select graded reading materials for pupils. Most primary teachers would teach spelling strategies as an integral part of composition, whilst many secondary teachers take the view that faulty spelling should be corrected and rehearsed out of context. On the other hand, primary teachers do give specific time to the practising of handwriting skills outside the context of writing for a genuine audience, which is not typical of secondary teachers. Primary teachers also give greater recognition to the value of activities which draw attention to rhyming and spelling structures in words. They are also much more likely to consider literacy as an integral part of teacher–child dialogues, whereas some secondary teachers see literacy as only indirectly related to their subject teaching, or the responsibility of the English department.

Overall, both primary and secondary teachers were, in the main, proponents of a negotiated literacy curriculum. What is clear from this study is that teachers cannot be simply categorized as falling into (or failing at) one philosophy versus another (such as 'real books' versus 'phonics'). Some of what teachers say they do is concerned with practising skills. Some of what they do is concerned with enjoyment and experience. At other times teachers have in mind processes such as composition. For the main part, teachers are mindful of the complexities of interactive literacy contexts.

An important conclusion, in the light of the official view that teachers do not have a conceptual map of literacy, is that teachers do have an organized understanding of literacy development in children, but it is not a simplistic conceptual map based on unitary methods, resources or skills. These findings are also important in refuting the argument that teachers have moved, in the last decade, away from traditional methods of teaching in order to adopt trendy but ineffective approaches.

Differences between subject specialists in secondary schools

Although we have identified a broad consensus of opinion amongst primary and secondary teachers (with some differences in emphasis), this study also highlights important differences between the subject specialists in secondary schools.

Table 2.3 Mean literacy questionnaire responses (out of 20) by secondary subject specialists compared with primary generalists

	A	B	C	D
Primary	1.7	3.8	4.6	9.9
Secondary				
English	0.8	2.5	3.9	12.8
humanities	1.8	4.9	4.5	8.8
science	3.7	5.2	4.3	6.9
All secondary	2.1	4.2	4.2	9.5

Despite the small numbers of different subject teachers involved in the study, contrasts between specialisms are apparent, and have important implications when issues to do with literacy across the curriculum are considered. Quadrant D responses to the questionnaire, which we have described as learning-driven, were much higher amongst English specialists than any other group, including primary teachers. Quadrant D responses were, however, lower amongst science specialists (1-way Anova, $F (3, 96) = 11.2$; $p < 0.0005$). Quadrant A responses, which we have described as 'teacher-driven', were much higher in science teachers than in any other group (1-way Anova, $F (3, 96) = 6.4$; $p < 0.001$).

What these findings demonstrate is that whilst many secondary teachers have a map of literacy development and teaching which covers very similar conceptual domains to primary teachers, points of difference do arise between subject specialists. Science teachers would appear to believe in more prescriptive, didactic approaches. For example, science specialists are much more likely to suggest that help with literacy is provided outside their subject area, rather than within it (1-way Anova, $F (3, 96) = 5.9$; $p < 0.001$).

It is apparent that many specialist teachers, with the exception of English teachers, are unused to thinking of literacy, of the functions and processes of reading and writing, as an important aspect of their subject teaching. They remain to be convinced of the power of texts as tools for thinking, organizing, problem-solving and communicating, within their subject areas. One explanation for this is that subject specialists have been trained to think about their subject areas in ways which emphasize the knowledge base rather than literacy. Or perhaps the issue is one of responsibility, whose job is it to promote literacy in the general scramble to cover Programmes of Study?

Teachers were given the opportunity to comment freely about any aspect of literacy covered by the questionnaire. This revealed qualitative evidence, particularly from primary teachers, of a flexibility in approach, tailoring strategies, resources and tasks to meet the needs of individuals and groups, rather than applying a method to all children. Some secondary teachers were prompted to write about their relative inexperience in teaching literacy, lack of training and opportunities for professional development:

As a secondary teacher ... I have had no specific training or development in literacy ... Maybe it has been assumed I do not need these skills or that I would acquire them as I went along ... I do not feel very confident in taking young people through the process of learning to read and have received no professional support in this.

SUMMARY

This chapter has considered what should be the proper site of literacy formation. We have seen that models of literacy generally treat reading or writing as essentially private or intimate activities, as bundles of skills, teacher moves or strategies for working in close reading encounters. However, most pupils' growing sophistication in using written language comes not from intensive reading-designated sessions, but from experience of using and constructing texts for different purposes, in different subject domains. This is increasingly the case as pupils move through the school system. What research we have suggests that there are not enough opportunities provided for developing literacy in a systematic and regular way, within the recurrent contexts of the mainstream curriculum.

The reason for addressing reading and writing in this way is because of the advantages for both pupils and teachers, in knowing more about the different literacies of subject areas such as science, history and mathematics. We shall be arguing that there are important implications in acquiring this range of specialized functions of written language for thinking, forming concepts, organizing and communicating within each subject discipline. Quite simply, more effective teaching and learning can be achieved by making explicit and working on these literacy functions as an intrinsic part of each subject discipline.

Authors such as Lankshear (1993) and Willinsky (1994) have argued that instead of thinking of reading or writing as isolated skills, we begin to consider them as socially constructed processes which are part of the 'daily landscape' of schooling. It is within the everyday, recurrent contexts of the classroom, that teachers introduce and encourage written language use, determining what pupils learn through what they model, exemplify, emphasize, denigrate or cherish. It follows that if schools want pupils to develop positive attitudes towards books and their own writing, to acquire certain forms of literacy in order to meet the intellectual, organizational and assessment demands of the curriculum, then it is everybody's responsibility to address these issues in their teaching, whatever age group or subject matter involved.

As a first step to analysing the literacy curriculum *in situ*, we have proposed a new, research framework based on adult–child proximation. The model examines teaching contexts in terms of adult control, management and mediation, together with degree of pupil initiative, engagement and active participation. Each of the quadrants in the framework is characterized by different emphases in teaching styles, how learning may be structured or formalized, how resources are used, the nature of adult intervention, the way questioning and assessment are conducted. We have indicated that these contrasting images of teaching and learning should be interpreted as signposts, not precision reference points. Some aspects of literacy experience, however, appear to be more closely associated with one kind of teaching than another, such as the practice of handwriting and spelling as decontextualized rote learning tasks, or the drafting and remaking of texts through shared partnerships. It is recognized that all these aspects may be upheld as important in some teachers' practice, with children moving in and out of these contrasting kinds of learning experience at different points in time.

A survey of primary and secondary teachers was conducted, using a questionnaire derived from the research framework. This investigation revealed, contrary to official statements, that teachers' views on literacy are complex but consensual. In the main, individual teachers do not espouse universal usage of particular resources or methods, but are rather more sensitive to the process of learning. Assumptions that teachers are predominantly child-centred and reject traditional skill teaching are also wrong. Teachers pay attention to a range of factors, such as the place of graded reading schemes, phonic patterns and spelling. There were many similarities, but also some differences, between subject specialists in the secondary sector. On the whole, teachers' conceptual maps defy simplistic description as belonging to one pedagogical approach or another.

It seems unlikely, given this evidence, that more effective teaching of literacy – raising of standards – will arise from a narrowing of the curriculum to particular traditional or formal methods, through more subject-specific teaching in the primary school, or by going back to basics. What rings through clearly, is that some of the professional development needs of teachers are focused on the practicalities of how literacy can be embedded within the curriculum, with a closer partnership between primary and secondary colleagues, and a sharing of responsibilities for literacy across phases and across subject boundaries. Above all else, we were impressed with the ability of both primary and secondary teachers, given understanding and encouragement, to examine and develop the conceptual basis for their literacy teaching and to reconsider how they conduct their classroom work. How we pursued these intriguing prospects is considered in the chapters which follow.

3 Auditing the literacy curriculum

> The classroom is the most important and complex place in the education system.
>
> DfE, 1993

> any theory must abstract from reality, none can capture it in its fullness.
>
> Hammersley, 1993

Much goes on in classrooms besides teaching and learning. There is also more to teaching and learning than literacy, although we have made out a strong case for the centrality of literacy in learning in all areas of the curriculum. We have also acknowledged that the complexities and subtleties of effective classroom environments are by no means fully understood or easy to describe. Notwithstanding the difficulties of the task, we set ourselves the research brief of examining how literacy is harnessed, within each classroom context, to the day-to-day business of school work. In Chapter 2 we argued that the development of literacy can only really be understood by examining encounters in which the different practices of literacy are introduced, modelled, shaped and encouraged.

Teachers create opportunities to explore aspects of literacy functions in the course of pursuing problems in maths or science, topics in history or geography, or constructing different forms of enquiry with pupils in drama, technology or English. In these encounters, recurring in what we have called the daily landscape of the curriculum, pupils are brought into contact with the complex conventions of written language. There are, of course, many other situations outside of school where children encounter print, but for most pupils, especially at secondary level, increasing sophistication in using literacy stems from using written language to cope with the demands made in different subject areas.

In planning our investigation of literacy in classrooms, we anticipated a rich variety of teaching and learning styles, with differences in emphasis and balance. The research framework introduced earlier was designed to provide a basis for examining the complex social milieux in which children's literacy practice is largely sited. Our use of this framework to model literacy teaching and learning takes account of the quality and purpose of adult–child inter-actions. In researching classroom environments we had three main objectives. First, to share a common, accessible language of analysis amongst teachers, school managers and researchers. Second, to provide a flexible framework for data collection, capable of being applied consistently across a range of classroom settings in different schools and involving children across the age ranges. Lastly, and most importantly, to inform and propel an extensive programme of in-service training and professional development focused on enhancing literacy teaching and learning. In subsequent chapters we report on all three of these issues in the contexts of primary and secondary schools.

CLASSROOM PERSPECTIVES

Educational researchers have looked at the classroom from a number of perspectives. Those with an interest in linguistics, such as Stubbs and Robinson (1979), Sinclair and Coulthard (1975), Edwards and Mercer (1987) or Barnes (1976) have emphasized and examined the nature and purpose of classroom conversation. Using various schemes for categorizing the patterns of classroom talk these researchers have provided valuable insights into the quality and range of teacher–pupil discourse. For example, commonly occurring exchange structures such as I–R–F have been identified: *initiations* by a teacher, which elicit *responses* from pupils, followed by evaluative comments or *feedback* from the teacher.

This teacher-managed sequence of events, which typifies many spoken exchanges between teachers and pupils of all ages, has led researchers to conclude that the properties and structures of much classroom talk reflect teachers' concerns to exert a high degree of control over what pupils learn and do (Edwards and Westgate, 1987). Although much of this research was conducted without the active involvement of teachers and pupils in inter-preting what was going on in classroom exchanges, linguists have usually drawn the conclusion that what is observed through stretches of classroom talk reflects power relationships in society at large, with teachers closing down pupils' thinking to received versions of events, and the handing over of prescribed bodies of knowledge.

In contrast, psychologists have often assumed that the purpose of schooling is to promote children's learning and personal development, with literacy a major component. Wood (1986, 1992) draws an important distinction between 'natural' and 'contrived' encounters where children are taught, which parallels the distinction we drew earlier between 'intimate' and 'collective' encounters in classgroups. Most interactions at home are sponta-neous and child-initiated, whilst classroom contacts are usually contrived and adult-controlled. When adults and children are working on the same kind of tasks in these two settings, the processes involved will be very different. Interactions follow different 'ground rules' and create different demands on the participants.

Wood (1992) points out that the archetypal maths question posed to children along the lines: 'If it takes 3 men 6 hours to dig a certain sized hole, how long would it take 2 men?', suspends the ordinary kind of pragmatic concerns with issues such as how soft the ground was, what kind of tools were available or how the men were to be paid, which would be explored in real life. In the contrived context of the classroom, pupils recognize this as a special kind of problem-solving with a defined outcome, the ground rules for which are typically only required in school. (See also, Sheeran and Barnes, 1991 for an account of ground rules in school writing.)

Wood (1992) goes on to suggest ways in which the discourse of classrooms can be made more challenging and effective. He argues that most of the dialogues that teachers hold with pupils do not promote reflection, enquiry, interest or motivation, although many teachers assume that they do. On the contrary, most verbal encounters in the classroom are very low in intellectual challenge, often dedicated to providing material for 'digestion'. Teacher strategies which are least effective in promoting learning are high in control or power, including posing frequent closed or display questions, fast turn round in dialogue with each participant's contribution kept very short, and trying to get children to repair, repeat or improve on what they say.

Wood suggests that teachers can adapt their styles by speculating, suggesting, surmising, interpreting, listening, planning and sharing their ideas with children more often. These features create an atmosphere of hypothesis-raising and collaborative problem-solving, where 'showing' and 'telling' replace 'demanding' and 'asking'. For Wood, the key issue is one of teacher control. These issues of management and control in classroom dialogue will reappear as we discuss our own data on teacher–pupil encounters with literacy.

It has often been pointed out (Desforges, 1988) that much advice to teachers about how children learn and how best to promote it has not stemmed from research in live classroom contexts. Many psychologists, influential in their own fields of research, have produced designs for ideal learning environments or conditions in schools. Eminent figures such as Gagné (1965), Skinner (1968) and Bruner (1968) have criticized schools for being too narrowly concerned with knowledge transmission: the handing over of information to those who know less by those who know more. In the work of Vygotsky, which we considered briefly in Chapter 2, schools are not expected to be places where children are closed down in their thinking by being told what they must know.

Instead, education is promoted as a communal activity, where children are *agents* of knowledge-making as well as the recipients. Hence, Vygotsky and other social constructivists pay attention to particular aspects of collaborative enterprise in schools, such as how adults enter dialogue with children in ways which provide hints and props to 'scaffold' new forms of thinking, before their significance is fully realized by the child concerned. These important notions of scaffolding, contingency, appropriation and the zone of proximal development, which characterize socio-constructivist accounts of learning, have recently come to prominence because they begin to address important questions of how children learn, but they have not yet been thoroughly tested in real classroom settings.

CLASSROOM REALITIES

Psychologists have often focused on individual learners and under-emphasized the powerful determinants of contexts on how teachers behave. Researchers who have spent time in classrooms (Desforges, 1988; Doyle, 1986) argue that classroom realities may be so demanding, chaotic and discontinuous, that teachers are preoccupied with imposing order on potentially volatile social contexts. A number of accounts describe teachers managing learners not learning, with a great deal of time spent organizing movement around the room, distributing resources, establishing and maintaining reasonable behaviour.

Strong emphasis is laid by teachers on talking at pupils, anticipating or neutralizing disruptions, cajoling pupils to do work set (Jorgensen, 1977; Desforges and Cockburn, 1987; Bennett et al., 1984). With order and cooperation as high priorities, the nature of learning engagement and the quality of adult–child encounters are often seen as secondary issues. We could also add that increased accountability, pressures to cover the prescribed curriculum and resource limitations, have all influenced teachers to become better managers of classrooms than of learning.

It is the here and now pressure of classroom life which explains some of the data we reviewed in Chapter 1, which accounts for how teachers use the available lesson time. We know that most work set for pupils demands practice of familiar routines and existing concepts, and only rarely are pupils given opportunities to construct something anew or generalize old skills in the light of fresh problems. Three quarters of the writing tasks observed in Bennett et al.'s (1984) study were geared to copying, neatness, punctuation and accuracy. When feedback was given to pupils about their work this was usually done in crisis moments on the basis of output, not on how a task had been tackled in relation to intended audience or purpose. Most classroom reading or writing events were fragmentary and occurred in bursts of a few seconds, whilst reading or writing were used predominantly for following instructions or completing set assignments.

It is on the basis of data collected across a wide range of teachers, classrooms and countries that the '*two-thirds*' rule has been formulated: for two-thirds of classroom time someone is talking; two-thirds of this talk is the teacher's; two-thirds of the teacher's talk consists of lecturing or questioning.

It is the demands of classroom realities which constrain teachers to work in the ways they do, and which in some instances may mitigate against effective learning. In other words, attempts to identify factors in classrooms which could be modified to provide a better learning atmosphere often fail because they pay too much attention to the learning needs of individual pupils and take no account of the demands made on teachers. Only through systematic study of the nature of joint activity, tutoring and discursive interaction, within the complex social environment of the classroom, with its myriad of conflicting demands, can we begin to find credible points of development for teachers.

CLASSROOM RESEARCH METHODS

There are just as many methods for observing and analysing what goes on in classrooms as there are motives for doing so. In Chapter 1 we outlined some of the difficulties involved in describing or capturing the evidence derived from classroom observation. This is partly because of the intricacies of interpersonal contacts and exchanges, and the rich composition of teaching and learning activities which characterize many busy classrooms. Problems also stem from the nature of the observer's theoretical perspective and how this determines the focus of attention. Data to be used for teacher appraisal purposes would be assembled very differently from information gathered as part of a study of the effect of seating arrangements on children's social contacts. For these reasons, methods of observation should be closely tailored to purpose (Croll, 1986; Pollard et al., 1994).

Issues involved in the systematic observation of classrooms include careful definition of procedures, and making highly explicit, what is to be looked at. Even so, many research studies adopt such broad categories for observation, such as 'reading', 'writing' or 'non-curriculum', that useful conclusions are difficult to draw about the quality of these experiences (Croll, 1986). In the terms of our own study, most previous research on classroom contexts has missed the vital element of how adults interact with children to structure learning. The purpose of our own audits of the classroom was to produce a much finer-grained account of literacy practices, than are to be found in the general categorizations of previous research.

The strengths and weaknesses of different approaches to conducting classroom research have been considered in a number of texts on educational research methods, such as Burgess (1985), Hammersley (1993b) or Wragg (1994). Reliance on quantitative measures, such as counting the number of questions asked of children by teachers, or estimating time spent by pupils in a specific behaviour category, such as unassisted reading, runs the risk of omitting important context factors, such as the effect of room layout and frequency of adult visiting on children's response patterns. Many researchers working in social contexts accept the need for flexibility, sensitivity, and the engagement of those who know or inhabit the context, in making sense of any data which are gathered (Reason and Rowan, 1981; Webster and Jones, 1990). In order to build up an accurate picture of events, a combination of techniques is often required, including direct observation of events, informal interviews, examination of resources and materials.

Part of the brief agreed with schools who took part in our own research, included the systematic collection of evidence across a range of classroom contexts, as a basis for reviewing current practice and informing a programme of professional development. To meet this need, both a questionnaire and a time-based observation framework were developed, based on our model of adult–child proximation. We also designed a schedule for taking field notes, and, in the primary phase of the project, a format for analysing the nature of adult scaffolding. Research instruments were discussed and piloted with the teachers involved, and training was given to teacher-observers. An important point to make about the research methods adopted in the study, is that teachers worked with the researchers in devising methods, collecting data, and making sense of the evidence.

AUDITING THE CURRICULUM

In a recent publication by OFSTED (1994), teachers are asked to consider where time is spent by pupils in the curriculum, with time highlighted as a most important but finite resource. Actually, the DfE's version of an audit is based on an accountancy model of stocktaking and balancing books, inspecting how resources are allocated and deployed according to government guidelines.

The word 'audit' derives from the Latin verb '*audire*': to listen or hear. The sense of audit we wished to promote was one of listening, of hearing without making judgements. The audits undertaken in our work were not single, self-contained instances or events, but part of formative processes of professional development carried out over a number of years. The listening stage of the research provided an opportunity to find out what was happening, to focus on teacher's concerns and anxieties, to understand prevailing attitudes, belief systems and intentions. We also wanted to describe how literacy was being used by teachers as a part of their method of working, to estimate differences in time spent engaged in a range of literacy-related tasks by pupils for different purposes, and to build up a picture across key stages, schools and subject areas within a school cluster.

The schools involved in the research wanted to be able to make an independent account of what was happening in classrooms and how this served the literacy needs of pupils. In the current climate of national inspection, measurement and accountability, many schools are determined to take the first steps towards this, for themselves. In so doing, schools give primacy to local contextual factors, in order to argue their achievements relative to the national picture.

The research was geared to identifying what made a difference, in terms of teaching and learning, to pupils' experience and achievement. All of the schools involved were committed to changing the culture of classrooms in ways which increase success in learning. In part, teachers were interested to compare whether current classroom practices fell short or measured up to stated intentions. In other words, the researchers were asked to compare *what people believe themselves to be doing* with *what they actually do* in the classroom. This contrast between teacher intentions and classroom practice was a particular focus in the secondary school research, in which teachers readily acknowledged the management and organizational obstacles which constrained how they worked.

The research team was asked, in the early phases of data collection, to be neutral observers. Opportunities were taken, during the data collection phase, to discuss the nature of classroom activities, the needs of children in groups, and specific events which had arisen during the course of each teaching session. The researchers were frequently asked, particularly by primary teachers, to give immediate feedback following a lesson observation. As part of the open dialogue we had cultivated with schools from the outset of the project, the data collection framework was discussed with teachers individually and the data interpreted. Importantly, we were able to take account of the teachers' own reading of events, near to the time of recording.

Subsequently, the representations of literacy learning and use which had been built from the audit data, were considered by the schools concerned in after-school meetings and whole staff in-service days, worked on in departments and faculty groups, and action plans prepared. The researchers supplied summaries of the data and drew out main implications for teachers to consider. Contributions were made to working parties which instigated and formalized action plans and policy documents. Later phases of the research plotted the steps taken by school staff to move beyond descriptions of current and future practice, towards actual development.

OBSERVATION FRAMEWORK

The research framework outlined in Chapter 2 (see Figure 2.1, p. 37) was used to generate both a questionnaire and a lesson observation framework (see Appendix 3). Details of how the questionnaire was constructed have already been considered. We also examined data from a preliminary trial of the instrument, involving fifty Year 6 and fifty Year 7 teachers, in a wide range of primary and secondary schools serving inner city, rural and urban environments in the southwest of England (Webster et al., in press).

Data from this phase of the research show that teachers' statements about their practice are complex but, in the main, consensual. Neither primary nor secondary teachers claim to be driven by particular methods or resources, but say they are concerned with approaching a range of literacy-related factors, such as handwriting, spelling or composition, in ways which are pragmatic and meet the demands of the curriculum *in situ*. There were some interesting similarities as well as some important differences between the views of primary and secondary teachers in response to the questionnaire.

On the whole, the views elicited by the questionnaire provide important evidence that teachers do have an organized understanding of literacy development in children. Teachers' conceptual maps are intricate but consistent. They are not predominantly child-centred, and they do not reject traditional skill teaching. However, this preliminary research confirmed our initial suspicions that many subject specialists in the secondary school, with the exception of English teachers, were unused to thinking of literacy, of the functions and processes of written language, as important and integral facets of their subject teaching. What remains unexplored in this initial study is the relationship between teachers' beliefs and stated intentions, and how they actually operate in the real time of their classrooms.

The second research instrument derived from the four-quadrant framework is a lesson observation proforma (see Appendices 3 and 4). This allowed a continuous time record of two-minute intervals to be drawn up during a lesson observation, together with field notes which describe the activities, events and progress of each lesson. Both teacher input and the behaviour of two or three selected pupils can be recorded in categories which were also generated by the four quadrants. Observation categories highlight aspects of literacy being used for learning, how tasks are set, the nature of texts used or generated, the quality of engagement, how pupils proceed with their work and how tasks are reviewed.

Quadrant A type activities, high in teacher management and control, include recording from dictation and copying from the blackboard. Quadrant B activities, dependent on occupier exercises and limited adult guidance, include working through set schemes, listening or watching whilst the teacher talks over prepared resources, off-task or hovering. Quadrant C activities, largely pupil-driven, include research, generating writing independently, pupil question-raising and individual engagement with written text. Quadrant D activities, characterized by active collaboration, include shared writing, reading or discussion, process reviews, reflecting on ways of knowing or doing.

Together with a continuous time line, observers were also provided with a list of descriptors, such as 'whole class' or 'small group' formats, 'second language' or 'mother tongue' teaching, 'manuscript' or 'textbook' resources, 'redrafting', 'reporting' or 'translating' functions. Observers were given prior training in how to complete the time record in order to provide a retrievable digest or *script* of each period of teaching observed, including details of staff and pupils involved, year group and subject area of the curriculum observed. Wherever possible, samples of the worksheets, resources and textbooks used were also collected. In Chapters 4 and 5, it is the lesson scripts recorded in different classroom contexts, at both primary and secondary level, around which much of our discussion centres.

Timed data can be extracted from each lesson record or script, showing, for example, how long an individual pupil spent copying from the board, completing a written exercise in a textbook, generating own writing, collaborating with a teacher, or off-task. Essentially, the technique allowed us to examine the nature of pupils' engagement with a wide range of literacy-related activities in the context of everyday classroom experience.

In the primary phase of our research, attention was given to the nature of adult interactions with children, particularly when texts were being read or generated. The primary classroom provided an important opportunity to study samples of dialogue which centred around teaching and learning issues, with specific reference to print. The primary scripts have enabled us to re-examine the components of scaffolding in relation to primary classroom contexts, and to reconsider the usefulness of paradigms such as the zone of proximal development.

In the secondary phase of the research we attempted to address some wider issues. Data derived from the literacy questionnaire were contrasted with evidence gained from direct observation of teachers' and pupils' classroom activities. This enabled us to pinpoint discrepancies between what teachers say they do, and how they work in practice. Such discrepancies will reflect the nature of classroom realities, the contextual factors which operate to constrain teachers and pupils to work in the ways they do. Analysis of these conflicting demands was fed back to the teachers themselves in order to generate possible solutions, to find ways of bringing stated beliefs and objectives closer to classroom practice. The final and all important stage was to share and discuss with teachers how literacy was currently being used in the course of classroom encounters across the curriculum.

The common quest, the purpose of conducting some form of systematic audit of a school's work, was to find growth points for teachers and ways of acting upon these in order to enhance the literacy curriculum. The data collection phase prompted a programme of sharing, reflection and action planning, as much through listening to staff as making observations of them. Given the time constraints under which the researchers operated, it could be claimed that not enough data were collected in our own study to be considered as a thorough audit. However, the data did highlight some important issues for reflection and development, which was our major research purpose.

TEACHING STYLE AND LITERACY EXPERIENCE

To what extent and in what ways are teaching style and pupil literacy experience related? We have made the case that to study literacy for learning necessitates capturing the nature of teacher–pupil encounters where written text is, or could be, a strategic component. To make observations of any one aspect of teaching style is not necessarily to provide an informative picture of literacy in use in a specific classroom context. For example, recording how a pupil is praised or disciplined, use of whole class teaching or small group work, whether a teacher tries to visit every pupil in the course of a lesson to check progress on a task or marks work handed in, of themselves may give only limited insights into literacy in action.

Similarly, to record the amount of time a teacher spends on giving instructions, setting tasks or interacting with a class group, is not a direct guide to how individual pupils use their time: how much and what kind of individual reading or writing takes place? However, it is our contention that the teacher's patterns of classroom management and organization do exert an important influence on pupils' literacy experience. This is particularly the case where aspects of writing or reading serve an executive function, realizing, reflecting or enacting aspects of the teacher's preferred style of working. An important part of the research project was to explore the links between teacher style and pupil experience, the *consequences* of one style of doing things in comparison with another.

We can describe the style of an architect or composer independently of the structure, texture, operation or impact of a specific building or piece of music. In teaching it is more difficult to separate out the process of construction from what is actually constructed. Learning is not done separately from the process of setting out a task, deciding how to tackle it, taking decisions about strategies and resources required, organizing information, solving problems and drawing conclusions. Pupils do not use writing or reading to make a point or access information, and only learn subsequently and separately how they went about solving these problems. Using literacy and learning to be literate *co-occur*. How teachers design and orchestrate teaching activities determines how and what children learn about reading or writing.

There are a number of components or cognitive steps which may be involved when pupils apply themselves to classroom tasks. We shall examine further what constitutes the fine detail of classroom thinking in the following chapter when we come to consider adult mediation in the primary classroom. However, the point to be made here is that what children learn is inseparable from the currency of classroom activity, what is bartered, haggled over and exchanged, what is held up by the teacher or pupils to be of value.

SUMMARY

In this chapter we have examined briefly some of the research issues involved in auditing the curriculum, in order to understand how literacy is currently used in classroom contexts, for different functions. When researchers look at school contexts, they do so from widely different perspectives. Linguists such as Sinclair and Coulthard (1975) have an interest in the properties and structures of spoken exchanges between adults and children, which often reflect power relationships in society at large. In contrast, psychologists such as Wood (1992), have considered whether the kind of dialogues which teachers hold with children in the 'contrived' contexts of school, are effective in promoting thinking and learning. Educationists sometimes complain that much of the advice given to teachers by researchers, ignores many of the exigencies which arise in real classroom settings and which constrain how teachers work.

In devising our own research project we were very much aware that teachers cannot always be concerned with effective teaching and learning, but that issues of order, resources and cooperation, may be paramount. Even so, for most pupils, especially at the secondary school phase, what shapes their development and use of literacy are those recurring day-to-day experiences of the classroom, however they may be organized and managed.

The sense of audit promoted in the project is one of listening in order to describe. Working alongside teachers, a number of research tools and strategies were devised, including a timed interval observation schedule, pro forma for field notes, and a recording sheet for scaffolding. The intention was to collect evidence on a systematic and objective basis, to draw on a range of information sources, and to involve teachers as co-researchers in examining their own classroom practice. An important issue, one which continues to drive our work with participant schools, is that of partnership between researchers and schools, not merely in data collection, but in establishing research questions, analysing evidence, and planning next steps.

4   Literacy and learning in the primary classroom

> Whatever else they do primary schools must accept overriding responsibility for teaching literacy and numeracy.
>
> Alexander Report, DES, 1992

Most parents and professional educators would expect that achieving competence in literacy and numeracy is at the heart of the primary school curriculum: its core business. Unlike secondary subject specialists, whose opinions vary widely on the centrality of literacy in different subject areas, primary schools have generally accepted that literacy and language are powerful components in promoting and reinforcing all learning. Even so, observations of primary classrooms which we reported in Chapter 1, suggest that some children may spend only a few minutes a week reading, whilst the amount of curriculum time devoted to literacy-related tasks diminishes in some cases to a fraction, as children move through the primary school (Raban, 1991; Allington, 1984; Galton et al., 1980). Reports which have recently been commissioned by the DfE (DES,1992; OFSTED,1994) confirm a considerable variation in the amount of time spent by primary teachers on literacy and numeracy.

Primary schools have come under criticism from a number of interest groups in recent years for apparently failing to meet their central responsibilities to teach basic skills. In the introductory sections of this book we set out our strong conviction that the falling standards issue was misinformed and misleading, distracting attention from the really important issues which make a difference to how teachers teach and what children learn. The issue is not simply that of teachers abandoning traditional tried and tested methods in favour of new, more fashionable approaches. There is no *unequivocal* evidence that spending much greater proportions of time on the mechanics of reading or writing would in itself raise standards of literacy. Similarly, retrieving (if they were ever cast aside) established methods of training basic skills, holds no guarantees for raising achievements. OFSTED (1994) confirm that the quality, management and organization of teaching, not methods, are the key factors in enhancing teaching and learning.

In this chapter, we examine the quality of encounters in relation to written text, how literacy is used as a vehicle for reflection and understanding, and how primary schools introduce children to specific ways of using print as a tool for thinking and enquiry. We shall look at what children are expected to know about literacy as they move through Key Stages and how well the primary school prepares children to meet the challenges which lie ahead in the secondary school curriculum. By focusing our research on the day-to-day tasks of the primary classroom, we are able to identify some of the consequences for children's learning of different patterns of organization and management. Elsewhere we have described this as the nature of pupils' critical practice within the social landscape of the curriculum. By examining the fine grain of adults' dialogues with children around print we are able to illustrate those features which allow strong literacy-learning environments.

DILEMMAS IN PRIMARY TEACHING

Primary teachers are now familiar with the call to consider themselves as reflective practitioners who question their own aims and actions, monitor, evaluate and revise their own practice (Pollard and Tann, 1987). Reflective teaching is typically addressed in terms of reconciling numerous demands and conflicts, in emphasizing one aspect at the expense of another, in exercising choices and resolving dilemmas. These dilemmas might be expressed in terms of discovery versus rote learning, intrinsic versus extrinsic motivation, cooperative versus individual problem-solving, formal versus informal teaching style.

These issues of how teachers choose to use the available time, what to stress and what to neglect, characterize much of the current debate about the primary curriculum. The recent Dearing Review (SCAA, 1993) of the National Curriculum and its assessment was charged with finding ways of slimming down the statutory requirements in order to free up some 20 per cent of teaching time for further work in the 'basics of literacy, oracy and numeracy'. Reports recently published as part of HMI's brief to monitor the impact of the National Curriculum in primary schools also pursue this line of thinking on how time – a 'finite resource' – is allocated. With an increased emphasis on accountability through testing and inspection, and the possibility that some primary schools will be identified as 'failing their pupils', many schools are beginning to review the way they teach.

In the most recent OFSTED (1994) survey of forty-nine primary schools, for example, the amount of time spent on English was said to vary from 15 to 33 per cent of the teaching week. OFSTED acknowledge that this way of summarizing a school's work must be treated with caution. Use of language and literacy cannot easily be quantified as disembodied elements of the curriculum. Despite urging caution, OFSTED recommend that all primary schools should make realistic estimates of the amount of time spent on different subjects in each class. HMI also point out some serious weaknesses in schools lacking clear policies in how to teach basic skills for learning reading, particularly the place and purpose of teaching phonics. HMI also highlight strong associations between teaching styles and organizational issues, such as use of questions, ability groupings or direct teaching, and standards achieved in English and other subject areas.

In lessons observed by HMI where pupils' achievements were felt to be poor, four major factors were held to be accountable. First, teachers avoided direct teaching and acted largely as servicers or supervisors of pupils' tasks. Second, time management was poor, resulting in too slow a pace for the tasks in hand and a drift off in attention. Third, that work was not sufficiently differentiated to match pupils' needs. Finally, that teachers relied on particular strategies, such as whole class teaching or individual work, which were rigidly applied and never varied. In contrast, good achievement by pupils was felt to be associated with high expectations and a close match of tasks to pupil needs. Teachers had a good grasp of their subject matter and were more skilled in asking relevant questions, and providing a single subject emphasis in topic work.

What are primary teachers to make of these data, couched as it is in general terms, with no specific evidence or illustration to support the criticisms? Presented as issues of choice and decision-making from a range of options, we doubt whether teachers are helped to reflect constructively on their classroom practice or enabled to change what they do. We doubt that children's achievements in literacy will be raised simply by making more time available to work on basic skills, or by any strategy which augments what teachers already do. Bolting on something new to extant practices does not promote change at the heart of the primary curriculum. Furthermore, the inspectorial role does not extend to supporting teachers to work more effectively. Perhaps the most worrying factor, however, is that data from HMI surveys of primary schools are presented to teachers in a form which allocates responsibility for change and improvement, without an underlying rationale which explains why some teaching strategies work better than others.

SOCIAL CONSTRUCTIVISM AND THE PRIMARY CLASSROOM

In the work of Vygotsky, revisited over several decades, researchers have found some very compelling accounts of the learning process which hold significant implications for teachers who are trying to promote and accelerate pupil learning. The social constructive approach treats learning as an interactive and communicative activity, whereby knowledge is shared and constructed in specific cultural settings. The primary school, for example, is a cultural institution which defines and constrains the nature of activities, relationships and programmes of study. Some of these constraints are more *explicit* than others, such as legal requirements for what must be taught, assessed, recorded and reported. *Implicit* rules govern how adults and children will address one another, form friendships and be grouped, how they will use books and computers, and how adults will question, direct, discuss and reflect issues with pupils.

Expectations may vary from one class to another, although differences in aspects of school life such as discipline, expressed in classroom charters, will still operate within a school or LEA policy framework and reflect societal norms, such as acceptable forms of reward and punishment. Similarly, whether parents are encouraged to read and write with their children, how children are heard reading and whether books go home, how books are shared and reviewed by class groups, the planning of readers' or writers' workshops, together with aspects such as displays of texts and children's work, are determined by the prevailing ethos in a school: how things are generally done.

Social constructivists argue that children's thinking is bound to these specific contexts of social practice and that learning is based on the mastery of the specific ways in which modes of behaviour, thinking and acting are defined by each context. The forms of language used in each context, including types of writing, text and talk, are tightly linked with particular social institutions. In order to study literacy, its teaching and learning, we must examine the social practices which organize them in the classroom.

It is through social interaction with the more mature that pupils are guided towards more systematic organization and independence in learning. In other words, children's thinking develops as a result of 'borrowing' ways of speaking, acting and problem-solving, which are first encountered in collaboration with adults or more capable peers. This borrowing or appropriation works both ways, in that teachers have to think about children's prior experiences, ideas and starting points, in order to adjust their interactions with individuals and plan appropriate challenges to move them on in their understanding.

In Chapter 2 we used the term 'scaffolding' as a metaphor for the kind of props which adults offer to children as they collaborate to learn. Scaffolding incorporates a number of strategies and is much more than just offering solutions or help to finish a task. Rather, scaffolding actively assists children to construct their own understandings. Scaffolding begins with outlining an area of enquiry and recruiting pupils to take part. It includes how tasks are clarified and represented, and how the teacher deals with aspects of procedure. When pupils are engaged in a task, scaffolding enables pupils to weigh evidence appropriately and to make choices about learning routes. Crucially, for literacy development, the teacher scaffolds the process of learning through the discourses and genres of written language: how to organize thinking through text and how to select appropriate formats for communicating the fruits of an enquiry in print. Finally, teachers scaffold learning by reflecting on the process and worth of a child's work, feeding back helpful suggestions prior to publishing or display.

How well teachers are able to scaffold learning in primary classrooms depends on a number of factors. In Chapter 2 we mentioned contingency: the timing and tailoring of assistance to keep the child on course without being too intrusive or controlling. Scaffolding and contingent teaching support the child's learning to the point where the child is able to take control over a problem and its solution: 'What a child can do in collaboration today, he can do by himself tomorrow.' The gap between what the child can achieve alone and in partnership with an adult is the area with the most productive teaching potential: the zone of proximal development. Despite the eloquence of his theory, Vygotsky's ideas may need to be reinterpreted as they are applied to real classrooms. Only recently have researchers tried to develop these ideas in the context of large groups of learners. Some kind of collective or interrelated zones of proximal development may have to be proposed for the theory to work (Forman et al., 1993). The theory needs to be illustrated and extended with reference to how adults respond to children in busy school contexts.

One important strand of the research we conducted in the primary phase is to examine the nature of teacher scaffolding and its relationship to various aspects of pupil activity and learning. Despite the current limitations to our knowledge of how scaffolding might be applied in classroom contexts, the social constructive approach is a new and potent source of ideas for enhancing effective teaching and learning.

NEGOTIATING THE RESEARCH BRIEF

In the primary school phase of the research, the project directors met with the ten head teachers of the nursery, infant and primary schools in the area cluster. All of the schools fed some, if not most, of their children through to the secondary school which had also taken part in the research. All of the schools shared a common concern to raise the literacy achievements of pupils and to become more effective environments for the teaching of literacy. Many of the schools, in fact, had already taken part in joint in-service days and surveys focused on teaching and learning styles in relation to literacy. None of the schools were complacent about their work. A quickly-reached consensus was voiced that the cluster schools wanted to be involved in the project, and arrangements were made to visit each of the schools individually, when further details could be explored with the staff concerned.

The researchers intended to make detailed observations of typical classroom activities across the age and ability range. We were interested to record how teachers habitually used written language, different text forms, books, worksheets and other print-based resources as part of their day-to-day classroom business. We were also interested to record the nature, frequency and purpose of opportunities created or seized in the course of learning activities, which served to model, shape or explore different types of literacies. The format for these observations (see Appendices 3 and 4) was a continuous time record of two-minute intervals, as described earlier.

Data could be collected using this observation framework on the activities of two pupils and the teacher in any one class session. Pupils were selected by staff for observation on the basis of being just above or just below average ability in the class group concerned, avoiding pupils at extremes of the ability range, pupils with special problems or identified needs. Some thirty-one hours of observation were spent in seventeen different primary classrooms involving thirty-four pupils. Observations were spread across reception, infant and junior groups, including several class groups where children were vertically grouped across the ages.

We also developed a technique for taking field notes alongside the time-interval recordings. This enabled records to be cross-validated against one another and for more detailed descriptions to be made of the activities, events, resources and classroom contexts. These summaries of the course and activities of lessons we refer to as lesson scripts. Each period of primary observation took a whole morning or afternoon session. The mean time for each session was 112 minutes, ranging from 86 minutes to 148 minutes. At the end of every observation period, the researchers discussed the lesson scripts with the teacher and we were able to take into account the considerations and reflections of the teachers involved. In some instances we had also talked with pupils in the lessons observed and this added to our understanding of the nature and purpose of activities, seen through different eyes.

For the primary phase of the research an additional research instrument was devised. This was a continuous time record designed to reflect the nature, frequency and quality of the teacher's verbal interactions with children. This schedule was coded according to five categories of intervention by the teacher. Notes were made of the teacher's verbal interchanges with children and later analysed. This technique was developed to provide supplementary evidence, cross-checked with the lesson scripts, which details how dialogues are held with children in the classroom context. For the purposes of the present study, the coding and analysis of the teacher's communications reflects and extends the processes which are collectively known as scaffolding. A sample coding sheet is provided in Appendix 5.

As in the secondary phase of the research, the data collection initiated an extensive professional development programme across the school cluster. Agreements had been drawn up with the heads of the schools involved, specifying confidentiality issues, time scales for data collection, which class groups would be observed, together with arrangements for feedback and follow-up training. The observation data served to launch and underpin a programme for reflection and change in the cluster of schools as a whole.

COMPONENTS OF SCAFFOLDING

Effective tutoring – the means by which an adult or more expert individual helps a learner to solve a specific problem or cope with a task – consists partly of the adult controlling elements of the task in order that the child can

1. Recruitment and management (to task)

Gaining attention
Directing to resources
Directing behaviour
Giving personal information
Monitoring and checking
Prioritizing progress through task

2. Representation and clarification (onto task)

Adding information
Identifying problems
Exploratory questions
Procedural questions
Paraphrasing
Reminding
Modelling

3. Elaboration (in task)

Locating and weighing evidence
Feedback during task
Marking critical features
Routes: alternative ways of proceeding
Assessing need for additional support
Taking stock: revisiting nature of task
Bridging: finding analogies, parallels and links
Maintaining child in field of enquiry

4. Mediation through print/text (about task)

Selecting appropriate formats and written genres
Finding ways with words
Thinking dialogues
Strategic listening to learners' accounts
Meeting conventions

5. Finishing (after words)

Celebrating, displaying, storing, sampling
Selecting the valuable
Publishing
Convening (drawing together)
Reflecting on process and worth

Figure 4.1 Components of scaffolding

complete it successfully. However, the process of tutoring is much more powerful than simply assisting a child to finish off work set, a point recognized in the early papers on tutoring when the term 'scaffolding' was first introduced (Wood et al., 1976). Potentially, teachers can help children to achieve competence quickly, and in so doing children gain valuable insights into adult ways of proceeding and managing learning which can then be applied generally to new situations. The transactions of tutoring – how the adult steps in to demonstrate, assist, confirm, correct or direct – serve to hand over responsibility for problem-solving to the child. In Wood's (1976) terms the tutorial function 'withers away' as the child becomes more independent in adapting procedures and achieving solutions.

Effective teaching depends upon both tutor and children modifying their behaviour in the course of learning to fit the perceived requirements and responses of one another. For Vygotsky and social constructivism, the domain in which these learning transactions most effectively take place, is the hypothetical space between teacher and learner, described as the zone of proximal development, at the current limits of the child's unaided competence. The degree of contingency exercised by the teacher, which is characterized by how well the adult judges the need for assistance, what hints, suggestions and feedback to offer which move children on in their thinking, depends on two factors. One is the adult's image or idea of the problem to be tackled: the theory of the task. The second is the teacher's image of the children, their prior knowledge, experience and capabilities: the theory of the learner. These two images or theories influence how the adult sets up activities, resources and expectations, and how learning transactions are conducted. In other words, these images determine how successful the teacher's scaffolding will be.

In the data which we present later in this chapter, we shall explore how different theories or images held by teachers of tasks and learners tend to coalesce around a limited number of major constructs. The intention is to demonstrate, through the classroom evidence collected, that there are predictable consequences for learning generally, and literacy in particular, of teachers' different constructions of their role.

Recruitment and management

The first aspect of the tutoring role is how the adult gets the child to focus on one task, rather than another: drawing attention from play activity, for example, to more formal or demanding tasks. In this stage of recruitment, the adult has to be a kind of spokesperson for the task, warming and inspiring children to its relevance or interest, even if this is not immediately apparent.

Teachers often begin a new topic or activity by stopping children in what they are currently doing, and insisting on full attention to new instructions. Strategies for achieving this may be simply directive, which we have earlier described as quadrant A style mediation, high in adult control and management. Examples of this kind of attention-gaining taken from our own observations are these: 'Cross your legs please, nice straight backs ... still waiting for Adrienne to face the board'; 'I can hear a voice and I don't know why'. Teachers have a wide repertoire of recruitment tactics including humour and bathos: 'This is really, really, really hard ... 10 plus 20' (Year 6 class).

An alternative strategy which some teachers use, which is much lower in control and conveys a sense of sharing and discussion, is to arrest children's attention with a compelling piece of personal information: 'One of my children was playing with the phone and rang up Australia by mistake'; 'Every year there's an argument in our house because I want to put a star on the top of the Christmas tree and my husband wants to put an angel'; 'There was a flood past my house when I was a child which swept most of the garden away'. This sharing of personal anecdotes has the effect of drawing children quickly into the topic.

In this initial orienting of children to the task ahead, adults may direct children to the resources required or set some main priorities: 'Get all your drawings done first'; 'You can try on the witch's hat when you've finished your story'. Teachers in primary schools often spend a great deal of time preparing interesting and attractive resources pitched at appropriate levels of interest and readability. Introducing children to activities may include firm statements about where to access information and resources, what to ignore and how to prioritize: 'You won't find the answer on my face!'; 'When you've finished with a book put it back on the shelf and line up behind hairy hat man'.

Representation and clarification

A second aspect of the tutoring role consists of helping children to represent tasks in terms they understand, clarifying what they have to do and how they can proceed. This might take the form of adding useful hints or information: 'If it's got big pieces it's a floor jigsaw, if it's got little pieces it's a table jigsaw'; 'Another name for a house like that is a cottage'; 'Writing on wax they wouldn't need rubbers, they could just scrape over it and start again'. This might involve checking out or correcting misinformation: 'What's an orphan? ... Someone who writes books. No, that's an author'; 'Cushions we put on a chair, pillows on a bed'.

The teacher may set out ways of organizing the task, such as allocating children to small groups, and in many primary classrooms, a number of different activities will be proceeding in parallel over the same time period. One way of helping children to manage themselves, observed in some classrooms with children as young as four years, is to assist them to draw up some form of learning plan or lesson organizer, aimed at developing independence. Importantly at this stage, pupils come to know why they are going to pursue an activity and what they are going to achieve as the outcome.

In helping pupils to construct problems for themselves, questioning is a strategy which, when used carefully, helps to elicit important process issues: 'Why do we always turn our maps to face the same point? ... So that we always know where we are ... it's called orienteering'; 'He got ill and they gave him a thermometer ... anyone know what a thermometer does?'; 'A force is a push ... where's that force coming from ... what's pushing the plunger in the syringe?' Representation is also achieved by discussing with children what they already know about a topic area, and what they might predict will happen during the course of an enquiry. Reminders may be very useful: 'You should all be on task now'; 'Remember to tell us your news, not jokes'; 'You don't need to copy it all out again, just the bits you want to save'; 'Remember to put in your title and your date'. Teachers at this stage may model how they would tackle a problem: 'You might write something like ... "Burglar Bill picked it up, it was a bomb ..."' An important aspect of clarification is to deal with pupils' questions about how to get started and how to proceed, paraphrasing and affirming children's oral accounts and intentions: 'Yes, that's right, we will assemble all the work into a book'.

In a group setting where children may come to a task with very different starting points, competences and prior experience, differentiation is a vital component. Teachers of very young children often find multiple ways of presenting and exploring issues. With immature children ways must be found of reducing the complexity or size of a task, so that the challenge which is offered is manageable. More able individuals are extended and expected to achieve more with less assistance. Reducing or increasing the steps involved in completing tasks according to children's needs is a significant part of the representation phase.

Elaboration

In this stage of the teaching and learning process, the adult assists children to develop or adapt their concepts. This may entail fitting new information into existing conceptual frameworks, or adapting and reconstructing previous ways of thinking to accommodate new learning. For example, in one classroom observed in our study, a teacher was asked to explain the term 'landmark' in the context of some notable event in history the children were writing about. She drew attention to a church steeple, visibly prominent from the classroom windows on a hillside overlooking the school. This kind of linkage with a feature in the children's immediate environment provides a visual analogy to support their understanding. The adult draws attention to similarities and differences between ideas being worked on and other previous episodes, information or events. These serve as strategic conceptual bridges.

There are many means which teachers utilize to mark or accentuate certain features of current tasks. This highlighting of similarities and differences helps children to make appropriate analyses of tasks and to map relationships between different areas of knowledge: 'That's the same letter which starts the story "Sarah Cockles"'; 'You've drawn one leg much shorter than the other, he'll fall over won't he?'; 'What can you tell me about this word ... it's both a letter and a word?'; 'The baby just seems to be saying the main syllables and missing out the other bits: "Boglaboll"'; 'Let's look at the word "every" ... what's the last letter?' In many episodes the teacher is not just giving away solutions but locating and weighing evidence with children so that they can draw conclusions for themselves: 'What are the three vowels in Wednesday? ... so what have we got in November?'; 'Where does it say Monday? ... and what day comes after that?'

Elaboration also includes considering alternative ways of proceeding through a task: 'What you could do now is match the pictures with the text'; 'Before you go any further, what colour will you choose to show that the fields on your map have been ploughed?'; 'We could use the cut and paste facility on the photocopier but it would be in black and white'; 'Write it on your own now without the help of the lines'. Selecting learning routes and accessing sources of information often depends on well-established class routines: 'You haven't written your name so go and get your name card'; 'Find the words you need on the wall'. How and where to look may be rehearsed many times and is part of the culture of a classroom context.

In support of common processes which are frequently required and deployed in a classroom, many primary teachers display posters and hoardings, such as worked examples of number operations, rules for colour mixing, word stores, charts of vowel sounds and letter mnemonics. For very young children, clear room labelling of resources and activity areas, with simple diagrams or instructions for operating computers, listening centres and other equipment, fosters self-sufficiency in locating and accessing required resources.

In this phase of the learning process it may be necessary to revisit the nature and requirements of a task, both to keep children on the right track and give feedback to sustain their engagement. Feedback may be offered at a macro level to the whole of a class: 'What a good group ... all working away ... all got their heads down ... beautiful'; 'Just to tell you: Darren's having his name in the book for working so well'. In many instances ongoing feedback while children are immersed in a task is work specific: 'You've got as far as you can on that'. How much ongoing feedback one teacher can offer to thirty or so children depends very much on how transactions are managed.

Mediation

Mediation is defined in the present context as using literacy to work through a learning process. This is the stage at which children's learning activity is brought into juxtaposition with the written language which both organizes and represents that activity. Put simply, these are the opportunities when appropriate ways are found with words. Helping children to externalize their thinking requires reflection with children during the task. Time has to be found for listening to accounts made by children of their own learning. This kind of strategic listening to how children are pursuing their learning activities is at the core of scaffolding and constitutes the dialogue of social-constructivism: 'If you put "I went at Sarah" it sounds like you're fighting with her. You could say: "I went to Sarah"'; 'Our writing has to make sense . . . you could put "Me and Josh" but you can't put a full stop after the "and" . . . a full stop means you've finished'.

It may be a very painstaking stage for some children as they meet up with the complex conventions of written language, exploring different purposes, devices and functions. Helping children to construct written accounts of their thinking may have to proceed step by step, helping children to find ways of extending their writing, of joining words together in a sentence, and of using language vividly and accurately: 'You liked the bright colours . . . OK let's use the word "bright"'; 'The flames go up . . . can you use another word . . . "shoot up"'; 'You mean "I like" or "I lick"?'; 'It actually made you put your fingers over your ears . . . we could use that . . . when I read that I immediately get the picture'; 'We don't have big letters in the middle of words . . . you've written a great big B in the middle of "robot"'.

The stages of elaboration and mediation are, in many ways, the most difficult middle processes to organize and manage effectively. What is required of the teacher is a succession of quickly and accurately gauged interventions to keep children thinking in the field of enquiry. The Vygotskian notion of interacting with a child in the zone of proximal development has to be reworked to be applicable to teachers in large class group settings.

Finishing

We have drawn an important distinction between closing in on pupils' thinking and closing down their thinking. The final component of teachers' scaffolding of learning is concerned with drawing together children's classroom activity, reflecting on process and worth. How teachers manage these transactions determines what children believe the teacher is looking for and therefore what holds value. Finishing can be perfunctory and focused on outcomes: the amount of work completed correctly. Praise can be social and general: 'Three or four weeks ago none of you could work together like this, well done', or move beyond general niceness to become more focal and work specific, recognizing aspects of learning: 'I like the way you put all your capitals in their right place and the spaces between words'. It can also include issues to do with how the pupil set out to tackle a problem and how learning activities progressed: 'You planned to paint a picture . . . how did it work out?' Children who have their work marked without personal interaction or reference to the wider class group obviously miss opportunities for learning indirectly from the feedback given to others. Some teachers regularly review the activities of the group with the group so that successful strategies and points of interest are shared.

At this stage, teachers highlight the child's or group's achievements, taking samples to celebrate, display, store or publish. Perhaps the most elusive but potentially significant moments are those when teachers attend to aspects of a child's achievements which signal changes in understanding. In Chapter 2 we described these instances of children's learning as pivotal in the sense that once having grasped the point there can be no turning back: it becomes added to or instrumental in a greater schema. The teacher who can identify these pivotal instances and hold them out for closer inspection, offers real support for learning.

HOW PRIMARY TEACHERS USED THEIR TIME

Data derived from the observations made in the primary schools have been summarized in Table 4.1. In almost all cases there was a distinct preference for teachers to find time to work in partnership with children, with approximately half the available lesson time allocated in this way. There were no teachers, in fact, who did not work collaboratively with some children, for some of the sessions observed. The nature of teachers' visiting of pupils and the character of their interventions varied between age groups and from one classroom to another. Details of the precise patterning of adult–child encounters we shall examine later in this chapter when we consider the lesson scripts and teacher scaffolding.

Characteristic of primary teachers in this study was for major portions of time to be given over to managing children, often instructing them as whole groups. Teachers paid a lot of attention to setting tasks and organizing working groups, to noise levels and movement around the room, to resources and pupils' conduct. In some classrooms teachers had deliberately set

Table 4.1 Teacher time in four quadrants across primary classrooms

Quadrant	Teacher time (mean mins per session)	s. d.	Minimum	Maximum
A	37.65	14.17	16	62
B	12.94	15.10	0	56
C	4.71	5.74	0	16
D	56.94	20.77	10	92

Note: Classrooms/teachers observed = 17; Mean time per session = 112 minutes; Range 86–148 minutes

themselves the goal of sorting out the behaviour of a class, such as lining children up in straight lines, entering and exiting rooms quietly, sitting still and working independently. These goals were sometimes made explicit in classroom charters pinned to the wall, so that pupils knew what they might be rewarded or punished for. In other class groups, behaviour was not tackled separately from the issue of pupils' learning activities. In these instances teachers channelled and shaped children's responses through specific, work-focused goals, such as how many items of an exercise the child was expected to complete within a given time scale, with the consequences clearly identified.

The amount of time taken up by teacher instruction, information-giving, questioning and task-setting, increased as a function of the year group. Teachers of Years 5 and 6 spent an average 49 minutes in quadrant A type teaching activities, compared with 32 minutes for teachers of years 3 and 4 (1-way Anova, $F(2,27) = 4.587$ p < 0.01). Similarly, there was a trend (though this did not reach levels of significance) for teachers of reception and infant classes to work more collaboratively with children (mean time in quadrant D $= 58.28$ minutes, s. d. $= 15.97$) than they did with older pupils in Years 5 and 6 (mean time in quadrant D $= 44.5$ minutes, s. d. $= 7.76$). It was not typical for teachers to occupy pupils with work schemes, exercises or resources, without engaging with them in some form of interactive dialogue (mean time in quadrant B $= 12.94$ minutes, s. d. $= 15.10$). Least frequent of all were those occasions when children were given time or space to pursue their own interests, with little adult structure, guidance or monitoring (mean time in quadrant C $= 4.71$ minutes, s. d. $= 5.74$).

These data complement the findings from the secondary school phase of the research project reported in Chapter five. Secondary teachers, like their primary colleagues, spent relatively high proportions of their time on management issues and didactic modes of teaching, with an emphasis on giving instructions, questioning and handing over information. Many second-ary teachers also said they would prefer to work in a participative way with pupils, emphasizing the importance of adult assistance, conferencing and interaction. Just as in the primary contexts, secondary teachers tended not to base their teaching on child-centred approaches or occupier resources, although this varied somewhat between departments.

HOW CHILDREN SPEND THEIR TIME IN PRIMARY CLASSROOMS

We might expect that in a typical primary classroom, where teachers spend a lot of their time giving instructions and managing pupils, that this would be reflected by children sitting to attention, being directed through prescribed teaching steps, drilled with information and rote content, in the absence of context, negotiation or interaction. In fact, children were rarely exposed to this kind of training or instructional regime. Mostly, our primary data show, teachers talked over a textbook, worksheet, or other prepared stimulus, whilst pupils watched, followed or proceeded with the tasks set. For the greater part of the time children worked individually, although they might be sat in groups, with minimal ongoing guidance on their exercises and assignments, whilst the teacher visited selected children briefly to monitor progress.

The data collated in Table 4.2 show that in an average session of just under two hours, more than half of the time (76.82 minutes) was taken up with what we have described as occupier-type activities. Averaging the times observed for the thirty-four children in the study, shows that some twenty-five minutes were spent listening, watching or following resources, such as video recording, audio tapes, worksheets and a wide range of text forms. A mean of thirty minutes was recorded when pupils were working unassisted on exercises such as illustrating a book cover, cutting out silhouettes, filling in speech bubbles, using a thesaurus or dictionary, completing vowel sound or phonics practice sheets. Many of these activities required some reading or writing, but of a fragmentary and restricted kind. It has often been said that most workbook-style prepared materials in use in primary classes are limited in challenge because they provide most of the context, information, format and vocabulary, for their completion.

Much smaller overall periods of time – just over eighteen minutes – were spent by children question-raising, pursuing their own research or personal interests, for example, as part of topic work time. Similarly, the average amount of time spent per lesson when pupils were working collaboratively with other pupils or adults, was no more than about fifteen minutes. Overall, children were observed off-task or hovering, looking busy but not really engaged in anything, for an average of seventeen minutes per session. In some classes, observed children were always on task. In other groups, much larger periods of time were observed when pupils evaded purposeful activity.

The nature and frequency of pupil engagement in primary classrooms varied as a function of age group. For example, children were much more

Table 4.2 Pupil time in four quadrants across primary classrooms

Quadrant	Pupil time (mean mins per session)	s. d.	Minimum	Maximum
A	1.76	3.10	0	10
B	76.82	26.69	20	130
C	18.35	12.41	0	48
D	15.29	13.00	0	50

Note: Children observed = 34; Total pupil observation time = 62 hours; Mean time per session = 112 minutes; Range 86–148 minutes

likely to be exposed to didactic, highly adult-managed forms of teaching, with an emphasis on drill and repetition, as they moved through the school (1-way Anova, $F(2, 27) = 3.5029$, $p < 0.05$). Conversely, collaborative activities were a much more predominant feature of early years' classrooms, than Years 3 to 6 (1-way Anova, $F(2, 27) = 10.05$, $p < 0.001$). On average, the child in an infant class might have spent some twenty minutes in total of a morning or afternoon session working with an adult, albeit in small interludes. This diminished to less than two minutes on average, in Year 6. Of all the year groups observed, children in reception and infant classes were less likely to be off-task (1-way Anova, $F(2, 27) = 4.4426$, $p < 0.05$). These contrasts between year groups no doubt reflect how teachers of younger children pace and organize their lessons, with more variation and differentiation of activities, and the greater availability of adults and assistants.

Analysis of both teacher and pupil data indicates clear associations between certain teacher strategies and pupil behaviour. Children were more likely to be off-task in lessons where they were expected to work unassisted for long periods of time with low levels of interaction ($r = 0.3582$, $p < 0.05$). More sustained literacy activities, such as generating writing, occurred in lessons where children were permitted to investigate and research their own topics for some of the time ($r = 0.5140$, $p < 0.001$). On the other hand, more formal, didactic teacher moves were not significantly associated with more sustained reading or writing, or for pupils being on-task, than collaborative or child-centred approaches.

TIME SPENT READING OR WRITING IN PRIMARY CLASSROOMS

Several observation categories in the research were focused specifically on aspects of reading, writing and critical reflection upon text. The primary classrooms in the study could all be considered to be print-rich environments. Teachers generally took great care to display reference and reading books, to label resources and equipment, to provide word banks and vocabulary charts with technical terms to signpost areas for listening, computers or writing, and to exhibit work in process or the fruits of pupils' enquiries. Many of the activities of the primary classroom brought children into contact with print, in some shape or form. The variety of these text contacts is richly documented in the lesson scripts which follow, particularly for younger children.

However, we wished to document a number of important aspects of literacy experience and use which constitute critical classroom practice for children, and which, in their absence, it is hard to see how children can make progress towards becoming proficient readers or writers. These include periods of time when children are actively constructing their own meaning from a written text, and periods when children are actively generating their own writing for a specific purpose. We were also interested to know how many opportunities were designed for reflective reading, and the drafting and remaking of written accounts with the assistance of adults.

We need to make clear that we draw a distinction between *transcription*, secretarial writing where children are simply transferring or copying text and its superficial features, and *composition*, where children are responsible for generating and assembling the components of a text (see Smith, 1982, for further discussion of this distinction). In reading, we distinguish between *passive engagement*, such as children following a text as it is being read over by an adult, and *active engagement*, when children control and assemble the making of meaning from a given text (see Meek, 1991, for a consideration of these issues).

We have argued throughout this book that literacy has a very powerful capacity, in all areas of the curriculum and for all children, to foster learning: to help children organize, represent, analyse, record and communicate their thinking. An important part of the role of the primary school, in many people's eyes, is to prepare children for the more complex demands of the increasingly subject-orientated curriculum of the secondary school. However, data from several previous studies (Galton et al., 1980; Lunzer and Gardner, 1979) suggest that pupils in both primary and secondary schools, spend only a minority of their time engaged with writing or reading processes, with a general 'retreat from print' from the age of 9 or 10 years onwards. Findings from our own studies of a secondary school show that pupils were not given many openings to read or write, or to look critically upon their reading or writing with adults or peers, as a regular and integral part of the teaching and learning process.

All of these previous findings find few points of contradiction in the data collated for the primary cluster. There were no significant differences by year group, in the time children spent in sustained reading or the generation of writing. Across the primary classrooms observed, a mean time of 2 minutes was recorded out of a mean session length of 112 minutes, dedicated to generating writing, with a range of 0 to 36 minutes. Similarly, time dedicated to reading engagement amounted to a mean time of 4 minutes, with a range of 0 to 26 minutes.

In reception and infant classes we would not expect all children to be mature or competent enough to read or write independently and for sustained periods of time. Lessons scripts denote a wide range of literacy-related activities where attention was being drawn to the structural components of written language, such as letter shapes, handwriting, vowel sounds, spelling, vocabulary, forms of expression and the conventions of print. However, expectations that older primary-age children would be more frequently engaged in independent reading or writing, or working on more advanced reading and writing processes for more of the time, were not in fact met. One other question which we shall raise later in this chapter when we consider the lesson scripts in more detail, concerns how far it is the primary teacher's responsibility to introduce children to the specific literacies of different subject specialisms, in preparation for the secondary school phase.

LESSON SCRIPTS

In this section we examine in more detail, samples of the observational data recorded in contrasting classrooms across the primary cluster. The lesson scripts should be read as case studies which illuminate how aspects of language and literacy are brought into use in different classroom contexts.

In each example, the data have been summarized according to the time frame of one hour of a teaching session, highlighting and selecting details of how the teacher and two pupils were occupied over two-minute intervals. We have coded the information according to the four-quadrant observation framework, together with the use made of literacy within each observed period of teaching. We have tried to illustrate the rich texture of the primary teacher's work, giving some indication of how the teacher introduced and set tasks, organized resources and materials, and what the children proceeded to do in response.

In each of the scripts we have tried to identify the consequences of certain patterns of teaching, and to establish under which social-interactive conditions of teaching and learning children move towards more adult forms of problem-solving, and behave more like adult readers and writers. Inevitably, given the emphasis we have placed on the making of dialogues around children's reading or writing, we shall pay close attention to the steps taken by teachers as they scaffold their interactions with individual pupils and groups. The teacher profiles and their associated characteristic ways of working, together with the implications of organizing learning in one way as opposed to another, formed the basis of subsequent in-service sessions with teachers from the cluster schools involved.

Year 3 script

Just after bonfire night, this Year 3 class were drawing pictures and making accounts of their firework parties. The children were grouped informally and moved around freely to retrieve wax crayons, erasers and spelling books. The teacher directed the activities from his desk at the front of the class, where he was also hearing children read from their reading books, occasionally visiting individuals around the room to check on progress, give advice and encouragement. Children also queued at the teacher's desk for assistance. The classroom had well-stocked displays of fiction and reference sources, clearly labelled storage and equipment areas, with a rich display of children's work from previous topics, such as an autumn leaf installation across one wall with colour poems.

The lesson coding shows the first forty minutes or so of an afternoon session. For some children this was a very interactive session, and almost all of the teacher's time was spent in brief exchanges with individuals about their work. Many of these fleeting contacts were instructional, aimed at keeping children on task: 'You know what you're doing? ... that's a good picture, now

The lesson scripts presented in Chapters 4 and 5 are derived from data collected during lesson observations. The teacher (T) and two pupils (P1 and P2) were tracked through each lesson, using the lesson observation formats described in Chapter 3.

In the centre of a person's script, we have given a brief *summary* (derived from field notes) of what each was observed doing over two-minute intervals. The code square to the **left** of the summary represents the *type of interaction* in which the person was involved; the square to the **right** represents the type of *literacy* use observed. Each square is given one of four shadings, representing the quadrants described in Figure 2.1.

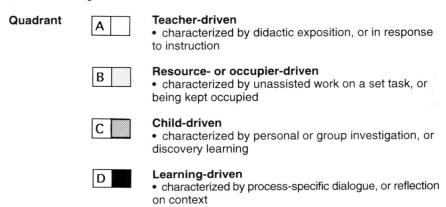

Quadrant

Teacher-driven
• characterized by didactic exposition, or in response to instruction

Resource- or occupier-driven
• characterized by unassisted work on a set task, or being kept occupied

Child-driven
• characterized by personal or group investigation, or discovery learning

Learning-driven
• characterized by process-specific dialogue, or reflection on context

Figure 4.2 Keys to coding of lesson scripts

we want writing.' Throughout the session there were many good examples, in scaffolding terms, of recruitment and maintenance through direction: 'Speed it up a little ... all I see there is rubbing out and no work ... colour that in green.' A table of boys was rebuked for being noisy and one child was asked to sit on the floor by the teacher's chair. On occasions instructions were given to the whole group as they worked: 'If you're doing the fireworks they need to be big ... the secret with these wax crayons is you've got to press hard.'

Many of the teacher's questions helped individuals to find information and to think over the problem ahead: 'What are the main things about bonfire night? ... how did it make you feel?', 'Do you think you might find the words you need in your wordbook?' Whilst children were engaged in their activities, the teacher interposed ideas and alternative ways of proceeding: 'You could try using more reddy/orangey colours.' However, the most frequent of the teacher's moves were geared to finding or affirming interesting things for children to write from their oral accounts. On the other hand, very few comments were given back to the children who were being heard reading at the teacher's desk. This was much more of a monitoring exercise than a

Literacy is described in terms of the quality of interaction in which its practices are generated, by the same system of shading. Literacy is defined either through listening, talking, reading or writing; since both verbal and textual practices are found in the learning context.

Although these four modes of language use underlie the curriculum for English, our *interactive* definition shows clearly that opportunities for learning through literacy arise in all classrooms and all subject areas.

LISTENING...	
to exposition or instruction	L
as audience to a reading, or viewing	L
as a respondent in a peer discussion	L
as a partner within a process dialogue	L
TALKING...	
to direct, order, manage, instruct	T
as an implicit task requirement	T
to discuss and explore	T
about reading and writing processes	T
READING...	
under direction or out loud	R
following another's reading	R
for personal or exploratory purposes	R
to learn about reading processes	R
WRITING...	
to copy or shift print	W
unassisted on a set task	W
to explore and generate ideas	W
to redraft text and review process	W

collaborative reading interchange. Although the teacher occasionally provided words for children when they got stuck, there were few instances of support to children to decode words for themselves, to discuss or reflect on their reading book stories.

In terms of the scaffolding process, we have highlighted the stage of transforming children's oral ideas into writing, as mediation through text: assisting children to generate, select and then draft out their work, using appropriate conventions: 'The flames go up ... can you use another word? ... shoot up ... did they go high? ... into the what? ... we could use that ... now when I read that I immediately get the picture'; 'Where are the finger spaces between your words?'; 'Let's think about the sparklers ... who lit them? ... exploding rockets? ... yes that's a goody ... do you want to use that?'; 'There's a "magic e" word ... you should have got that'; 'I saw bright colours

YEAR 3 TEACHER (M)

mins	Activity	Code
0	Visiting groups	T
	Queue of pupils at desk	T
	Directing from desk	T
	Working on individual scripts	W
	Assessing, correcting, advising	W
10	Stays at desk, marking	W
	Shouts at some noisy boys	T
	One-on-one assistance	W
	Marking description of bonfire	W
	Six pupils in queue	W
20	Seven pupils in queue	W
	Disciplines and moves boy	T
	Continues one-on-one	W
	Seven pupils in queue	W

PUPIL 1 (F)

mins	Activity	Code
0	Completes illus./ writes 'on bonf'	W
	Talks to me about her writing	W
	Gets out home reader	T
	Goes to get spelling book	
10	Gets out home reader	R
	Off task	ot
	Shows me credits in writing book	T
	Continues writing	W
	Helps friend with spelling	W
20	Off task/ chatting	ot
	Off task/ writing on rubber	at
	Teaches boy about vowel sounds	W
	Discovers idea for story	W
	Asks me to spell 'loud'	W

PUPIL 2 (M)

mins	Activity	Code
0	Visited by teacher	T
	Drawing story illustration	W
	Copies opening sentence	W
	Copying from board	W
	Helping friend/ queues	T
10	Queuing	ot
	Queuing	ot
	Queuing	ot
	Sees teacher/ returns and writes	T
	Queuing/ thinks better of it	ot
	Off-task/ playing with bag	ot
20	Queuing	ot
	Queuing	ot
	Queuing	ot
	Queuing	ot

	Code	Activity
	W	Ten pupils in queue
	R	Listens to individual readers
	R	Ten pupils queuing
	R	Reading with single pupil
	R	Reading/ deals with one writer
40	T	Tells off reader
	R	15+ pupils around desk

	Code	Activity
30	ot	Queuing
	ot	Queuing
	W	Gives up queuing/ writing
	W	Writing
	ot	Queues for spelling
40	ot	Queuing
	ot	Queuing

	Code	Activity
30	ot	Queuing
	ot	Queuing
	ot	Queuing
	ot	Queuing
	W	Teacher spells 'shooting'/ writes
40	T	Looks at friend's work
	ot	Queuing

Figure 4.3 Sample of Year 3 script

in the Catherine wheel . . . write that for me.' Much less time was spent in this session on finishing: reflecting on the lesson or the work that was completed, although one or two individuals were given feedback: 'That's colourful . . . I like that'; 'You've really got the hang of these fireworks . . . what a clever boy.'

The coding of the lesson script also gives an indication of how two children spent their time, in parallel with the teacher. From the perspective of these two pupils, despite the energy expended by the teacher throughout the lesson on keeping a number of activities going, much of these two individuals' time was wasted. Both the girl and the boy worked in short bursts and were frequently distracted, often by other children who were working alongside. Only the boy was visited briefly at the outset of the lesson, whilst more than half of his time was spent queuing for spellings or to check that his ideas for what to write were acceptable. In establishing a culture of authority and control, the teacher had also created a high degree of dependency in the children. In managing the class from his desk, the teacher ended up being visited continually by large numbers of children for help.

In terms of literacy, several of the children in this class were given assistance to reflect on their experience, and to turn their recalled mental images into words. The teacher helped to sift and filter these ideas to find things worth communicating to others. What the teacher liked and valued was made clear, so that the children had a sense of the kind of language and expression which could be turned acceptably into print. The proper conventions of writing were also introduced, corrected and affirmed, as the children found ways of transforming their ideas into print: 'You mean "I like" not "I lick"'?; 'What letter does "screaming" begin with?'; 'The fireworks is noisy . . . what's wrong with that?'.

The teacher's weighing of children's ideas ('That's a goody . . . you can use that') is an example of how, in the daily landscape of the curriculum, children are gradually exposed to the teacher's own concepts and attitudes about the nature of the writing task. In other words, the children's writing is gradually shaped by the culture of the classrooms in which they participate.

Interestingly, within this teacher's classroom organization, there were few occasions when the content or outcomes of these micro-dialogues were shared around the wider group. The teacher's choice of allowing children to visit him for information, advice and feedback, meant that many children were unable to proceed without his dispensations. To queue, de facto, is to be disengaged and off-task. More frequent visiting of individuals, working at individual work stations, and the communal sharing of ideas and critical commentary, would have exposed many more children to the process of turning ideas into writing.

Year 4/5 script

In this Friday afternoon session, a Year 4/5 group were finishing off activities which they had been occupied with during the week, including making cartoon strips with cut out sticky shapes and speech bubbles, writing stories about discovering and exploring caves, colouring a maths work sheet according to a number code, and creating Egyptian tomb decorations using hieroglyphics. Pupils were grouped informally but worked mostly alone. The teacher worked intensively for much of the time with one boy who needed a great deal of help to write, but moved around the room from time to time to give instructions or feedback. A classroom assistant was also available for part of the session to keep this range of diverse activities going.

The coding for the teacher shows some time given over to explaining and exploring issues with selected pupils, but the greatest proportion of time was spent collaboratively, in this case offering one-to-one support. Whilst engaged with this individual, the teacher also held brief satellite conversations with other children as they visited her for advice or commentary. Coding for the two observed pupils indicates that both were mostly on task, interspersing writing activities with talking and reading, although neither had any extended interchanges with the teacher.

Analysis of the teacher's dialogue reveals a wide range of scaffolding functions. As in most of the other primary classrooms observed, scaffolding took the form of a rich texture, with the teacher's moves responding contingently to meet children's needs as they arose. Scaffolding did not occur sequentially, as though moving through a series of steps or stages. For example, recruitment and maintenance of children took place throughout the session, in response to perceived levels of concentration and application: 'Okay, working quietly now'; 'I'm going to put the timer on your work now'; 'I'm getting a chair and then I'm going to get it out of you somehow'.

As the nature of the exercise was being set out, affirmed or interpreted, the teacher rephrased the task, established that the key vocabulary was comprehended, and posed questions which led the child into the problem. We have described this aspect of scaffolding as representation and clarification because the child is helped to take responsibility for the task in terms which are personally meaningful. Rather than reducing the complexity of the problem or handing over ready-made solutions, the teacher finds ways of helping the child to manage, although the process may be a fairly painstaking one: 'You know what you want to say but you're having trouble with the writing . . . get it straight in your head first and then I'll help you set it down'; 'You have got to talk about things that make you sad or jealous . . . what does jealous mean? . . . and how would I know when you're happy, what would your face look like?'; 'So what did you do when you found the cave . . . come on, the suspense is killing me . . . I want to know what happened'.

Some of the teacher's dialogue serves the function of taking stock, weighing what the child has begun to do and how to proceed, perhaps

Classroom observation chart — Year 4/5

YEAR 4/5 TEACHER (F)	Code
mins 0	
Register/ 'Good afternoon'	T
Instructs class to finish off tasks	T
Sorts out desks and groups	T
Monitoring	T
Explains what cartoon strips do	T
10	
Checks each group	T
Sits with one pupil	T
Dirty chair: goes to clean stain	
One-on-one assistance: detailed	T
explanation to support writer	T
20	
Stays with pupil, advises table	T
Gets writer to explain what he	T
is doing, planning each step	T
Asks for general quiet	T
Picking out gaps in spelling	W

PUPIL 1 (F)	L / Code
mins 0	
Brings picture: asked to finish it	T
Talking to friend/ sees Ms.	T (ot)
Changes activity> reading corner	T
Blank A3 and coloured hexagons	
Cutting out shapes	
Gridlines on A3	W
Starts strip cartoon with shapes	W
Writing speech bubble	W
Shows Ms./ settles down again	T
'This is Cinderella and she works	T
from morning to night...'	T

PUPIL 2 (M)	L / Code
mins 0	
Drawing at table: filling in	W
sum picture	W
Multiplying quietly & marking	W
different areas to be shaded	W
Goes to get felt tips	W
Head on arm and colouring in	W
Very absorbed and detached	W
Continues	W
Talks to assistant	T
20	
Momentarily off-task	T (ot)
Moved on to quieter table	
Wanders round collecting books	(ot)
Shows work to teacher	T

	Continues one-on-one support	T
	Pupils begin to visit	T
	Individual conversations	T
	Advice and appraisal	T
	Satellite conversations: quickly	T
	responding to needs> shifting on	T
	Reviewing with individual	W
	Helping writer to finish piece	W
	Stop and listen	T

30		Planning discussion with 2 girls	T
		Cuts out Fairy godmother	
		Cuts out ballgown	
		Cuts out Two Ugly Sisters	
		We talk: the 'patches' are boots!	T
40		More writing in speech bubbles	W
		Another girl starts 'The 3 Bears'	W
		Collaborative work	W
		Stops working to listen	L

30		Colouring in	W
		Half on task: helper at table	W
		Adding and colouring	W
		Helping another pupil/same task	T
		Returns to chair/colouring in	W
40	ot	Pops out of chair/returns	
		Colouring in and finishing	W
		Finishing off	W
		Stops working to listen	L

Figure 4.4 Sample of Year 4/5 script

modelling what the adult might do next. In these terms, scaffolding is a form of elaboration of the task, checking out its boundaries, adding detail and signposts: 'That's your cave entrance ... I'd like you to put something else around here so I can see clearly what it is ... this is very exciting ... you could say something about who you followed ... remember we want to know what you saw in there.'

Perhaps the most critical aspect of this teacher's scaffolding, for the child with literacy difficulties, is the point where the child's ideas are constructed in writing. In the lesson observed, the teacher's mediation centred around conventions of handwriting, spelling, punctuation, including where to find information and the consequences of treating words and sentences in one way compared with another: 'Going left into the cave ... "going" will be in your wordbook, find the page with "l" on ... "l-e-f-t" ... Yes, good boy, well done ... do you think we should have a full stop, otherwise we'll run out of breath? ... "other" ... no that's "over" ... "th" instead of "v" ... "train"? ... you need an "i" between the "a" and "n" otherwise it's "tran" ... cross the "t" and dot the "i" ... "walk" you've made harder than it is: only four letters'.

The scaffolding moves which select the valuable and draw attention to positive and weak aspects of a piece of work or aspects of the lesson as a whole, also occurred throughout the session. Here the teacher's concern was to fix those learning issues which had moved on in the group or individual's repertoire: 'Three or four weeks ago none of you could get all your capital letters and full stops right ... now you can.' In terms of literacy, almost all of the dialogues which were held around pupils' writing, were concerned with the structural components of personal narrative.

Year 1 script

In this lesson, a Year 1 infant class were completing follow-up work to the story which they had shared earlier: Jill Murphy's *Whatever Next!* In total the session lasted almost two hours (see Appendices 6 and 7 for the full lesson script). What propelled the session was a series of carefully organized activities around a central theme. The children had watched a television programme based on *Whatever Next!*, when the story had been read as a voice-over to the illustrations from the book. Part of the programme was interactive, highlighting 'r' words from the story using a magic pencil, such as 'rocket', and requiring the children to finger-write letters in the air. Subsequently, children examined pages from the book itself, found other words in the dictionary beginning with 'r', and were shown flashcards with 'r' words and other vocabulary from the story. Worksheets had been produced using the main characters from the book, requiring words such as 'robot' to be transferred as labels to the pictures. There was also a row of dotted 'r's for practising letter formation, and a cloze exercise with words provided to fill in the blanks. Some children wrote words on star shapes which were then strung behind model rockets. Whilst one group designed rockets on the backs of their worksheets, others made rocket models from cardboard tubes. Given the opportunity for free play with construction toys, other children chose to build yet more rockets.

All of the children moved in and out of a number of representations of aspects of the story using different media. The coding of the teacher's interactions with the group demonstrates a careful attention to constructing learning with individuals and small clusters of children, moving children's thinking along in a variety of ways. The extract begins at the point where the teacher outlined to the whole class, working in groups, what activities should be pursued, following the television programme. She showed how to fix the stars to rockets, each star bearing an 'r' word. The words 'ramp', 'rabbit', 'reindeer', 'red', 'rocket' and 'roundabout' were written up on a flip chart. The teacher drew attention to significant features of some of the words, exposing similarities and differences, and words within words: 'See a little word at the end of rabbit?'; 'What's the first letter of reindeer? ... it does sound like rainbow, but it's got an "e"'; 'If you do your words before you do your rockets you won't get glue all over the place'. At this point the teacher moved over to another group who were thinking about the sounds which fireworks make, using picture stimuli: 'What do you think that one says ... cr..cr..crackle!'; 'Oh that's very good ... what's that letter and noise? ... bbb – what's next? ... ang!'

This extract also illustrates the rich texture of the teacher's scaffolding, with quick strategic shifts between managing or recruiting children to tasks, asking questions and adding information to clarify issues, elaborating learning routes, and celebrating the valuable: 'Wash your face for me and hang up your pinny ... Do you know what a rat is? ... Like a mouse only bigger ... Excuse me please I'm talking to Hayley ... You don't say "me need the loo" you say "I need" ... Could you put a few more words on the back of there please? ... Damien you could use glue to put that on ... What does "butterfly" start with? ... Yes "Bouncy Ben!" ... Tracy that's beautiful ... can you hurry? ... No, sweetheart, you need some string.'

Important, in terms of literacy experience and development, were those frequent occasions when the teacher brought the children's activities into contact with appropriate spoken language and print formats: '*Whatever Next!* ... there's something on the end of that word ... How come the rain is coming through the holes? ... It's not a real helmet! ... Does anyone know what a sieve does? ... What's another word for that?' The teacher responded to some children's oral accounts with feedback about standard syntax, requesting a repetition: 'Jane, it's not "where to is", it's "where is the string" ... can you say that please?' Predominantly, dialogue centres around the literate conventions which the children are grasping at in the context of their assignments: 'Sand on my ... begins with "b" ... b-o-d ... body ... body ... Let's go back over that ... How many letters can you see? ... You've written that upside down, but altogether it's pretty good.'

YEAR 1 TEACHER (F)

Code	Activity	mins
T	demonstrates making a rocket	0
T	'r' sound: word-starts & ends	
W	r-words written: ramp, rocket	
T	task order/advises, suggests	
T	soundscape for drawn image	
T	collects together other group	10
T	working with individuals	
R	predicting & shaping process	
T	assessing/suggesting	
T	standardizing spoken syntax	
R	predicting/cuing/sounding	20
R	letter-word building/managing	
T	empathizing/inquiring/defusing	
T	ordering speech turns/feedback	
T	standardizing syntax/checking	30
W	modelling/familiarizing	
T	comparing/advising/grouping	
T	intervening/demonstrating	
T	redirecting/founding idea	
W	spelling/organizing/comparing	

PUPIL 1 (F)

Code	Activity	mins
L	sat in front of teacher, listening	0
T	rehearses, copying teacher	
W	watching, finger-tracing writing	
	collects stars made in morning	
W	writes ' my star' on paper slip	
R	sticks label on star, looks at list	10
	cuts out 'yellow' from list	
W	writes name on label for star	
	finds piece of cardboard tube	
	constructing rocket	
T	'Miss, can I cut my paper out?'	20
	cutting out wing shapes	
	cutting out	
W	helping neighbour with label	
T	visited by teacher, needs glue	
	resumes work on rocket	30
	sticking wings on	
	sticking down tail fin	
	colouring rocket in felt tip	
	finishes quickly	

PUPIL 2 (M)

mins	Activity	Code
0	at table, joining in talk	T
	sounding out 'rabbit'	R
	draws roundabout on paper	W
	copies 'roundabout'/leaves aside	
	goes to find star	
10	finishes colouring it yellow	
	writes 'star' on label	W
	sticks label to star	
	cuts out square for making tube	
	won't stick/gets sellotape	
20	tapes tube... ends up with cone	
	takes tape off, paper tears	
	watches other activity in group	
	asks pupil 1 to help spell 'rocket'	L
30	writes label, cuts it out	T
	looks at how partner built hers	W
	finds length of cardboard tube	
	gets scissors/talks to partner	
	draws wing shapes on tube	T
	starts working alone	

Figure 4.5 Sample of Year 1 script

Panel 1

Scale	Tactic	Code
40	suggesting tactic	T
	keeping/owning through words	T
	contextualizing/affirming	R
	querying convention/prompting	W
	retracking/modelling/causality	T
50	sound-spell check/reconsidering	W
	praising/summative affirmation	T
	workplace process/name-keeps	T
	reflective & conditional prompts	T
60	labelling/recalling process	T

Panel 2

Scale	Action	Code
40	moves to writing corner	
	reads prompt sheet with helper:	R
	'Today we made....' thinks/talks	T
	through last activity/ reflects	T
	starts writing/helper moves	W
50	continues prompt: a star and...	W
	a r (looks to flipchart) ocket	W
	reads through/continues	W
	the star is/goes off	W
60	(copies) yellow/finishes/moves	W

Panel 3

Action	Code
cuts tube to better length	
cuts notches in end of tube	
cuts out triangle, tries out as fin	
cuts a bigger triangle	
fixes tail-fin/colours rocket	
uses base of can to draw circle	
cuts out circle	
colours circle red/gets glue	
sticks circle on end of rocket	
shows teacher/finds label	T

SCAFFOLDING AND THE CULTURE OF PRIMARY CLASSROOMS

It has been claimed that classroom tasks form the critical link between the teacher and the child (Bennett et al., 1984). Obviously, some of the variability in children's learning in any classroom context is accounted for by the nature, relevance and pitch of tasks. The differentiation of tasks to meet the individual needs of learners is an important component of any attempt to increase the access of all children to the curriculum. However, data from the lesson scripts show that a common task can be mediated in different ways by different teachers and for different pupils, even within groups in the same class. Study of tasks which pupils are set is insufficient to determine how well, or what, children learn. Rather than tasks, it is the nature of scaffolding which mediates understanding, and which must be considered as the critical link between teacher and child.

Teachers are used to thinking of their work in task terms. At the point where tasks are set up and presented to pupils, some teachers explore how to proceed through it, for example, as a series of investigative steps. Much less frequently, teachers focus on the learning issues involved, specifying appropriate ways of developing an understanding. Scaffolding is the complex set of interactions which shape and promote children's thinking through a task. Effective scaffolding focuses on the *working minds* of children, rather than the nature of the work in hand.

In order to be good at scaffolding teachers must develop a precise knowledge of the characteristics of learners and their starting points in terms of experience and understanding. This is just as important as a thorough knowledge of the field of enquiry. Earlier we described these elements in terms of the teacher's theory of the child and theory of the task. In our research into patterns of teacher–pupil interaction in the primary classroom, scaffolding is instantiated in forms of dialogue.

Scaffolding is not a linear or sequential process. The lesson scripts demonstrate that scaffolding is often recursive and that aspects of the scaffolding process, such as recruitment or elaboration, may overlap. Put simply, we observed teachers engaged in multi-faceted acts of discussion and elicitation, attempting to scaffold various children in different ways. In many instances, scaffolding is an intimate event, confined to an individual's enquiry. However, there are occasions when collective events are shared, as the teacher holds out a critical issue for group inspection, such as an invitation for a class group to reflect on one child's achievement in a writing task.

The zone of proximal development – the hypothetical space between adult and child, within which scaffolding takes place – requires reinterpretation in the context of a primary classroom. One might be forgiven for conceptualizing a zone as a singular place and a uniform act which describes all adult–child interactions in general terms. We would suggest that, when observing classsrooms in detail, and contrary to the general view, there is little evidence of either one zone, or one uniform type of interaction. Pupils and teachers do not enter a zone, collaborate, and then leave; they construct multiple zones with different levels of proximation, or closeness. For example, a teacher may be attending to a reader at her elbow and involved in dialogue with that pupil, whilst becoming aware of the needs of another pupil at the other side of the classroom. The reader continues his dialogue, whilst the teacher addresses, or *closes in on* the needs of the more distant pupil. What in spatial terms still seems peripheral, has fleetingly become central: another zone of development is being opened.

Zones of proximal development are best thought of as overlapping or intersecting networks of working minds, sharing an enquiry situated in a communal, social context. The concrete, spatial or territorial images evoked by the word 'zone' are misleading.

THE TRANSITION FROM PRIMARY TO SECONDARY SCHOOL

One important aspect of our literacy research, rarely examined hitherto, is the relationship between children's experience of teaching and learning in separate phases of schooling, and how children cope with this transition. One of the questions we set out to examine in the study was how primary teachers prepared children to meet the forthcoming literacy demands of the secondary curriculum, or, conversely, how secondary teachers took account of children's literacy competence as they entered the more subject-orientated curriculum.

Whereas we observed, in both primary and secondary classrooms, a range of opportunities for using literacy in order to sustain different modes of enquiry, there were few examples of consensus over the purpose and relevance of literacy, and how best to recognize or promote literacy development in the context of the classroom. In consequence, there was no identifiable system which enabled teachers to discuss literacy, to reach a common agenda, to rehearse alternative strategies for individual needs, to set goals for different Key Stages, and to evaluate children's progress. Teachers in the main, do not have a language for thinking about literacy as a dialogue of minds.

One of the transitional hurdles for children moving between primary and secondary schools, is the change in patterns of interaction between pupils, teachers and tasks. Primary children often experience, as our lesson scripts show, highly interactive learning contexts in which scaffolding is prominent. Primary teachers build learning around a detailed knowledge of learners and tasks, frequently constructing and matching a range of learning opportunities around a conceptual centre. In the secondary school data, which we present in the chapter which follows, what drives teaching is often a need to fulfil the content demands of the subject.

An important question addressed in this research is how well one phase of schooling prepares children for, or builds on, another. All children face a culture shock which is inherent in the contrasting size, organization, expectations and curriculum focus, as they move between school phases. We have argued throughout this book, that aspects of literacy cannot be studied in isolation from the social and institutional contexts which nurture and define them. Children are generally not prepared by primary schools for the changes ahead. These include the shift from close, and various, encounters where individual needs are sometimes understood, to loosely coupled learning experiences, where secondary teachers are largely preoccupied with delivering their subject contents. At primary school, literacy, learning and the classroom context often form a composite; in the secondary school they become parted for the first time and allocated priorities. Literacy shifts from a privileged to a peripheral position across schooling.

In many primary classrooms, building literacy competence is seen as an important aspect of all activities; whereas the diversification of subjects and teachers at secondary level leads to general expectations that pupils already possess such competences, or that the responsibility for this basic provision rests elsewhere. Primary teachers seem to draw literacy out through their teaching, particularly with younger children, where the classroom is the context for literacy development. In contrast, many secondary teachers assume that learning about their subject is the main priority and literacy must be constructed outside of their classroom contexts. These issues become clearer within the detail of the secondary school research.

SUMMARY

In this chapter we have considered aspects of literacy in the context of the primary classroom, with a particular focus on the quality of adult–child encounters around text. This research was undertaken at a time when teachers were being 'warned' by various quarters, including HMI, of the dangers of topic work, of child-centred discovery methods of teaching, and of neglecting traditional approaches to the teaching of basic skills. These issues have been presented to schools as a matter of how they choose to spend the available time. In our view, improvements in children's learning will not come simply from electing to spend more time on one area of the curriculum at the expense of another. We can throw some light on what makes for more effective learning by examining social contexts in which teaching is organized, looking at the quality of children's learning encounters around text, rather than methods of teaching or classroom tasks.

Our own research is based on some compelling accounts of learning processes, derived from socio-constructivism. Scaffolding has been explored in terms of various components: recruitment of children to the topic in hand; helping children to represent tasks in terms they understand; elaborating concepts to make links with existing conceptual frameworks; mediating ideas through different forms of written language; and the finishing of an enquiry through some form of review of the process of learning and its outcomes.

Each of these forms of scaffolding involves transactions or dialogues between adult and learner. The lesson scripts which we reported in some detail, show the richness of texture of many teachers' interactions with children as lessons unfold. Typically, teachers visit children and groups, deal with many issues in parallel, make quick strategic shifts between maintaining children on task, questioning and clarifying, directing children to resources and planning next steps, or celebrating the valuable. Scaffolding is recursive and multi-layered, not linear or sequential. Children move in and out of zones of interaction with adults in the classroom, sometimes interactions are close and individual, occasionally, critical incidents are held out for sharing with a larger community of learners. The spatial imagery associated with zones is best replaced, in the context of the primary school, with a notion of overlapping, multiple networks of active minds.

Data for scaffolding and lesson scripts need to be interpreted alongside summary data, such as time spent by teachers and class groups overall, in certain kinds of activity. Characteristic of primary teachers in the study was for major portions of time to be spent working collaboratively with children, although this tended to involve selected children only briefly. Children were often instructed as whole groups, with teachers paying a great deal of attention to organizing resources and managing issues such as movement or behaviour. Data collected across a range of primary classes, show an emphasis on collaborative-type activities, especially with reception and infant groups. More didactic styles of teaching, such as giving instructions, questioning and handing over information, are also prominent, especially with Years 5 and 6. Child-centred activities, such as children pursuing their own topic work with little adult guidance, was unusual, as was relying on set schemes or worksheets, without engaging children in some form of interactive dialogue.

Looked at from the children's perspective, the child in an infant class might spend some twenty minutes in total of a morning or afternoon session, working collaboratively with an adult, albeit in small interludes. This diminished to less than two minutes for the children observed in Year 6. Children were more likely to experience highly adult-managed forms of learning, with an emphasis on drill and repetition, as they moved through primary school; they were also much more likely to be off-task. By far the greatest amount of pupil time is accounted for by occupier-type activities, such as listening, following or working through resources, as teachers talked over a textbook or other prepared stimulus. Many children worked unassisted for long stretches, very rarely engaging in question-raising or researching their own projects.

We have highlighted time spent reading or writing as highly significant for children's literacy growth. Reading and writing were defined in strict terms, relating to the active involvement of children in constructing their own meaning from a written text, and generating their own writing for a specific purpose. These processes we have distinguished from transcription, or secretarial forms of writing, and from passive forms of reading led by a teacher. The data reveal limited amounts of time engaged in more active and independent reading or writing activities – a few minutes per day – and these moments tended to be fragmentary and unsustained. These data confirm earlier accounts in the research literature and complement the findings from the secondary phase of the research, which we discuss next.

Finally, this chapter has considered the important issue of transition between primary and secondary phases, and the nature of children's literacy experience as children move between the two school cultures. The schools involved in our study were unused to thinking about the demands made on children across phases. There was no evidence of a systematic approach to introducing children to the specific reading and writing functions of different subject areas. Primary children face something of a culture shock as they move from the more interactive settings of the primary school where literacy is constructed, or scaffolded within lesson contexts, and on to the loosely-coupled, content-driven secondary curriculum where literacy competence is expected or dealt with peripherally.

5 Literacy across a secondary school curriculum

The facts show that the majority of children are born capable of acquiring impressive levels of expertise in most spheres of competence, if the circumstances of their lives make this possible.

Howe, 1990

The data reported in this chapter were collected over a period of time in one secondary school setting. The school concerned is a long-established 11–16 LEA maintained school of 700 pupils, serving predominantly council housing in a city in the southwest of England. The cluster group to which the school belongs includes feeder primary and infant schools which were also centrally involved in the research. The nature of the cluster's catchment area means that there is a large proportion of one-parent families and a high level of socio-economic deprivation. In the secondary school concerned, some 46 per cent of pupils receive free school meals. Standardized reading tests administered to all pupils in Years 7 and 8 indicated that only 13.7 per cent of pupils had reading quotients which were at or above the average for the age group. The school is regarded as being highly successful in fulfilling the potential of its students. In recent work with the NFER on 'value-added', the school had three out of ten departments in all schools in the same city which were identified as adding 'more than expected'. As part of the school's improvement strategy, enhancing literacy teaching had been identified as a high priority in the institution's development plan.

Although the school had initiated the research project, permission to enter and observe the work space of others needs to be negotiated very carefully. Both observers and observed have to trust the aims and objectives of the research. The research team met the senior management to outline a possible theoretical framework for the research, to explain interests, share experiences of other projects undertaken, and negotiate practicalities. A brief contract was drawn up outlining who would be involved, methods to be adopted, how information would be fed back to staff and further development work undertaken in the school.

Given that the research would require extensive observation and information-gathering in a wide range of classroom contexts, the issue of ownership was crucial. Importantly, three of the five individuals who were involved in the observation phase of the research were members of staff nominated by the school. This went some way to reassuring teaching staff that the research would involve the school directly, raise questions relevant to their work, and share data collection, analysis and action planning with them. Anonymity of the members of staff observed was assured, although the school saw the publication of data amongst other professionals as being an important testament to their commitment to change. The importance of management lead in conducting some form of audit of the literacy curriculum, as a basis for professional development within the school, cannot be underestimated.

RESEARCH METHODS

Details of the research strategies developed in the project have already been given in Chapters 3 and 4. Both a questionnaire and a time-based observation framework were designed around our model of adult–child proximation. As in the primary phase of the research, the intention was to make detailed observations of typical classroom activities across subject specialisms, and involving children of different ages and abilities. As in the primary phase, we were interested to see how teachers habitually organized their classroom business, how print-based resources, such as textbooks, worksheets, handouts and other evidence sources, such as newspapers or documents, were examined and worked on. We were also interested to observe the quality, frequency and purpose of opportunities designed or seized by teachers, which modelled, shaped or explored specific types of literacy within specific subject domains.

By contrasting data derived from the literacy questionnaire with evidence gained from direct observation of teachers' and pupils' classroom activities, we can examine a number of interesting issues. Principally, we can pinpoint discrepancies between what teachers say they do, and how they work in practice. In this way we can begin to understand the nature of classroom realities, the contextual factors which operate to constrain teachers and pupils to work in the ways they do. As in the primary phase of the research, the data collection phase was the beginning of a process of analysis, reflection and development, as schools planned how they might respond to some of the issues which had been highlighted.

The observation framework was designed to record data on both the teacher's patterns of organization and management, as well as the nature of pupil experience, with specific reference to aspects of literacy. Observations were deliberately focused on those features of the teacher's style which impinge directly or indirectly on aspects of literacy used for learning. These include preferred ways of setting out lines of enquiry, how questions are raised and discussions managed, how resources and materials, particularly written text, are used together with strategies for interacting with pupils. We have acknowledged that to focus on *any* aspect of a teacher's style is not necessarily to observe literacy in use. Relevant aspects of teaching style are those which bring individuals or groups into juxtaposition with the formal language and written conventions of the contrived tasks of classroom contexts.

Without revealing the underlying four-quadrant research framework until the fieldwork was completed, all the staff of the secondary school concerned were asked to complete the literacy questionnaire. Lesson observations were made by two researchers and three members of staff across all departments in the school. Findings discussed here include questionnaire data and observations of thirty-nine teachers from ten faculties, including science, English, maths, special needs, modern languages, humanities, music, art and design, information technology and physical education. Observations were made over a two-week, mid-term period.

Data were also collected on how eighty different pupils across the secondary age range were occupied during some seventy hours of the lesson observations. In each case where pupil data were collected, the class teacher had been asked to identify individuals who were either just above or just below average ability in the class group concerned, avoiding pupils at extremes of the ability range, pupils with special problems or identified needs. Observers used the pro forma provided to collect data on two pupils and the class teacher within the same lesson time frame (see Appendices 3 and 4). These lesson scripts for each teaching period observed constitute the corpus of evidence collected in, and then presented back to the secondary school involved.

TEACHERS' CONCEPTUAL MAPS AND OBSERVED CLASSROOM PRACTICE

In the questionnaire phase of the study, secondary teachers made frequent reference to collaborative styles of teaching, with twenty-one out of thirty-nine staff (approximately 54 per cent) allocating responses to quadrant D on at least 9 out of 20 items. These findings are very similar to the data reported in Chapter 2 from the pilot phase of the questionnaire, when a wider sample of secondary and primary teachers was involved. There is a very clear tendency for teachers to stress participative, negotiated ways of working. In thinking about their preferred approaches to aspects of reading, writing, spelling and handwriting, teachers are strongly orientated towards active roles for both pupils and teachers, drawing up appropriate tasks with pupils, helping pupils to plan and carry out their work with assistance and supportive intervention, modelling processes and practising skills within the context of purposeful, meaningful activities. Process issues are high on the agenda, including reviewing, reflecting and making links between current and future learning. Teachers identify very closely with what we have described as contingent teaching: sensitivity to the needs of learners and the requirements of the task.

Observational data show that teachers spend high proportions of time working collaboratively with individuals (average of 22 minutes out of 50).

Table 5.1 Percentage of secondary teachers (n = 39) identifying questionnaire items in four quadrants

No. of items (out of 20)	Quadrant							
	A		B		C		D	
	n	(%)	n	(%)	n	(%)	n	(%)
0–2	27	(69.2)	5	(12.8)	9	(23.1)	3	(7.7)
3–5	9	(23.1)	18	(46.2)	20	(51.3)	7	(17.9)
6–8	2	(5.1)	14	(35.9)	6	(15.4)	8	(20.5)
9+	1	(2.6)	2	(5.1)	4	(10.3)	21	(53.8)

Table 5.2 Correlations between time observed in lessons (average 50 minutes) and questionnaire responses

	Quadrant			
	A	B	C	D
Mean time (in mins) observed	23.04	3.56	1.13	22.27
s. d.	12.43	7.85	2.77	12.39
Median time (in mins) observed	21.41	0	0	21.36
Inter-quartile range	12.36–35.14	0–3.53	0–0	12.18–32.05
Correlation between questionnaire responses and classroom observations (r)*	0.39	–0.259	–0.108	0.313
Significance (p)	<0.05	<0.05	ns	<0.05

*critical value of r (for 37 df) = 0.268 (p < 0.05)

Furthermore, there was a significant, though weak, correlation between teachers identifying quadrant D in the questionnaire phase and subsequent observed behaviour. This can be understood as indicating a connection between what teachers say about aspects of literacy teaching and what they do in practice. Field notes indicate a wide range of learning-driven moves, such as dropping in on groups, helping pupils to restructure a problem and then melting away again, meeting enquiries, making suggestions, indicating short cuts, keeping interest alive, identifying parallel situations met before to help solve a current problem, reviewing implications and adopted methods, rounding off lessons with discussion centred around 'What went well or not so well?'

We should point out that the data under analysis here concern the *teachers'* moves, strategies and responses. How teachers spend their time shapes, but may be very different from, how pupils spend their time. For example, a teacher may work collaboratively with four or five pupils during the course of a lesson, but the majority of a class group may be engaged unassisted, in completing set tasks in isolation. Data from observation of the teacher need to be set against parallel data drawn from observing individual pupils in the same time frame, in order to build a more complete picture of the teaching and learning experience. This is precisely what we have attempted to do in later sections of this chapter when more detailed analyses are made of lesson scripts.

Teacher management and structure

Out of the twenty items on the questionnaire, 70 per cent of respondents identified quadrant A statements as close to their own practice on two occasions or less, with a third (33 per cent) identifying quadrant A only once, and a quarter (23 per cent) not at all. Since this domain is concerned with high teacher management and structure, we can assume the teachers in the study are generally not in favour of working in this mode, which supports the earlier findings from the pilot study when responses from both primary and secondary teachers were analysed. Although there are differences between departments, which will be considered subsequently, overall the staff involved would prefer not to be didactic, not to decontextualize learning, not to practise skills in isolation or to base their teaching on drills, repetition or prescribed tasks without negotiation.

In contrast, the observational data show that, for an average 50-minute lesson, almost half of the time (23 minutes) was spent by teachers using highly didactic strategies. The small correlation between quadrant A responses on the questionnaire and observational data shows a clear tendency for those who mentioned quadrant A in the questionnaire to be observed using quadrant A teaching strategies. Conversely, those who rarely mentioned quadrant A were less likely to use didactic strategies. In other words, those teachers who conceptualized some aspects of their teaching in quadrant A terms, were also more likely to act in similar ways in practice. The important discrepancy here is between the relative amounts of time spent by all teachers in the classroom in the kinds of teaching typified in quadrant A compared with other styles, bearing in mind how teachers indicated they would prefer to work. Although teachers express a preference for avoiding didactic methods, they nevertheless spend much of their time in this mode: what teachers say about their teaching is not borne out by what they do.

Field notes made during lesson observations document a wide range of management activities: writing instructions on the board, giving out exam information, reading out questions, dealing with application forms, explaining dance steps from a choreography sheet, introducing terms such as 'radius', 'right angle', 'orbit', taking pupils through a spreadsheet and expanding cells in a computer program. In these instances, aspects of reading or writing are used as an intrinsic part of administrative or organizational tasks. As we pointed out at the beginning of this chapter, to observe every aspect of a teacher's classroom organization is not necessarily to observe literacy in use. However, these are clear examples of teachers shaping pupils' experience of literacy as an executive and organizational tool: assisting in getting things done.

There were many other instances, also documented in field notes, of teachers using their lesson time on management issues, where literacy played no part, such as finding keys to locked cupboards, retrieving exam papers from another school site, printing out documents from a computer, photocopying worksheets, reorganizing furniture, allocating tasks to groups, dealing with phone calls, selecting writing equipment and other instruments, setting and collecting homework, clearing up after other groups and packing things away. Teachers also had to deal with outbreaks of verbal aggression, racist remarks to other pupils, refusals to work, interfering with other's property, pupils having their own conversations and interruptions at the door.

Apart from occasionally sending pupils out of the room, most of these instances were minor ones, dealt with by reminding pupils about the job in hand, possible consequences of negative behaviour for having to complete tasks after school, cajoling and neutralizing, quietening down or shouting over, or questions with managerial intentions: 'Have you read the poem, Roy?' 'Can I just call you to order again please?' These findings confirm the literature cited earlier on classroom realities and the priority which teachers give, in the real time of the classroom, to establishing and maintaining order and cooperation (Doyle, 1986; Shipman, 1985).

Occupier or resource-driven activities

About 60 per cent of the sample allocated five or fewer questionnaire items to quadrant B, described as resource-driven learning, characterized by low levels of interaction, pupil initiative or engagement. Teachers occasionally acknowledged the need for structured resources such as key words for spelling or coded reading schemes, but were generally reluctant to conceptualize aspects of literacy in terms of dependency on occupier resources or worksheets, where there is limited consideration of purpose, process or function. During the observation phase of the study, teachers were very rarely identified as operating in quadrant B, which accounts on average for less than four minutes of teacher time in a 50-minute lesson. We can say of this kind of resource-dependent teaching, that although infrequently mentioned, teaching time identified as falling into this quadrant was even less obvious in practice.

There is no positive correlation between teachers who mentioned quadrant B at the questionnaire stage of the study and later classroom observations. Of those who allocated questionnaire items to quadrant B on six occasions or more, 91 per cent never used it in practice. Field notes indicate that some teachers used time to patrol, monitor and oversee particular activities, occasionally replicating exam-type conditions to work independently through an exercise with no conferring, question-raising, negotiation, assistance or feedback. Pupils were sometimes supervised without an activity being set, or the teacher got on with marking or preparation. Despite teachers' concepts of the periodic usefulness of quadrant B for certain aspects of teaching, there is little evidence from our classroom observations that this mode of teaching actually played much part. In other words, teachers rarely use occupier resources or strategies which are low in interaction.

As we shall see from a closer examination of some of the lesson scripts from the secondary school research, teachers tend to take much more active control of lessons and use resources such as textbooks, handouts or worksheets as part of teacher-led management, instruction and transmission.

Pupil-led learning

Quadrant C is characterized by informal, pupil-led learning, where individuals structure their own learning routes with little guidance or management from the teacher. Questionnaire data suggest that this domain was least preferred amongst the sample. Three quarters (74 per cent) of respondents mentioned quadrant C on five occasions or less out of the twenty items. Data derived from lesson observations indicate that little more than one minute on average of the fifty minutes available lesson time was spent by the teacher providing space, resources or opportunities for pupils to get on with their own topic work, reading or assignments, such as a free-choice reading or study period.

There were two members of staff who mentioned quadrant C in the questionnaire in more than ten instances out of the twenty items, but there was a negative, though non-significant correlation between questionnaire and observation data. In other words, those who considered some aspects of their teaching in quadrant C terms, rarely used it in practice. Over the sample as a whole, however, teachers express low preference for pupil-centred methods and this is reflected in how teachers work in the classroom.

Inter-departmental differences

Data given in Table 5.3 show how teachers working in different departments of the school conceptualize their work in literacy teaching. The formal, heavily prescribed and adult-structured mode of teaching represented by quadrant A, was favoured by special needs staff. They were predisposed to strategies such as the rote teaching of grapheme–phoneme rules; to the introduction of different types of writing, such as poems, diaries and letters as an object lesson; to the rehearsal of spelling rules and correct English grammar; to the use of formal tests for making quantitative assessments; and the support of pupils through intensive remedial programmes in one-to-one or small group settings outside of main classes. They also saw much of their work as dependent on resources, and were least likely, of all the departments in the school, to perceive their work in pupil-centred terms, or, with the exception of science staff, in collaborative, learning-driven terms. Given the correlation between how teachers view their practice and the lesson observation data for quadrant A, the work of special needs staff is likely to sustain

Table 5.3 Percentage of questionnaire responses allocated to four quadrants by teachers in different departments

| | Quadrant | | | | Total |
Department	A	B	C	D	responses
Special Needs (n = 3)	30.0	28.3	15.0	26.7	60
English (n = 3)	1.7	8.3	25.0	65.0	60
Drama, Music, Art (n = 4)	2.5	17.5	28.8	51.2	80
Modern Languages (n = 3)	13.3	31.7	16.7	38.3	60
Humanities (n = 5)	12.0	36.0	15.0	37.0	100
Science (n = 6)	10.0	28.3	36.7	25.0	120
Maths (n = 6)	12.5	27.5	20.0	40.0	120
CDT/Technology (n = 6)	7.6	21.2	17.8	53.4	120
PE (n = 5)	5.1	26.3	25.3	43.4	100
TOTAL (n = 39)	9.9	25.5	22.9	41.7	780

Note: Chi square = 97.42 (24 df) $p < 0.00001$

this adult-structured, direct teaching of skills outside main classes.

In contrast, English teachers were very much more disposed towards collaborative styles of teaching than any other teaching mode, with approximately two-thirds of questionnaire responses allocated to quadrant D. English teachers were not in favour of teaching rules for decoding or spelling divorced from the context of book reading experience or the process of composition. They saw assessment in terms of monitoring and discussion, leading to a profile of student abilities. Rather than the deliberate teaching of handwriting, presentation and writing formats as an object lesson, they were more concerned with investigating writing conventions and genres as an integral part of writing for specific functions and audiences. They stressed the shared responsibility across all subject areas for developing literacy as tools for learning. Many other departments, such as CDT and technology teachers, drama, music and art specialists, also perceived their work in collaborative, learning-driven terms.

Informal, pupil-led learning with an emphasis on practical discovery methods was the prominent focus of responses made by science teachers. They stressed the value of experience and of research in stimulating children to write appropriately for tasks encountered. Without exception, the six science teachers in the study expressed the view that for pupils with literacy difficulties, lack of help or support at home accounted for poor progress, whilst they believed that additional help should be given *outside* of mainstream lessons. As a group this department did not share the view that science was an important vehicle for developing pupils' literacy, a finding which supports the earlier evidence from the pilot phase of the questionnaire reported in Chapter 2, to which science teachers contributed. Pupil-centred learning also figured highly in the collective views of drama, music and art teachers. For example, there was a consensus of opinion on the importance of pupil enthusiasm and motivation in determining whether pupils became literate, more important than how literacy was constructed or worked on in different subject areas.

Resource-driven learning was characteristic of many of the views expressed by modern languages staff, humanities and maths teachers. They valued structured teaching materials and prepared schemes, with appropriate resourcing of lessons. These groups of teachers also paid attention to active collaborative styles. Only three out of twelve teachers in these departments felt that literacy was not the responsibility of subject specialists; many acknowledged the importance of taking opportunities to extend pupils' reading and writing in different subject contexts. Overall, Table 5.3 indicates that most departments showed a balance in their preferred modes of teaching, with collaborative styles figuring most prominently, and didactic styles least in evidence, with the exception of special needs staff.

SECONDARY TEACHERS' CONSTRUCTS AND CLASSROOM BEHAVIOUR: AN OVERVIEW

To summarize briefly this phase of the secondary school research, we began by examining teachers' constructs on the teaching of literacy, across different departments. Questionnaire data revealed strong preferences amongst the majority of staff for collaborative, contingent styles of working, including such issues as reflective and formative assessment, questioning, and the negotiation of tasks within meaningful contexts. English teachers were very disposed towards collaborative, learning-driven strategies, typified in quadrant D of our model. Many other departments said they would prefer to work in this way, including design and technology teachers, drama, music and art specialists.

Resource-driven learning (quadrant B) characterized many of the questionnaire responses of teachers in humanities, modern languages and maths departments, evidenced, for example, in the value placed on structured schemes and materials. Informal, pupil-centred learning with an emphasis on practical work and research (quadrant C), was more typical of science teachers, but also figured in responses of teachers of fine or performing arts. Exceptionally, special needs staff were predisposed to more didactic, adult structured approaches, including quantitative assessment, skill-focused teaching and rote learning methods. Special needs teachers favoured the intensive support of pupils with literacy difficulties outside the mainstream curriculum, a view shared also by science teachers.

Most departments presented a balance of views on the most appropriate ways of developing literacy across the curriculum, including the proper use of structured resources, practice of skills, opportunities for pupil research, together with more active, collaborative styles. In this respect, it is not true that teachers would prefer to adopt specific methods exclusive of others, or that they eschew more traditional skill-focused teaching, although there are clear differences in emphasis between departments. However, it cannot be assumed that all teachers accept responsibility for teaching aspects of reading and writing as part of their subject brief.

The second stage of the research examined contrasts between teachers' stated preferences and observed classroom practice. Observational data and lesson scripts reveal a wide range of challenges and tasks, evidence of widespread engagement of pupils in using a diverse range of functional literacy. However, there is a clear mismatch between teachers' stated values and classroom behaviour. For an average 50-minute lesson, almost half of the time was spent by teachers using highly didactic strategies. In some instances, literacy was included as part of the teacher's attention to organizational factors, such as setting tasks through instruction sheets. The lesson scripts also identify long periods of time when teachers are occupied in managing resources, behaviour and disruptions.

A major conclusion is that many teachers are constrained to work in ways which prioritize order, cooperation and adult control, even though they might prefer to tackle things differently.

Many teachers who expressed preferences for resource-driven or pupil-centred learning at the questionnaire stage of the study, rarely used these modes of teaching in their observed practice. Subsequent discussion of these findings with teachers suggests that styles high in adult management, such as setting rote tasks, group questioning of children, teacher exposition and direction from the front of class, are 'low risk'. Offering opportunities for pupils to pursue their own self-chosen routes, experiential and collaborative learning styles, has possible consequences for a breakdown in order and control.

THE NATURE OF PUPILS' LEARNING EXPERIENCE

So far we have considered our observational data from the perspective of the teacher: the nature of the adults' constructs, classroom moves and interventions. As we have already indicated, to gain a more complete view of the teaching and learning process requires the pupils' parallel perspective, within the same time frame, to be taken into account. The lesson scripts which follow give a clear visual representation of how time was spent by both teachers and pupils in different areas of the curriculum, how lessons proceeded, how teachers conducted their interactions and the quality of pupil engagement.

The typical script of a lesson includes a high proportion of teacher exposition and organization, with pupils consequently spending much of their time listening and responding to exercises set. Table 5.4 gives details of specific pupil observation categories and summarizes those activities most likely to occur in a lesson.

Although we have indicated that teachers spend large amounts of their time in didactic mode, working from the front of the class to give instructions

Table 5.4 Percentage of pupils (n = 80) by time spent in different classroom activities

Activity	Never	Time observed in minutes			
		>0 ≤5	>5 ≤10	>10 ≤15	>15
QUADRANT A					
Reading to a group (passive audience)	97.5	2.5	—	—	—
Copying from board/teacher's notes	87.5	5.0	5.0	—	2.5
Recording from dictation	97.5	2.5	—	—	—
Drill/repetition of an activity	92.5	2.5	—	1.2	3.7
QUADRANT B					
Working through set scheme	78.7	6.2	2.5	7.5	5.0
Reading or copying from textbook or worksheet	88.7	2.5	1.2	1.2	6.2
Listening/watching prepared resources	12.5	5.0	23.7	12.5	46.2
Unassisted work on set task	61.2	5.0	11.2	3.7	18.7
Pupils off-task/hovering	31.2	18.7	21.2	17.5	11.2
QUADRANT C					
Pupils decide for themselves how to carry out task/practical work	57.5	20.0	12.5	1.2	8.7
Pupils allowed to pursue own interests/activities	92.5	5.0	2.5	—	—
Question raising	87.5	10.0	—	1.2	1.2
Researching through reference	91.2	2.5	6.2	—	—
Generating/redrafting writing	76.2	3.7	8.7	3.7	7.5
Individually engaged with text	78.7	7.5	6.2	2.5	5.0
QUADRANT D					
Shared discussion	95.0	—	5.0	—	—
Purpose/objective/hypothesis raising	97.5	2.5	—	—	—
Reviewing process	97.5	2.5	—	—	—
Pupil–teacher on task collaboration	56.2	22.5	12.5	3.7	5.0
Critical recording: making accounts	87.5	7.5	5.0	—	—
Critical reflection: rethinking accounts	92.5	7.5	—	—	—
Reflect ways of knowing/doing	92.5	6.2	1.2	—	—

or information, gain and maintain attention, establish orderly procedures and keep things moving, the pupils' individual experience adds another dimension. Pupils were not often engaged for sustained lengths of time in carrying out rote, structured tasks, drilled by the teacher. The straightforward explanation for this we have already considered: teachers expend much more time and energy organizing, directing and managing resources, rooms and pupils, than pupils do in pursuing their learning. Few pupils were observed for any length of time occupied by these kinds of drilled or rote activities, even if this is what the teacher intended.

Most teachers were not predisposed to use didactic methods of teaching, although, as we have seen, almost half the teachers' time in any lesson was spent on managing pupils in this way. An important issue is whether sufficient learning time is given over to quadrant A type activities. In this way, effective classroom management could be accomplished through the nature of tasks set.

The major portion of curriculum time was accounted for by resource-driven activities: completing set exercises, unassisted with minimal interaction. This contrasts with the data for how teachers themselves operate: rarely designing lessons around occupier resources, with limited opportunities for class group interactions. Yet when individual pupils are observed, whatever the teacher intended, it remains the case that much of the lesson time is taken up with watching or listening, working with minimal ongoing guidance on exercises and set tasks, completing assignments in isolation, off-task or hovering: looking busy and occupied but doing very little.

Of the pupils observed in the study, some 46 per cent of cases were recorded listening to or watching resources for more than fifteen minutes in a 55-minute lesson. Nearly one in five pupils were working unassisted on set tasks for more than fifteen minutes of the lesson. About a quarter of cases involved using set schemes for variable amounts of time, whilst 11 per cent included working from textbooks. Off-task behaviour and hovering were observed in 11 per cent of cases for more than fifteen minutes per lesson, and in 38 per cent of cases for between five and ten minutes per lesson.

A frequent quadrant C activity involved pupils carrying out their own assignments or practical work, which appeared in some 42 per cent of cases, and in more than 8 per cent of cases occupied more than fifteen minutes of lesson time. Question-raising, pupil research or pursuit of own interests, occurred only rarely and even then, for brief periods of time, generally between 0 and 10 minutes.

There were, in fact, wide variations in how pupils spent their time, even in the same lessons. Despite the fact that the majority of teachers were in favour of collaborative, negotiated methods of working and spent relatively high proportions of time teaching contingently – guiding and interacting with individuals – at the pupil level only a minority of a class group were so engaged. The practical realities of classroom contexts dictate that pupil–teacher on-task collaboration can only occur relatively infrequently and for small numbers. Opportunities for critical reflection and review are also very infrequent.

Quadrant D, or participative activities involving adult–pupil or pupil–pupil collaboration, occurred in some 44 per cent of cases. Of these, 22 per cent were brief encounters which lasted less than five minutes, with some 5 per cent of cases showing an extended working together of more than fifteen minutes in a lesson. These data show that teachers adopt collaborative teaching styles for much of available lesson time, but that this generally involves moving around a teaching group, working briefly with a few individuals. The most frequent kind of pupil activity observed in this study involved pupils working individually and unassisted on a set task, or pursuing some kind of prepared exercise. Moments of shared discussion, hypothesis raising, making some form of critical account of proceedings, reflecting on how tasks had been tackled, what went well or needed to be modified for next time, were infrequent and brief.

Overall, there were no gender differences in the number of cases recorded in one quadrant compared with another. In other words, there is no evidence in this study that female teachers compared with male teachers, or girls compared with boys, tend to spend more time in collaborative activities as opposed to resource-driven, pupil-led or highly structured activities. More detailed analyses of those activities most likely to occur show no differences in frequency of cases observed in relation to the gender of the pupils. For example, girls are no more likely to be observed off-task than boys, or to work unassisted on set tasks.

This present study complements earlier data on how teachers spend their time in classrooms. Teachers often say they would like to work in the participative, collaborative mode described by quadrant D and many succeed in doing so. However, in many lessons teachers talk at pupils, set tasks which occupy but do not necessarily challenge, expect pupils to work independently, collaborate briefly with pupils to check progress and sustain engagement, avoid pupil-centred pursuits, shared discussion, reflection and critical review. This we have accounted for by the desire to be in control, to actively instruct and maintain order.

Many teachers saw more collaborative styles of working as 'high risk', with the possibility that pupils would not cooperate or take advantage of informality. Pupils themselves might resist tasks which required them to deal with unfamiliar, intellectually-demanding problems. In this sense, teachers organize learning environments in ways which are well-adapted to the demands of the social context of the classroom. Many previous researchers have concluded that teachers are more concerned with enlisting pupil cooperation, maintaining order and discipline, than with learning (Jorgensen, 1977; Doyle, 1986; Desforges and Cockburn, 1987).

TIME SPENT READING OR WRITING

One of our observation categories is specifically focused on pupils constructing their own writing, whilst another category focuses on engagement with different text forms, such as personal reading, or reading a text for information. In the primary school chapter, we defined fairly strictly those periods of active engagement in constructing meaning from text, and those instances of generating and composing writing, as distinct from passive reading led by a teacher, or secretarial forms of writing.

In 76 per cent of cases, generating or redrafting of writing was never observed. In 12.5 per cent of the cases when pupils were generating their own writing, this was for less than a total of ten minutes out of a 55-minute lesson. Reading engagement was never recorded in 78 per cent of cases, whilst in only 7.5 per cent of cases were periods of reading for more than ten minutes in total recorded.

Quadrant D includes categories where pupils and adults are reflecting on their reading and writing, but in approximately 90 per cent of cases these activities were never observed. Not only do pupils have very limited opportunities for sustained reading or composition in the course of their lessons, but there are even fewer opportunities for critical, reflective reading, and the drafting and remaking of writing with adults or peers. These data support and extend previous investigations where researchers have looked at curriculum time spent engaged with writing or reading, and which report only fragments of time devoted to literacy, in the sense of sustained reading or the construction of writing (Galton et al., 1980; Lunzer and Gardner, 1979).

The present data suggest that in the majority of the secondary school lessons we observed, pupils were not given many opportunities to read or write as part of the teaching and learning process. When those opportunities did arise, they were likely to be brief and discontinuous, amounting to no more than about ten minutes in total. In the introductory chapters of this book we considered the role of literacy as a tool for thinking, as a powerful means of enabling pupils to organize their thinking, seek information, represent problems, record, analyse and communicate the fruits of their enquiries across all subject areas. We have argued that a key challenge for all teachers is how to shape learning experiences and teaching contexts so that all children share the power of literacy, its scope and application. Perhaps one of the most important findings of this study of secondary school classrooms is that, for many pupils, teaching and learning proceeded without literacy taking a major part.

Summarizing the data on observed pupils' experience across subjects obscures certain areas of the curriculum where literacy played a more strategic role. Many teachers designed lessons in which all of the pupils read or wrote for specific purposes, for much of the available time. In the following section of this chapter we will consider some of the lesson scripts we recorded in greater detail, identifying how teachers achieved this attention to the processes of reading or writing construction.

For the secondary school which took part in the study, significant shifts in practice would be required if the whole curriculum was to become the ground in which literacy development was situated: the school would need to develop clear and coordinated systems which support literacy. The next phase of our work with the school involved every department in examining how aspects of literacy could be used more frequently, in more sustained and challenging ways, for a much greater range of learning-focused functions. In effect, all subject teachers were required to ask themselves what constitute the specific literacies of their subject specialisms, and how and when these could be fostered.

LESSON SCRIPTS

In this section we examine samples of the observational data recorded in different lessons across the subject areas of the secondary school (see Figure 4.2). These provide extracts from the wealth of information collected in the research programme, in the form of case studies, which demonstrate typical ways in which aspects of language and literacy were brought into use in contrasting lesson contexts. In each example, the data have been summarized according to the time frame of the lesson, documenting how the teacher and two pupils were occupied over two-minute intervals.

Read in parallel, the summaries give an indication of how the teacher managed the lesson, what resources were used, how activities were set out and what the pupils proceeded to do in relation to the teacher's moves. We have tried to illustrate the rich texture of lessons, coding the information according to the original four-quadrant observation framework. However, the main focus of the lesson scripts is on the use made of literacy within each observed period of teaching. An additional coding at the end of each two-minute interval specifies literacy-related activities, whilst data are also provided on the range of printed materials available and what functions these served. Essentially, the scripts provide evidence on how subject specialists introduced or extrapolated the specific literacy requirements of their subject areas for the pupils involved.

The humanities script

In this humanities lesson, a Year 8 mixed ability group worked on a geography topic tracing urban development through the years. Pupils sat in pairs at tables facing the front, and had largely assigned themselves to seating positions according to friendship patterns. The teacher had chosen to work from the blackboard using a prepared diagram to which notes were added during the course of the lesson, occasionally moving around the class to inspect pupils' work and offer comments or encouragement.

It can be seen from the coded teacher moves that the lesson began with a few minutes of shared planning, as the previous day's work was recapped and current activities explained. The teacher then embarked on a long period of exposition, making reference to the diagram on the board, clarifying the terminology used. Instructions were given on copying the diagram into folders, although one pupil had already started, whilst another alternated between raising a question, listening, chattering and fetching equipment. The teacher's visiting in the middle of the lesson was used to praise, prompt and discuss progress with a handful of students, followed by whole class instruction when the previous day's writing was added to with further notes, which the pupils copied from the board. Finally, more explanations were given about the work in hand and equipment was collected.

In terms of literacy, the pupils explored some of the specialist terminology and visual formats of a geography exercise, although the writing

HUMS. TEACHER (F)

Time	Activity	Code
0	explaining & recapping	T
	yesterday's lesson in detail	T
	uses diagram on board	W
	describing terminology	T
	referring to board	T
10	explanation of task	T
	explaining diagram	T
	continues	T
	continues	T
	completes	T
20	visiting individuals	T
	encouraging	T
	praising	T
	instructing individuals	T
	instructing individuals	T

PUPIL 1 (M)

Time	Activity	Code
0	listening	L
	listening	L
	copies diagram (not told to yet)	W
	copying	W
	copying	W
10	listening	L
	listening	L
	asks to borrow crayons	T
	copying from board	W
	borrowing from other pupils	
20	sharpening pencil	
	talking to peer	ot
	talks to teacher about progress	T
	copying diagram	W
	copying diagram	W

PUPIL 2 (M)

Time	Activity	Code
0	listening to teacher	L
	listening	L
	asked question about shopping	T
	chats	ot
	chats	ot
10	listening	L
	listening	L
	out of seat to get pencil	ot
	copying diagram from board	W
	chatting to peers	ot
20	copying from board	W
	continues copying diagram	W
	continues slowly	W
	continues copying	W
	continues	W

Table 1

wholeclass command: continue	T
yesterday's written task	T
writing notes on board	W
writing notes on board	W
tells class to stop chatting	T
writing notes on board	W
writing notes on board	W
explaining what to do next	T
collecting in resources	
collecting in pencils & crayons	

(time markers: 30, 40, 50)

Table 2

asks: continuing from yesterday	T
listening	L
copying notes from board	W
copying notes	W
continues	W
continues	W
continues	W
continues	W
continues	W
packing away	

(time markers: 30, 40, 50)

Table 3

continues	W
continues	W
continues with diagram	W
continues copying	W
borrows Tippex	
correcting error	W
completes diagram copy	W
starts copying notes	W
copies and breaks off	W
packing away	

(time markers: 30, 40, 50)

Figure 5.1 Humanities script

component was largely restricted to copying and transferring prepared print. The majority of the time was taken up by the teacher instructing the whole group with some teacher-directed discussion around diagrams and notes on the board. In this teacher-led lesson, the pupils mainly entered the teacher's own subject discourse, spending much of their time listening, whilst written text was used without discussion of the process or context.

Content issues predominated in this lesson, but content was not linked to pupils' own experience or understanding, or situated in a live or recalled experience. There were brief moments of negotiation as the teacher visited pupils and inspected their work, but most pupils completed the set task without any critical feedback. The task was about urban development, but there is little sense in which these pupils were making their own enquiries into urban growth, or simulating actual problems in the classroom to use the tools, documents and text resources of such an enquiry.

The maths script

In this lesson a Year 11 mixed ability maths group were working on area and circumference, using a textbook, diagram and formulae displayed on the blackboard. Pupils were seated at tables in pairs or alone, facing the front and the teacher's desk. Textbooks were given out at the start of the lesson, as pupils settled to the task. A set of questions was read out from the book and the maths concepts modelled. The teacher divided her time between exposition and monitoring, with some brief checking and prompting of individuals around the class.

This was a very teacher-centred lesson, requiring high self-motivation from pupils to stay on task. One of the observed pupils spent almost half of the time interesting himself in other things, playing with his calculator, discussing films and work experience. The substance of the topic was presented in a way which made few links between the mathematical processes under consideration and their application in the real world: this is a good example of the special kind of self-contained activity associated with the contrived contexts of school.

Pupils proceeded through the task at varying rates using the same materials and activities. Because the pupils were expected to listen and absorb the information which the teacher generated, with a minimum of discussion, involvement or negotiation, the degree of compliance varied from pupil to pupil. For those individuals who wanted to mark time or found interest in other things, the teacher was required to use manoeuvres such as patrolling, prompting, reiterating instructions and checking work rate.

In terms of literacy, the pupils were introduced to some of the written symbols of mathematics, the conventions of diagrams, textbooks and the nature of school-based maths enquiry, most of which would be highly familiar. They listened as the teacher directed their attention to relevant aspects of diagrams, labels and textbooks. There was some teacher-led discussion and dialogue around the text, whilst the two observed pupils spent most of their time either responding passively to the demands which were made, or off-task. Importantly, the textbook was used as a support to the teacher's presentation, not as a source of information, which would have allowed pupils to explore for themselves how maths is represented in text formats. As in the geography script considered previously, there was little extension of the pupils' expertise in using literacy for learning: what pupils practised during this lesson in relation to the reading of textbooks for information, or the construction of writing for a specific purpose, was what they already knew.

The science script

During this science period, a Year 10 mixed ability group worked through a laboratory experiment on using acids and alkalis in different strengths of solution. The teacher began by reviewing points from the previous session, drawing up hypotheses arising from pupils' comments and responses to questions. A brief experiment was set up which pupils organized for themselves, with advice and direction from the teacher, who gave specific deadlines for completing aspects of the task. The range of activities included the group challenging some of the outcomes of the experiment, using a textbook as an information source and to address a related problem, and generating ideas from the pupils' own experience on the uses of neutralization in everyday contexts.

The pupils moved quickly and enthusiastically through this sequence of learning activities, and although they were given a lot of initiative, expectations were made clear. The pupils had collaborative experience of hypothesis-raising, defining specialist terminology, collecting data, querying results, speculating, proving points, revising arguments, relating classroom data to everyday life, recording evidence and drawing conclusions. Significantly, this wide variety of tasks had a common *conceptual* centre: all of the activities were linked to the main focus of the topic. Despite the teacher's organizational skill, the learning experience was disrupted in various ways, for example by the visit of another teacher to discuss exam timetables and an appointment for a music lesson.

A number of opportunities were taken when pupils were engaged orally in following and acting on instructions. There was discussion of some of the specialist terminology and forms of enquiry in science. In relation to written language, textbooks were used as sources of evidence and pupils were given explicit instructions not to copy from them. Most of the pupils worked on the same set tasks with no differentiation of activity or outcome. However, periods of time were allocated when all pupils were writing personal accounts. The coding for this lesson script highlights the emphasis placed on dialogue and discussion around the science processes involved. In contrast, very little attention was given to issues of literacy *process*: how to take notes,

MATHS TEACHER (F)

Time	Activity	Code
0	settling class	
	resources & books given out	
	register / 'nice, new books'	T
	reads out questions (no page ref)	R
	'draw a diagram'>draws on board	W
10	'pi times what?' / models	T
	leads investigative talk	T
	reads out how to find circum.	R
	patrols class	
	'make sure you have these 2	T
20	formulae written down'	T
	visiting / reads text for pupil	R
	explaining process	T
	'please read the questions.'	T
	'read it twice, three times."	T
30	restates / 'big 3 and little bits'	T
	visiting / monitoring	T
	working with small group	T
	individual assistance	T
	'check your answers up to q.5'	T

PUPIL 1 (M)

Time	Activity	Code	ot
0	settling down		
	resources out		
	getting ready		
	listening	L	
	copying notes from board	W	
10	copying/listening	W	
	watching second example	L	
	looking at textbook	R	
	starts chatting		ot
	chats to boy behind him		ot
20	listens to teacher talk behind	L	
	no engagement with text		ot
	fiddles with calculator		ot
	watching late arrival		ot
30	workbook closed/isolates self		ot
	workbook open/text opened	R	
	talks to boy about placement	T	
	Loch Ness monster&Jurassic Pk.	T	
	flicks thro' text/writes answers	W	

PUPIL 2 (F)

Time	Activity	Code
0	settling down	
	resources out	
	opening book	R
	listening	L
	copying from board	W
10	explains how to find area	T
	copying end of first problem	W
	looking at text/sharpens pencil	R
	starts writing in silence	W
	silent writing	W
20	silent writing	W
	silent writing	W
	silent writing	W
	pupil in front explains process	T
	'Ms. what questions need we do?'	T
30	silent writing	W
	conferring with two peers	T
	collaboration/teacher visits	T
	checking/confirming answer	T
	referring to answers	R

Time		Activity	
40		h/w sheet given out	T
		writes up worded definition of	W
		area and circumference formulae	W
		patrols	
		checking pupils' work / no talk	W
50		chats about exam technique	T
		explains moderation process	T
		expository talk	T
		hovering / meeting enquiries	T
		packing away	
60			

Time		Activity	
40	ot	work experience	
	ot	fed-up/'done h/w already'	
	ot		
		starts h/w, solving q. rapidly	W
		praised by teacher	T
50		gets on with h/w	W
		no proofs, answer straight down	W
		from calculator	W
		packs away	
60			

Time		Activity	
40		attempts to finish off task	W
		continues	W
		continues	W
		continues	W
		completes	W
50		starts h/w	W
		checking with pupil behind	T
		verifies process/'that's right.'	T
		helps pack away	
		helps pack away	
60			

Figure 5.2 Maths script

SCIENCE TEACHER (F)	
reviews last lesson / IRF	T
hypothesizes from pupil feedback	T
setting experimental task	T
monitoring pupil response	L
walking around visiting	L
supportive discussion with	T
individual pupils and groups	T
monitoring, advising, directing	T
monitoring and advising	L
monitoring and advising	L
sets completion time	T
challenging outcomes	T
introduces textbook task	T
recaps task	T
explains key terms	T

PUPIL 1 (F)	
listening	L
listening	L
listening	L
setting up experiment in pair	T
organizing ingredients	T
planning	T
talks to new teacher in room	T
discusses exam timetable	T
checks exam timetable	T
returns to experiment	T
wanders	ot
listening, preparing for new task	L
listening	L
listening	L
goes to music lesson	

PUPIL 2 (F)	
listening	L
listening	L
listening	L
setting up experiment in trio	T
organizing ingredients	T
collaborating with partner	T
discussion during experiment	T
completes experiment	T
clearing away equipment	
clearing away	
notes down results	W
following in textbook	R
listening	L
listening	L
listening	L

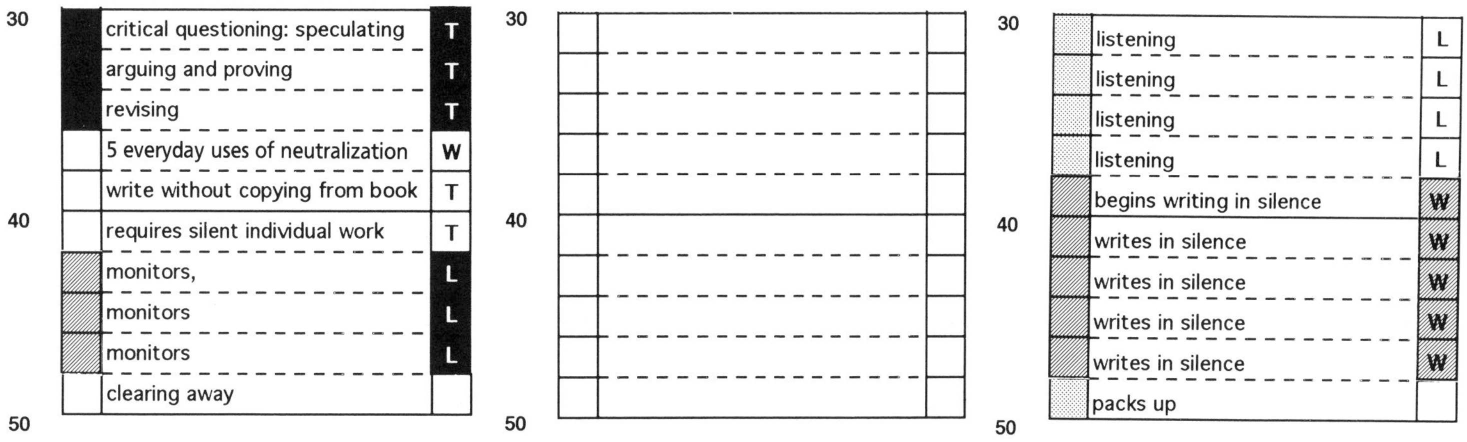

Figure 5.3 Science script

the construction of a written analysis as opposed to a personal account, how to set out a sequential argument and draw conclusions, appropriate grammar, spelling, punctuation and presentation.

The English script

A Midsummer Night's Dream had been at the centre of much of the term's work for this Year 9 mixed ability group. This particular lesson began with a few minutes' wait as activities were drawn to a close with a previous class. The room was organized with linked conference tables around the periphery of the room. Pupils sat at the inner edge of the tables facing outwards for private reading or writing. At various times chairs were turned around so that pupils faced inwards for a group discussion. The text of the play being used had both Shakespeare and a modern translation.

The lesson proceeded with a teacher-directed discussion on how the characters in the play might look – their clothes, hair or faces – followed by small group work when pupils conferred and then wrote their own accounts of how characters had been visualized. The teacher visited individuals, reframing questions and assisting with their writing. Pupils were selected to read from their work to the whole class. The teacher then turned to the original Shakespearean text and read whilst pupils followed. The next activity involved pupils tagging the text at important points of evidence, locating those parts which had helped them to draw up a picture of the characters.

The lesson coding depicts this as a highly collaborative session. There was a mixture of individual work, small group and whole class discussion around the text, although all pupils worked on the same task. The two observed pupils spent most of their time exploring or responding to the questions set, either individually or with a partner. Even so, one pupil managed to feign being busy for ten minutes or so. In terms of literacy, most pupils had by the close of the lesson, read silently or aloud, reflected on their reading, and been introduced to the idea of supporting arguments with specific reference to a text. The writing opportunity was of a limited, personal/ imaginative kind, but some assistance was given with the process of writing construction to a few in the group.

The drama script

In a lesson related to the English one above, the same Year 9 class worked in a drama studio equipped with a stage, gantry and rehearsal space, improvising extracts from *A Midsummer Night's Dream*. The drama activities had been planned with the English faculty, using the same text. Pupils began by refamiliarizing themselves with the plot, spending the first half of the lesson in collaboration with the teacher, thinking around the possibilities for improvization. Prepared handouts were available in the form of a rehearsal plan and a cue sheet. Issues were raised and dealt with, regarding on- and off-stage perspectives, dialogue, stage movements, characterization, idiom and register.

In the second half of the lesson, pupils worked in one of four groups around a prepared set of notes, on either lighting, make-up, staging or acting. The class convened to watch the acting group before the end of the session. Much of the teacher's time was spent visiting and encouraging the groups, discussing progress and setting specific, short-term objectives.

The lesson coding shows the high degree of interaction between the teacher and the class, with interspersed periods dedicated to silent reading or listening. Most of this teacher's preparation and organization was related to managing the learning activities, supplying relevant resources at different phases, guiding pupils towards independent activity. In terms of literacy, pupils were required to explore and interrogate texts and the teacher's notes, in order to complete the performance objectives. However, none of the pupils transposed their oral enquiries into any form of written notes, and the personal contributions or needs of individuals were concealed in the group format of the lesson.

The modern languages script

This Year 8 modern languages lesson was centred around a textbook and magazine, including two crosswords, word jumbles and a wordsearch activity. The teacher opened the lesson by describing himself in French and modelling key vocabulary and phrasing. Individuals were then selected to answer questions with descriptions about themselves, followed by a textbook exercise which required drawings of people to be matched to their descriptions given in French. A quick spelling test was given and then a question and answer session, questions in French, writing in English. Pupils spent most of this part of the lesson listening, responding or writing to teacher-directed questions or set tasks.

In the second half of the lesson the magazine activities were explained and pupils worked with partners to solve the language puzzles, whilst the teacher monitored progress and rounded off the session with a brief review and some more questions posed to individuals in French.

In terms of literacy, the pupils handled the written equivalents of oral language which they had explored earlier. Most of the exercises set came in the form of cloze-type activities, locating and assembling small chunks of text to complete linguistic puzzles. There were brief occasions when pupils read for information in the given text, worked collaboratively with a partner or with the teacher. Many interesting ways were found for pupils to manipulate French vocabulary and phrases, using extracts from genuine literacy artefacts, such as a magazine. In the classroom setting it is very difficult to create situations which produce a live momentum to use a second language: this is perhaps the subject domain where the issue of decontextualization is felt most acutely. Nevertheless, pupil-pairings and group work helped to make many of

English classroom observation chart — three parallel timelines (minutes marked 0, 10, 20).

ENGLISH TEACHER (M)

Activity	Code
finishing off with Year 11	T
finishing off with Year 11	T
'chairs around to face centre'	T
teacher-led discussion	T
visualization of characters	T
'did Puck look clean?'/review	R
into groups/discussion & writing	T
visiting groups and individuals	T
elicits questions/talking through	T
portrayal in modern translation	R
assisting analysis into writing	T
pupils feed back personal account	L
whole group listening to each	L
member's account	L
individual narration/listening	L

PUPIL 1 (M)

Code	Activity
	waiting
	waiting
L	listening as whole class
L	remembering cartoon version
R	scanning modern translation
L	listening
ot	hovers/avoids settling to task
ot	talks off task
ot	pretends to be busy
ot	silent
ot	distracted
L	listening to group
	listening, adding notes
L	listening
L	listening

PUPIL 2 (F)

Activity	Code
waiting	
waiting	
turned to centre/listening	L
scanning play/recalling cartoon	L
reading/offering ideas	R
listening/visualizing aloud	L
using prompt sheet to compile	R
describing Oberon, Puck, Titania	T
imagining/writing down ideas	W
reading for cues and clues	R
writing/discussing/selecting	W
reads out her notes/describes	R
listening to another account	L
listening to another account	L
listening/adding to notes	L

Panel 1

	R/W/L/T
30	
reading into original Shakespeare	R
finding original ref. from trans,	R
supporting groups to read aloud	L
modelling pronunciation/cadence	R
visiting/listening/explaining	L
40	
supports groups to 'tag' evidence	R
matches written notes to original	W
insistence on proof & explanation	T
visiting/closing activity	L
'next time we meet...'	T
50	

Panel 2

	R/W/L/T
30	
whole class attends to original	R
group familiarization/reading	R
reading aloud/scanning	R
modelling/practising Sh. language	T
matching original to translation	R
40	
tagging evidence/group talk	T
discussion/writing notes	W
finding proof	R
turns back to centre	L
listening/projecting	L
50	

Panel 3

	R/W/L/T
30	
locating and reading original	R
reading two lines aloud	R
matching versions and evidence	R
working with partner/talking	T
researches/pinpoints key words	R
40	
tagging evidence/ collaboration	T
amplifying account	W
scanning text/amplifies notes	W
completing/turns back to centre	L
listening/projecting	L
50	

Figure 5.4 English script

DRAMA TEACHER (M)

Time	Activity	Code
0	seating pupils	T
	register / recaps.	T
	direct and review / questioning.	T
	talking through account.	T
	contextual references	T
10	presents real life analogy	T
	follows pupils' suggestions	T
	'visualize it as a piece' / models	T
	on- and off-stage perspective	T
	imagine how we want it to look	T
20	hands out cue sheet	R
	chance to read through	R
	hands out impro. sheet	R
	be positive and practical	T
	rough> instructions> record	T

PUPIL 1 (F)

Time	Activity	Code
0	sitting on bench	
	gives out texts	
	reviews / retells plot	T
	corrects teacher from text	T
10	scanning text to prove point	R
	reads aloud	R
	marking text	W
	listening	L
	attentive to teacher	L
20	listening	L
	reading / listening	R
	reading / listening	R
	listening	L
	listening	L

PUPIL 2 (M)

Time	Activity	Code
0	sitting on bench	
	throws away chewing gum	
	tells teacher act and scene	T
	recalling plot	T
	context empathy	L
10	listening	L
	offering information	T
	listening	L
	listening	L
	listening	L
20	listening	L
	reads, laughing with enjoyment	R
	reading / listening	R
	listening	L
	listening	L

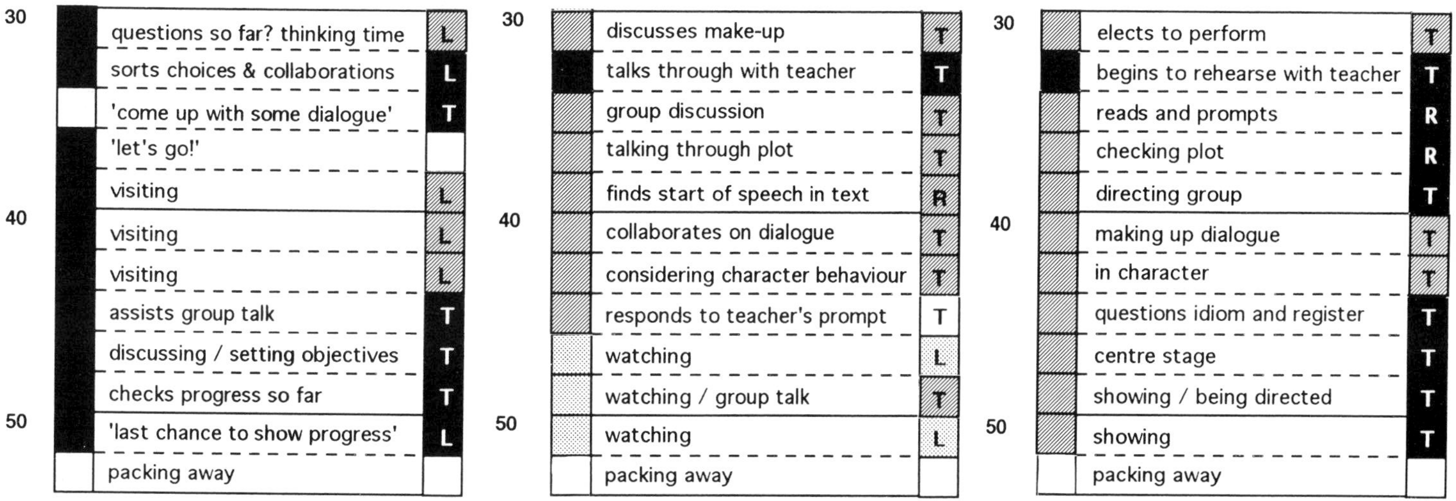

Figure 5.5 Drama script

MFL TEACHER (M)		PUPIL 1 (M)		PUPIL 2 (F)	
register and oral questions (Eng)	T	waiting/listening as whole class	L	waiting/listening as whole class	L
describing self (Eng)	T	listening	L	listening	L
describing in model language (Fr)	T	listening	L	listening	L
questioning pupils (Fr)	T	answers teacher with description	T	listening	T
handing out textbooks		receives textbook		receives textbook	
drawing attention to written task	R	individual reading of text	R	individual reading of text	R
setting exercise: match person	T	listening to teacher/following	L	listening to teacher/following	L
to description (reading French)	R	familiarizing/reading/following	R	familiarizing/reading/following	R
spelling test/write French term	T	begins closed test/writing	W	begins closed test/writing	W
spelling test	T	writing/following teacher	W	writing/following teacher	W
eliciting individual answers	T	listening/practising aloud	L	listening/practising aloud	L
writing answers/explains in Eng.	W	answers closed question/marking	T	marking from model answer	T
writing in Fr/questions in Eng.	W	self-marking from model answer	W	marking from answers on board	W
eliciting response and correcting	T	marking from board/listening	W	not involved in discussion/adrift	ot
completing feedback	T	evaluating/correcting mistakes	W	evaluating/correcting mistakes	W

Panel 1 (Teacher activities)

Time	Activity	Code
30	setting magazine activities	T
	reading through tasks	R
	explaining tasks	T
40	visiting pupils/monitoring	L
	advising, encouraging	T
	explaining to a group	T
	checking individual progress	L
	checking individuals	L
	checking individuals	L
50	finishes monitoring	L
	reviewing task	T
	individual questions to pupils (Fr)	T
	closed questions (Fr)	T

Panel 2 (Pupil activities)

Time	Activity	Code
30	looking at magazine/scanning	R
	listening/discussing in group	T
	listening to teacher/familiarizing	L
	solving jumbled words/writing	W
40	into c'word grid/discussing	T
	teacher visit/explains correction	T
	working with partner/writing	W
	discussing/writing up together	T
	completes c'word in collaboration	T
50	packing away text & magazine	
	listens to teacher review	L
	packs away ex. book and pens	L
	following final descriptions (Fr)	L

Panel 3 (Pupil activities)

Time	Activity	Code
30	looking at magazine/scanning	R
	listening/discussing in group	T
	listening to teacher	L
	listening to partner/translating	L
40	discusses crossword (Fr. clues)	T
	losing interest/drifting	ot
	explaining crossword to partner	T
	solving together, completing	T
	word-search, using key to task	T
50	packing away	
	listens to teacher review	L
	packs away ex. book and pens	L
	following final descriptions (Fr)	L

Figure 5.6 Modern Languages script

the exchanges interactive. It remains the case, however, that the individual who talked, read and wrote the most French, was the class teacher.

SUMMARIZING THE LESSON OBSERVATION DATA

The data which we have considered from the secondary school phase of the research confirm many of the findings from previous studies. Most classroom reading or writing opportunities were brief and occurred in fragments, rather than extended time blocks. As we have already indicated, reading or writing events did not occur at all for more than three quarters of the pupils observed, and when time was given over to reading or writing, this was unlikely to be reflective or assisted, to explore a wide range of functions and genres, or to last more than a few minutes.

Despite their strong commitment to collaborative styles of working, all of the teachers we observed spent a lot of their time organizing and managing learners, giving out information and setting tasks, interacting only briefly with individuals to sustain their involvement and check on progress. In some instances, resources had been prepared or chosen with great care, in order to provide an arresting entry into a new topic. Teachers based their lessons around stimuli as diverse as newspaper extracts, advertisements, poetry, letters, video and television recordings.

However, the characteristic pattern of these management-led lessons generally constrained the nature of any literacy-related tasks to the function of writing or reading in order to complete a set exercise (see Appendix 8). Literacy served the purpose of setting and solving problems, mostly by copying or moving information from one place to another. Negotiating tasks, setting up contexts which emphasize relevance and make bridges to the pupils' own experience, encouraging pupils to actively pursue their own lines of enquiry, were not typical.

A highly characteristic format, occurring in almost all of the lesson scripts, was for two or three teacher-controlled tasks to be introduced with supporting information in a textbook, blackboard notes, handout or work-sheet. In the lesson contexts we observed, reading and writing were most likely to be used for following or responding to the teacher's instructions. Occasionally, pupils read as they followed the teacher's exposition, listening to new ideas in science, maths or humanities, whilst looking over a text.

There were few opportunities to pre-read texts, to read continuously or to interrogate textual evidence. Very rarely were pupils able to read critically: analysing and evaluating the reading sources. When analysis did take place, this was usually the teacher exercising critical power, with pupils witnessing. The classroom data suggest that the individual who spends most time actively practising and reflecting on reading is the teacher.

There were very few occasions when attention was drawn to the use of reading as a form of enquiry, specific to a subject domain. In the English script, pupils were involved in visualizing characters from a play, substantiating their portrayals with close reference to the text, identifying the evidence they had used in constructing their portraits. Here, the strategies of reading for a specific subject purpose were made explicit, modelled and rehearsed by all the pupils. In the science script, learning enquiries included discussion of hypothesis-raising, data-collection and analysis, together with the recording and reporting of findings. However, these processes emphasised oral, rather than written language.

There may well have been other occasions, unobserved by the researchers, when pupils were introduced to specific reading processes intrinsic to science, history or design: weighing evidence, sources or arguments which constitute the very essence of working as a scientist, historian or designer. However, this cannot have occurred very frequently or for many pupils. For the most part, pupils used whatever reading strategies and experience they brought with them into different subject domains, which remained unchallenged and unextended.

On the occasions when pupils were required to write, they mostly got on with this independently, in the form of completing set exercises, copying or transferring. In almost all cases, the context, form and purpose of writing were handed over by the teacher. For example, in a PSE lesson, students completed a worksheet on personal characteristics, filling in spaces in sentences, completing stem sentences or responding to questions with single words. Examples of this kind could be found in almost every lesson across the curriculum and are highly familiar to secondary teachers. When pupils were able to generate their own writing, as in the English script, this was typically for descriptive purposes in the form of personal accounts or narratives.

Some pupils were visited briefly in some lessons by teachers who gave assistance to the drafting of writing. However, in the majority of cases pupils wrote unassisted, without attention to the process of construction, and without critical reflection or feedback. As in reading, what pupils used as they came into different subject areas, were the writing strategies and experience they already had, and which were unchanged by the teaching or learning activities.

There were one or two exceptions to this. In information technology, for example, all the pupils were given opportunities to write extended personal accounts using word processors. Help was provided on the drafting of sentences and paragraphs; with spelling, punctuation and grammar; in revising and publishing written work. Ostensibly, these lessons were meant to foster keyboard competence, but they achieved far more than that. This was an isolated case: most subject specialists requested writing in closed contexts prescribed by a worksheet or textbook, requiring short, step-by-step responses. They did not seem used to thinking of the functions and processes of writing or reading as important aspects of their subject teaching. There were very few occasions when teachers made explicit the processes of enquiry which are strategic to science, maths, design or the humanities, and which are supported and shaped through specific kinds of reading or writing.

Earlier in this chapter we discussed some of the differences between natural and contrived contexts in which individuals operate. We said that in contexts which have been fabricated, such as classrooms, ordinary pragmatic concerns are often suspended as people pose questions and respond to them, set problems and find solutions. Participants share ground rules and common knowledge in relation to the system of the classroom, what is normally expected and how people behave. To a greater or lesser degree, teachers succeed in transforming the classroom into a forum of genuine challenge and investigation. Whilst very little of what pupils do in school can be considered to be creating new information or pursuing real lines of enquiry, some teachers did manage to turn classrooms into real research laboratories, publishers' offices or design studios. In these settings, aspects of literacy found a natural form and function, as tools for the job.

AN AGENDA FOR CHANGE

The immediate purpose of the research study was to provide direct observational evidence – how literacy was currently approached by different subject teachers across the curriculum – as the starting point for a professional development programme within the school. The success of the whole project would be judged by how well different departments were able to create teaching contexts where literacy played an important and strategic role. The long term outcome envisaged was the raising of student competence in all aspects of written language, through more literacy-focused learning encounters. The school had embarked, with the help of outside research support, on a process of becoming a more literacy-orientated community.

The research team adhered to the principle that literacy practices should be examined within the complex social contexts of the classroom. Any recommendations emerging from the study would pay attention to the constraints inherent in managing groups of learners, as well as managing learning. It was also important that teachers were helped to implement practices which they viewed as pedagogically sound, but were unable to act upon because of real or perceived obstacles. As agreed in the contract drawn up at the outset of the research, in-service training with individual faculties and in whole staff meetings, began to address the following issues.

Common practice for composition and presentation

Lesson scripts from different subject areas showed very little consistency in the way aspects of pupils' written presentations were shaped and modelled. Both teachers and pupils needed to share a common set of expectations, operating across all subject areas, which would eventually be synthesized in a policy document for the whole school. It was important to stress that these expectations were not demands which would be imposed on pupils and staff, but conventional features of schooled literacy which required explanation and negotiation. Teachers and pupils would be encouraged to consider why, how and when conventions were used, in order to explain what purpose such conventions served. Broad areas for consideration included:

1　*Layout:* the placing of print on the page, including titles, headings, underlinings, information blocks, diagrams, illustrations, page numbers.
2　*Language:* specialist subject vocabulary and terminology, appropriate written genres supported by relevant spoken registers.
3　*Editing:* investigation of error and the process of reconstruction to make a final draft, including acceptable methods of adult intervention and correction, positive analysis of superficial and structural understanding in children's written language, and quality of feedback.
4　*Banking:* common storage and retrieval procedures, such as 'rough books', 'process books' and 'portfolios'; process sheets and topsheets; progress or content records.

Quality and duration of reading events

One important need identified in the study was more frequent and sustained opportunities for reading for a variety of purposes across the curriculum. Faculties were asked to consider the nature and quality of reading to accomplish the demands of lessons, or series of lessons in each scheme of work and before modules ran, including the range of resources and texts required. Teachers were asked to construct tasks which focused critically on specific texts, and to require pupils to take the initiative for reading. Some lessons would be planned to incorporate reading episodes of approximately fifteen minutes, with an emphasis on reading for a specific purpose in relation to teaching and learning.

It was also important that subject specialists began to ask themselves questions about the specific literacy formats, processes and demands, required of specific subject areas. What was distinctive in the reading functions and strategies which characterize history or science in contrast with design, technology, maths or English? Whose job was it to ensure that pupils were given appropriate experiences and when should such specialized teaching begin?

Quality and duration of writing events

More frequent and sustained opportunities for writing were also required. A key concept to explore with staff was the construction of written context. Lesson scripts from the research phase of the study indicated that many teachers tended to give the context for writing too readily, particularly to pupils lacking in confidence or initiative. Whilst all writers need to learn how to contextualize their composition appropriately, any form of unthinking reproduction through copying or transferring, or over-reliance on a given model, impairs literate initiative.

In particular, teachers were asked to include more opportunities to develop continuous writing, where they supported pupils' intentions without doing all the conceptual work in their stead. As a basic entitlement, each module of work across the curriculum would entail one written outcome in which the writing process would be given equal weight to written content. Pupils would be praised and assessed through their developing understanding of process issues involved. Subject specialists were required to articulate what the specific writing demands of their subject domains consisted of, and how these might be translated into practical teaching ideas in the contexts of science, geography, mathematics or history.

Literacy in the daily landscape

For the most part, the literacy curriculum is hidden amidst the daily demands and expectations of different subject domains. We asked teachers to reconsider the centrality of literacy within their subject teaching and to find more opportunities to teach process issues. Data from the lesson scripts show that the teacher's attention was usually paid to how well pupils had derived accurate information or correct answers, rather than strategies for reading and recording. In one important sense, the pupils' existing understanding and use of literacy processes was neither challenged, nor extended, in the tasks which were frequently set. Since the focus was often fixed on content, pupils used their existing competence to complete tasks: what they took away from lesson experiences, in terms of literacy competence, was mostly what they arrived with in the first place.

Collaborative work

Lesson scripts showed that teachers habitually grouped pupils in certain ways, without addressing the relationship between groupings and learning outcomes. Collaborative work, involving pupils as reading and writing partners, in investigative crews, as reviewers and consumers, are some of the ways in which reflective practice can be developed. We asked teachers to consider, alongside rules for behaviour, codes for pupils working together and what functions these would serve.

Information technology

Using information technology, especially word processors, as a more familiar part of different subject teaching, for research, reference, composition and presentation, was also seen to be an important way of promoting active learning and enhancing students' thinking through written language. Given the amount of time spent by pupils during observation, using prepared resources and other technologies, such as video or tapes, ways of using these technologies in a more active, mediated way, are also important areas for professional development.

SUMMARY

In this chapter we have presented data collected in one secondary school setting, as part of an extensive professional development programme focused on enhancing literacy teaching and learning across the curriculum. We have argued for the centrality of literacy in every subject area, although there are wide variations in stance and practice, with regard to how literacy is used for learning within different subject specialisms. The research methods adopted, based on our framework of adult–child proximation, allowed us to compare teachers' conceptual maps with observed practice, identifying those factors which constrain teachers to work in certain ways, and providing signposts for change.

From the questionnaire phase of the study we concluded that the majority of secondary teachers, like their primary colleagues, have strong preferences for participative, collaborative teaching styles. Many departments said they would like to work in this way, including English staff, design and technology teachers, drama, music and art specialists. Other teachers valued structured schemes and materials, such as in modern languages and maths, which we have termed 'resource-driven' teaching. Informal, pupil-centred activities, were more popular amongst science and art teachers, including performing arts. Special needs staff, exceptionally, favoured more didactic, adult-structured approaches which emphasize rote or drill methods. Importantly, most departments presented a balance of views; it is certainly not the case that secondary teachers (or indeed their primary colleagues) eschew more traditional, skill-focused teaching, in favour of pupil-centred approaches. However, it cannot be assumed that all secondary teachers accept responsibility for teaching literacy within their subject specialisms.

A second phase of research examined contrasts between the beliefs expressed in the literacy questionnaire and observed practice in the classroom. Despite what they say, many teachers work in a way which prioritizes order, cooperation and adult control. This we have interpreted – advised by teachers themselves – that styles high in management and control are 'low risk' in the potentially volatile social contexts of many secondary classrooms.

From the pupils' individual perspective, the classroom experience may look very different. Pupils were not often engaged in carrying out rote tasks drilled by the teacher, even though the teacher might be expending a great deal of time and energy directing pupils and activities. The major portion of curriculum time was accounted for by resource-driven activities, such as completing set exercises in isolation, with little adult help or guidance. The practical realities of classrooms dictate that teachers can only guide, or interact with, a selection of individuals for brief moments in time. Instances of shared discussion, reflection and review, were rare.

An important area for observation was focused on time spent reading or writing. As in the primary research, we defined reading strictly in terms of the active involvement of pupils constructing their own meaning from text. Writing was defined in terms of generating and composing. Other kinds of reading or writing, such as following a text read by a teacher, or transferring print from one place to another in order to complete a worksheet, were coded separately. In more than three-quarters of lessons, generating writing or active reading engagement, were never observed. In the majority of observed lessons, pupils were not given many opportunities to read or write as part of the teaching process, nor were they able to spend much time critically reviewing their reading or redrafting their writing. Opportunities that did arise were usually brief and fragmented.

Although we have argued for the importance of literacy as a tool for thinking, analysis, recording and communication in all subject areas, for many pupils in this study, teaching and learning proceeded without literacy taking a major part.

Data from the lesson scripts provide a more detailed account of the rich texture of lessons, how activities are organized and resources deployed, and the use made of aspects of literacy. Teachers often based their lessons on stimuli as diverse as newspaper extracts, videos, letters and advertisements, in order to make an arresting entry into a new topic, to *recruit* pupils to the task. Literacy tended to be restricted to writing or reading in order to complete an exercise, rather than reading to pursue an enquiry or to exercise critical power. Occasionally, pupils were introduced to reading or writing strategies which embody the underlying forms and purposes of enquiry in specific subject domains, such as supporting an argument with reference to the text of a play, or recording data in a science experiment.

One key finding from this secondary phase of the research is that in the main, the process issues of reading or writing, were rarely examined or developed within the contexts of different subject areas. Most subject specialists requested reading or writing in closed contexts prescribed by a textbook or worksheet, requiring a limited response. There were few instances when pupils were introduced to the enquiry processes strategic to science, maths, design or the humanities, and which are supported and shaped by specific kinds of reading or writing. We concluded that, very largely, pupils used whatever literacy strategies and experience they brought with them into different subject areas, which remained unchallenged and unextended.

All of these ideas were fed back to the school staff concerned, as part of agreeing an agenda for change. Questions were asked about how the secondary school could build on pupils' earlier experiences in the primary school, and how to manage the transition from highly interactive contexts, to more loosely-coupled, content-driven classroom settings. Issues which were considered included common practice for writing conventions, such as layout, banking, editing. Teachers were asked to incorporate into their lesson designs, reading and writing episodes which explored the specific literacy formats, processes and demands of different subject areas. They were also asked to consider aspects of group work, such as writing crews, and to bring information technology, especially word-processing, more prominently into the daily landscape of all areas of the curriculum. Most important of all, secondary teachers were asked to consider how literacy could become the focus of learning in different subject domains, paying attention to how classrooms are organized to promote good quality interactions around text, where literacy process issues are raised, challenged and expanded.

6   Managing the literacy curriculum

Not all adult–child interactions embody the idealised view . . . of adults eager
to instruct and children eager to learn.

Forman et al., 1993

In this chapter we set out a number of steps which will enable schools to
become more powerful communities for literacy teaching and learning. In
many instances, particularly in primary schools, the literacy curriculum is
already well-developed and successful, with very careful attention paid to the
major partners involved: children, parents, teachers and texts. Simply stated,
our major concern in the research undertaken with primary and secondary
schools has been to identify those aspects of teaching and learning contexts
which can be managed selectively in order to strengthen the literacy
environment.

The evidence we have presented in this book has formed the core of a
working partnership between researchers and teachers, in a shared momentum
to examine and improve current practice. In the present political climate,
schools find themselves under pressure to become more publicly accountable,
whilst also exposing themselves to market forces through mechanisms such as
league tables. Many schools have begun to make moves to manage inspection
and report issues for themselves. Auditing the literacy environment is one facet
of a school cluster's attempt to account independently for pupils' learning and
achievement, to identify what makes a difference in successful classrooms as a
basis for raising the quality of teaching and learning from within.

The neutral evidence base of our dialogue with schools has enabled a
wide-reaching set of ideas to be generated, to enlarge and inform the choices
which teachers make in their day-to-day work. We must stress that this
collaboration between researchers and teachers was not a single, self-
contained incident or summative event, but a formative process of professional development carried out over a number of years. Changing
long-held beliefs and generating new understandings of how literacy may be
tackled by a school cannot take place instantaneously. Change at the
classroom level has to be justified, modelled, supported and coaxed into place
over a period of time.

From the outset we wished to move away from older models of reading or writing as rule-descriptions, stages or skills, which have in turn spawned a wealth of suggestions on how to teach the mechanics of literacy through attention to basic skills or rule-performance. Most of these models of learning to read or write ignore the complex constraints of the classroom, which is where most children and teachers spend their time. Instead, we have posed the question of how to raise the literacy levels of cohorts of school children at all ages, as a challenge for the whole curriculum and for every class or subject teacher. Within the curriculum, we have begun to address the quality of learning encounters in relation to written text: how literacy is used as a tool for wider enquiry and understanding. In other words, we have begun to examine under what conditions children acquire literacy most effectively, and the consequences for literacy of organizing classrooms and activities in certain ways.

STEP 1: UNDERSTANDING LITERACY WITHIN THE WHOLE CURRICULUM

Teachers are unused to thinking about literacy as a set of interlocking systems. In one sense, literacy is a system of symbols for moving between spoken and written language codes. In another sense, literacy enables individuals to represent their ideas and to develop disembedded forms of thinking. In school, literacy is located in a system of classroom encounters which may change markedly from class to class and school to school. Depending on how these are managed and organized, literacy may be shaped as an inert system of decoding and recording, or reconstructed between adults and children as a powerful resource and means of enquiry. Specific subject specialisms bring teachers and learners into contact with specific conventions and specific functions of written language. Literacy has the power to facilitate children's classroom practice in terms of planning a programme of work, originating hypotheses, evaluating and questioning, data recording and analysis, weighing of evidence, drawing of conclusions, and communicating the fruits of their enquiries to relevant audiences. These systems of learning we have described throughout the book as the site of literacy formation, with differences in emphasis arising between teachers, subjects and schools.

In order to address the central relationship between developments in children's literacy and what teachers require of them in the classroom – the nature of their critical practice or experience – we have considered teaching and learning in terms of mediation or proximation, with an emphasis on relevance, purpose, meaning, planning, self-regulation, and critical reflection. What is handed over or learned is not simply information, but procedures and strategies leading to independence in the learner. In both primary and secondary school contexts, the quality of children's literacy encounters is explored through social interaction and dialogues held around text.

The key components of socio-constructivism we surveyed in Chapter 2:

scaffolding, appropriation and the zone of proximal development. These concepts provide metaphors for the quality of teacher intervention in learning. A crucial part of scaffolding is the teacher's contingency: how well the adult paces help given to children, maintaining interest, allowing room for initiative, stepping in before pupils veer off course, restructuring problems with children and weighing findings, including how the task was tackled and what can be carried forward to the next time. Appropriation refers to how adults adjust their teaching to meet the needs of the learner during classroom interaction. The zone of proximal development refers to the gap between what children can achieve on their own and what they can manage, given adult assistance. Many previous studies, and much of the data collected in the present research, show that classroom activities are often repetitious and occupy rather than challenge children, with children out of the zone of proximal development for much of the time.

To stretch children in large group settings, to move all children on in their understanding, places enormous demands on teachers and requires a critical examination of the utility of the zone of proximal development in relation to school contexts. Evidence from the primary sector indicates that there may be several zones operating in many classrooms, which children move into and out of. Most teachers create learning opportunities which have a rich texture, offering different quality interaction to different pupils, for different purposes and at different times. Whether pupils move in any or all of these potential zones varies widely from child to child.

In order to understand more clearly the dynamics of teaching and learning in contrasting classrooms, we devised a framework for analysis building on concepts of social interaction. However, not everything which happens in schools is geared to effective learning. Much of what transpires is concerned with managing behaviour, order and cooperation. To assume that the finite resource of teaching time can be allocated selectively to one aspect of the curriculum as opposed to another, misses the point that classroom time is often purloined by the exigencies of busy, demanding and sometimes volatile social contexts. Hence, the framework we fashioned embraced different images of the roles of teachers and pupils and is capable of accommodating some of the complexities of classroom life. Aspects of literacy, such as group reading, talk around text, generating and redrafting writing, we have studied as intrinsic parts of the day-to-day business of the classroom, in different subject domains. This is what we have referred to as literacy within the daily landscape of the curriculum.

STEP 2: TOWARDS A SCHOOL POLICY FRAMEWORK

An important issue is how far teachers can become better managers of classrooms and pupils, whilst at the same time also becoming more effective managers of learning. The production of policy frameworks for schools has been a growth industry in recent years in the belief that policy statements, of themselves, lead to more concerted enterprise, to clearer goals. It is well recognized that many aspects of school life such as behaviour and discipline, child protection, information technology, learning support, language and literacy, depend on staff sharing some common values and strategies, which are consistently applied. In order to achieve a whole school approach, the generation and publication of a policy document is often seen as an important component. Policies imposed from outside schools are unlikely to be viewed with the same commitment as policies generated by a school staff working together to meet an identified area of need. Furthermore, as many teachers recognize, the act of writing things down is insufficient in itself to ensure that objectives are shared or fulfilled.

The policy framework which the schools involved in the research study began to work on was distinctive in several ways. First, many of the school teaching staff took part in the phases of data collection, analysis and subsequent training. Policy decisions emerged from the combined efforts to review the curriculum, out of a process of ideas' generation and discussion, rather than being imposed by senior management or outside agencies. Any changes which were decided upon were at least partly in response to internal rather than external initiatives. Second, having decided as school teams to pursue a literacy audit and to invite observers into classrooms, teachers had invested a great deal in the research, trusted its intentions, and were prepared to act on the findings.

The third, perhaps most important factor which underpinned the policy framework, was the recognition of a common principle: the commitment by all teachers in the schools concerned to share responsibility for extending and enriching the use of literacy within every classroom context. As we have seen, this undertaking required a less radical shift in the primary than the secondary school where more diverse curriculum and organizational demands have to be faced. Within the cluster of schools and in each school context, the sharing of the research models and its language of analysis promoted consistency and momentum. The action plans drawn up by teachers and, in some cases, whole departments, during the follow-up training sessions of the project, translated the policy objectives into specific priorities for each school concerned. An important question to ask about policy statements in schools embarking on changing practice, is whether management objectives reflect or predetermine initiatives generated by teachers themselves.

STEP 3: PROMOTING PROFESSIONAL DEVELOPMENT

Many approaches have been recommended by specialists in school management and staff development for enabling teachers to improve teaching and learning (McMahon and Bolam, 1990; Oldroyd and Hall, 1991). Many recent accounts of efforts to change schools as learning environments have begun to regard schools themselves, rather than policy makers, LEAs or external agencies such as the DfE, as centres of change. This view of the school as an institution which identifies its own needs, thinks about possible solutions and then tackles its own problems in a systematic and sustained way, is consistent with the philosophy we have adopted in this research project.

Embodied in the notion of a thinking or learning school are some important assumptions. For the school to become a centre of change, recognition has to be given to what most teachers spend most of their time doing. So a curriculum focus is critical, examining the internal conditions of classrooms, and the school's procedures for managing, resourcing and supporting teaching and learning activities. This is not to ignore the important role which outside agencies, such as advisers and inspectors, may play. All schools operate within wider political and cultural contexts which attempt to define, constrain and interpret how schools should function. However, at a practical level, it is recognized that to raise levels of pupil achievement by improving teaching and learning, requires changes in the culture of classrooms.

How do adults change and learn? We see no crucial differences between the processes of mediation involved when adults engage with children in learning encounters and the professional development of adults. In both situations individuals are challenged in their existing understanding and are helped to move forward, to reach new concepts and competences. We could just as easily apply the model of adult–child proximation we devised to account for teaching and learning in the classroom, to our staff development work with teachers in the project. Choices can be made between information-giving within a transmission model, experience-led approaches which allow individuals to find their own solutions through trial and error, or contrasting approaches which are interactive and collaborative. Throughout this book we have argued for a broad range of learning activities, but permitting dialogue, exchange and good quality interactions with others.

In the literacy project, we took for granted, since the schools invited our participation, that some teachers saw the need for change. Many teachers shared a broad conceptual basis on important aspects of literacy, as evidenced by the questionnaire study reported in Chapter 2. However, there were great individual differences in levels of confidence and expertise between teachers in primary and secondary schools, and in different subject specialisms, in relation to the teaching of literacy within the curriculum. These differences came to light in some of the feedback sessions when teachers commented freely on the research project. We pursued the research, therefore, with some teachers feeling ambivalent and uncertain, others holding dissimilar expectations about what would be gained from the project. Involving teachers as co-researchers in the data collection phase went some way towards establishing shared ownership of the proceedings and the outcomes. Even so, we knew that for many teachers, to achieve any long-term impact on classroom practice would entail shifts in attitude, some disagreement and debate, much persistence and a long time span.

An important part of the research was concerned with awareness-raising or *problem-sharing*. The audit phase of the project gathered data directly relevant to the schools concerned and imparted information. Some of what we did was focused on *problem-coping*: designing training opportunities where teachers could react, assess their own positions on the issues raised, and interact with colleagues to form their own opinions. Some of what we did was geared to *problem-solving*: helping individuals to construct practical ways forward in the presence of facilitators. It is this last phase of supporting teachers to change what they do in the classroom, which is the most difficult, but arguably the most significant, in relation to long-term professional development.

In the remaining sections of this chapter we set out some of the main issues which were worked on by the schools involved. A range of staff development opportunities were dedicated to these literacy issues over time, including whole staff in-service days, department workshops, preparation and analysis of key documents, discussion of critical incidents, generation of action plans, mutual lesson observation, modelling of lesson procedures and resources. A key factor is that the school management team made time available for the work, acknowledged the complexities of the change process, and involved themselves directly in the research, for example, by being observed teaching.

The main lessons we have drawn from this project in relation to staff development are that the need for change has to be clearly and neutrally demonstrated; ownership and commitment have to be won and not assumed; management support must be demonstrated, for example, by allocating time and resources for the work involved; and a wide range of training activities should be available over a long period of time. Teachers, especially subject specialists, start from different points in terms of their awareness of the literacy needs of children, depending on the kind of training they have previously had. In schools where English departments have traditionally been looked to for expertise in areas such as children's spelling, handwriting, written language or reading, there may be a reluctance in moving towards a greater sharing of responsibilities.

Teachers can be helped to change what they do through interactive and mediated approaches which keep a steady focus on the realities of the classroom. Most people, however much they appear to agree in principle, start from different understandings and levels of competence. Any attempt to improve practice across a whole curriculum or group of schools is bound to meet resistance, to progress slowly and piecemeal, and to require a driving force behind it.

STEP 4: CONDUCTING A CURRICULUM AUDIT

One of OFSTED's current concerns, expressed in documents such as *Primary Matters* (1994), is that there are very wide variations in the amounts of time spent on individual subjects in different schools. Time on task, including the length of the taught week, has been identified as an important variable affecting educational achievement. Furthermore, schools rarely make effective or systematic estimates of how time – 'a finite resource' – is used. As part of the burgeoning list of responsibilities which school managers now shoulder, organizing, monitoring and evaluating the curriculum are high priorities.

In the course of this book, we have pointed out the complexities of classroom contexts and the difficulties involved in describing the nature of classroom transactions. Only superficial data can be gained from analysing the prescribed timetable *per se*, whilst the proportion of pupils' time spent in productive engagement with any subject area cannot easily be measured. In the primary school, particularly, there are genuine problems in quantifying time spent on language or literacy, since these areas may be taught through topic work across the subject boundaries. In fact, we have made out the case for not viewing language or literacy as discrete areas of the curriculum, but as central to all learning in all subjects.

Our own approach to data collection has taken the form of lesson observations, focusing on the quality of adult–child interactions around written language. In both primary and secondary school contexts, teachers decided to make their own accounts of pupils' learning and achievement, isolating those factors which made a difference in successful classrooms, as a basis for enhancing the curriculum. The researchers' role was to facilitate the long-term development plan which the schools had embarked upon, with literacy as a central issue. Importantly, the curriculum audits which were carried out during the research project were designed to inform the schools' own debate and reflection. Accordingly, the sense of audit we wished to promote was more that of listening than of accounting. The listening stage depicted literacy as an intrinsic part of teachers' styles of working, within a diversity of subject domains and classrooms. The evidence of how teachers worked and how pupils responded, informed a professional development process in the participant schools, over a long span of time.

Schools considering making their own independent audits may wish to adapt some of the methods and resources we have developed. There are some important issues, in terms of developing schools as literate communities, to do with how literacy is perceived by teachers in different departments of a school, and how literacy is effectively used within different classroom contexts. Attitudes vary on the value of teaching literacy within different subject domains and how responsibilities should be allocated. All teachers, whatever their subject expertise, invest in literacy as a means for learning, to a greater or lesser degree. It is the task of a school manager to take account of prevailing attitudes amongst staff, and to find growth points. However, to conduct a representative audit of classroom practice requires a commitment of time and personnel. The drawing up of an agenda or informal contract specifying *who*, will do *what*, by *when*, goes some way to ensuring that steps will be taken. But the most important factor, if an audit is to inform whole-school developments, is that all staff trust the purposes and intentions of such an approach. Answers will come from efforts to investigate the questions which, collectively, staff want to ask.

STEP 5: INCREASING TIME SPENT READING AND WRITING

One of the issues thrown up by a number of research investigations, including our own, is the limited amounts of time when pupils are actually engaged in writing or reading, through the school day. Time spent by pupils in literacy-related activities appears to diminish from infant school onwards. Furthermore, when pupils do read or write, these instances are likely to be fragmentary and discontinuous. In the primary school, personal reading and narrative writing predominate, so that pupils have very little experience of different formats associated with different subject areas. It may also be difficult to ascertain in what ways reading and writing strategies are expected to advance over time, what is expected of Year 6 pupils which is different from Years 4 or 5? In the secondary school, literacy is mainly used for following instructions and the completion of set exercises. When children are given time to read or write, the majority of ideas for writing, the contexts for engaging with print, generally come from the teacher.

Findings from our own research confirm that many teachers appear to be suspicious of the value of pupils reading or writing in class, increasingly so as pupils get older. Many secondary teachers remain to be convinced of their responsibility, as subject specialists, for creating teaching contexts where literacy plays a significant and strategic role. Other staff simply feel unskilled or lack confidence in how to tackle this dimension of the curriculum. Teachers (including English teachers) cannot look to the National Curriculum documentation for advice on these issues.

An immediate step which can be taken by primary and secondary schools is to increase the time which is purposefully given over to aspects of literacy in the classroom context. Lesson scripts from the research phase of the study bear out the limited opportunities for constructing writing or for sustained reading. Many of the schools involved in the research study, including subject departments in the secondary school, reached a consensus on a number of expectations for literacy teaching: common formats for layout, presentation, editing and banking of children's work. Perhaps, most importantly, schools reached agreement on basic entitlements for all pupils to be supported to produce a minimum number of written assignments per work module, across the curriculum. Similarly, schools can set expectations for incorporating reading episodes of a given duration in every lesson, which some schools call ERIC (Everybody Reads In Class) or DEAR (Drop Everything And Read) time, although this tends to be confined to private reading of fiction.

Obviously, the quality of reading and writing encounters is also highly significant, but time and space have to be made available in the first place. We are not suggesting that more time added on, or switched from one activity to another is sufficient. Impact on literacy experience will grow from a refocusing and redesigning of how literacy is used to promote enquiry within different subject areas.

STEP 6: CREATING CLASSROOM CONTEXTS WHICH BRING LITERACY ALIVE

We could reformulate this step as the creation of classroom contexts in which both adults and children must use print *to live* successfully. One observation, frequently made in our classroom research, is that the individual who spends most time identifying problems, negotiating learning routes, constructing writing, exploring reading sources, analysing and reflecting on literacy processes, is the teacher. In a real community of learners, print contact is frequent, varied, relevant and extensive for *all* participants, whilst the amount of coasting by children is minimized. Our data indicate that there are very wide variations from one teacher to another, in the situations or conditions which are created for children, where they most closely resemble mature readers or writers.

A fundamental aspect in designing a teaching space to promote literacy for young children, is room organization. Key experiences can be either enhanced by, or in conflict with, room management. For example, in one infant classroom, a teacher wanted the children to assume more responsibility for their own learning, to take initiatives, plan and regulate their own work, to be more independent in pursuing their own enquiries. Accordingly, the room was designed for several kinds of interaction, including areas for planning and reviewing with small groups; defined areas for individual work, such as writing stations, listening centres, computer tables; and storage areas for reference sources, books and materials. Each of the areas was clearly marked with an overhead sign. Book areas were well-stocked with covers visible. Non-fiction books were arranged by subject, whilst collections of current topic sources had been extracted and were displayed separately. Writing areas contained a range of implements, paper, envelopes, clips, stapler and adhesive tape. Hoardings around the room displayed concept maps and useful word lists. There were other clearly labelled resource banks where children could retrieve letter templates and vocabulary cards.

This print-rich, process-friendly environment also included a range of 'Big Books' on stands, flip charts, alphabet friezes, dictionaries, magazines, newspapers, yellow pages, calendars, junkmail and catalogues. A bulletin board was available for children to mount messages, jokes, memos, announcements, invitations or postcards. Routines had been established over time, whereby children convened at the beginning of sessions to share ideas, discuss and plan. Work or learning plans were usually written down. Evidence of group brainstorming, question-raising and work in progress was also displayed. Children requiring a lot of help were given small, manageable targets to complete within given timescales and frequently visited. Children never had to queue for advice, information about what to do next, feedback or resources. The point to be made about this teaching context is that the boundaries to different work areas, traffic flow, labelling and resources access, routines for planning and sharing, all promoted the children's growing independence as learners. The teacher had designed the learning environment to promote a range of interactive opportunities.

Another key issue for all teachers, in both primary and secondary phases, is the idea of basing a range of teaching activities around a *conceptual centre*. Successful lessons, those teaching contexts in which all children were engaged for extended periods of time in activities with a high literacy focus, were often built around a number of analogous themes, practices and processes. For example, a Year 2 lesson script showed a succession of overlapping activities, following a television story, which was also examined as a 'Big Book'. Homing in on 'r' words from the story, children researched dictionaries and word banks, used flip charts and flashcards, completed worksheets and stem sentences, labelled diagrams and drew pictures, built rockets and robots. Whilst most of these activities concerned word recognition and letter formation, everyone was clear about the relevance and meaning of the various tasks. There was no sense of activity for activities' sake.

In all school contexts, much depends on how successful the teacher is in transforming the classroom into a *virtual* writer's workshop, design studio, laboratory or office. Maintaining such virtuality in the daily round of lessons is very demanding. Children will be bringing into lessons varied and complex notions of representation and production, often drawing on their own experiences (Reed, 1986; Reed and Beveridge, 1993). In Chapter 3 we discussed some of the distinctions between natural and contrived settings where individuals learn. In the contrived context of the classroom, pupils come to recognize a special kind of teacher-managed problem-solving, with implicit ground rules and prescribed outcomes, which suspends the pragmatic concerns of real life. The data we gathered in the secondary school phase of our research indicate a very characteristic pattern of lesson organization across the subject areas, which is high in teacher management and control. The typical script of a lesson included a high proportion of teacher exposition and instruction, with pupils spending much of their time following or responding to set exercises. Reading frequently took the form of pupils looking over a text as the teacher directed attention to points of interest. Scripts showed very few opportunities to pre-read, to research sources, to read continuously, or to reflect on reading processes.

In fact, in the majority of the classrooms observed, learning proceeded without literacy taking a major part. In writing, for example, pupils were frequently asked to provide short responses to prescribed, closed tasks, or to transfer print from one place to another. When pupils were asked to generate their own writing this was typically for descriptive purposes in the form of personal accounts or narratives. The function of writing, its form and structure, was almost always determined by the teacher. To complete set tasks, such as a work sheet on lifestyles in PSE, or a comprehension exercise on equal opportunities in history, pupils generally drew on the literacy resources they already possessed. Pupils were often introduced orally to specialist terms, conventions and procedures in different subject areas, but with little extension of their expertise in relation to reading or writing for specific subject purposes. Frequently, ideas were not written up by the teacher or down by the pupils. Not using literacy to think or record thinking results in a lack of literate currency.

There are, of course, very few school situations when pupils are uncovering things which are new, which have not been replicated thousands of times beforehand. In many instances pupils are simply exposed to information which the teacher may feel to be important, but which has few links with the pupils' own lives. However, many teachers designed activities where class groups did make their own enquiries into real issues, such as researching a neighbourhood in geography to estimate employment prospects, or surveying a shopping mall to identify gaps in goods or services. In these lessons, when actual problems were simulated in the classroom, pupils were prompted to use the tools, documents and text resources of such an enquiry.

For the teachers who took part in the project, the point at which literacy across the curriculum began to take shape, came from recognition of what was distinctive about the literacy demands of history or science, compared with technology or maths. An art department devised process sheets to assist pupils who needed more information on light and shadow, 3-D effects and techniques of drawing. The sheets provided a series of hints, in the form of explaining techniques and terms, including diagrams and illustrating effects, to assist pupils' making. A special needs department worked on story maps, reconstructing the main elements of different story structures in visual terms, indicating sequences through a topography captured through symbols, keys and annotations. A technology group examined the literacy demands of a cross-curricular activity involving reading a designer's plans for constructing a kitchen. All of these examples highlight textual means of modelling and deconstructing aspects of enquiry, which are representative of different subject domains. Taking this step forward enabled teachers to begin to look at tasks where these literacy processes could be explicitly supported.

STEP 7: SCAFFOLDING

Classroom tasks form an important link between the teacher and child. We know that the nature of tasks, in terms of interest, relevance, degree of difficulty and level of abstraction, accounts for some of the variability in children's learning. However, many of the lesson scripts we examined in the research project show that similar tasks can be mediated in different ways by different teachers and for different pupils in the same class groups. In other words, study of the tasks which pupils are set by teachers, is insufficient to determine what or how children learn. In our view the most powerful determinant of children's learning, the difference which makes the difference, is how teachers construct the learning process itself, instantiated in adult–child interactions in the social context of the classroom.

Scaffolding is the complex set of interactions through which adults guide and promote children's thinking. We considered how scaffolding, or dialogic teaching, might be investigated in some detail in relation to the primary school data of our study. In order to be good at scaffolding, we suggested, teachers must have a precise knowledge of the characteristics and starting point of the learner, together with a thorough knowledge of the field of enquiry. These two *theories* of the problem and the learner, influence how the adult sets up a topic, organizes groups and resources, and how learning transactions are conducted. The components of scaffolding include recruiting pupils to a particular activity, and helping them to represent or construct the problem in terms they understand. At the elaboration stage the adult negotiates ways of proceeding, finding links with existing concepts or prior experience. Children are helped to find ways of representing their thinking in a wide range of print formats in the mediation stage. The final stage of scaffolding we outlined is concerned with finishing: drawing together the fruits of children's learning, reflecting on process and worth.

Our data show that scaffolding is not a linear process which moves sequentially from one stage to the next. Rather, the stages overlap and are cyclical, with teachers tailoring their interventions to the needs of individuals and groups. In many situations the various kinds of scaffolding are applied contiguously, to support learning in different ways, for different pupils or groups. Contingency – the timing of assistance without being too obtrusive or managerial – is arguably the most important quality for teachers to have in enabling children to take control of their own learning.

Similarly, we must reconsider the notion of the zone of proximal development: the hypothetical space between the teacher and the learner in which these transactions most effectively take place, at the current limits of the child's unaided competence. In the reality of classroom contexts, there are weak and strong fields of interaction, which groups and individuals move in or out of. Proximity to the adult is not a guide to the quality of a child's encounters, since in some instances, a child reading by the teacher's elbow may be simply monitored. In most teaching contexts, moments when children are challenged, either individually or in groups, at the limits of their current understanding, will be few and far between.

Teachers exercise a number of choices in their work. From the research data of our study we can identify those consequences for children's learning of managing transactions in one way as opposed to another. Inevitably, since all of the classrooms we studied were mixed ability, effective teaching reflected this diversity by sustaining a range of individual and collective zones of interaction. In terms of literacy, those adults who were most useful to children were those who facilitated reading and writing processes, rather than simply instructing them in the mechanics of reading and writing. A crucial factor concerned those dialogues with children which helped them to construct written accounts of their thinking, and to use print as sources of evidence, not simply as instructions for what to do next.

Some teachers in our study organized learning around themselves, overseeing children reading or writing, acting as custodians of resources, managing learners. Others focused more on managing learning: their scaffolding consisted of a succession of quickly and accurately gauged interventions, which kept children in the field of enquiry, encouraging them at all points to become more independent and reflective.

STEP 8: WIDENING THE RANGE OF FUNCTIONS FOR READING AND WRITING

Very few of the teachers we observed in the research project made any explicit reference to the specific text forms associated with different subject areas or different forms of enquiry. Much previous research has suggested that when teachers do highlight aspects of literacy in their work, they are likely to concentrate on 'word attack' skills in reading and the procedural aspects of writing: neatness, accuracy, spelling and presentation. Whilst these are important, there are also significant conceptual processes involved, which pupils need to know about, which mark the distinctive forms of literacy used in science, technology, history or mathematics.

Our work with primary and secondary teachers indicates that, in the main, teachers are uncertain about how the specific literacy demands of different subject domains should be taught and when this work should begin. These are not issues which primary teachers discuss with their secondary colleagues, or vice versa, so progression and continuity in children's experience is also lacking. We have to say that, from our own research data, neither primary nor secondary teachers have an organized system for preparing children to use literacy across the curriculum.

In Chapter 1 we drew attention to the power of literacy for changing children's thinking. We suggested that schools introduce children to a wide range of very specific ways of using print, which embody the processes and functions of different subject domains. Writers, such as Donaldson (1989) and Wood (1988), have argued that literacy fosters the ability to plan, to self-regulate and to think objectively. Learning to use the functions of print in different subject areas, expands children's powers of analysis and problem-solving: they acquire the tools of systematic and objective thought, together with the terminology, routines and strategies associated with different forms of enquiry. Both these authors assert that teaching children the flexibility of written language for thinking cannot simply be left to chance. On the contrary, it must be planned for and actively fostered, from primary school onwards.

The specific literacy demands of different subject areas increase as pupils move through the school system, particularly at secondary level with subject specialization. However, the amount of time spent teaching literacy decreases over the same time period. The particular discourse forms associated with different subject areas of the curriculum are known as genres, examples of which include texts which narrate, explain, persuade, argue or amuse. Genres which encourage pupils to organize their thinking in particular ways can make different information-handling demands (Beveridge, 1989).

Not everyone agrees on the amount of explicit instruction which should be given to genres, since there is a danger of 'boxing things up' too early, of handing writing formulae over to children, which are only partially understood. However, a balanced approach could plan to include experience and discussion of different genres, drawing attention to some of their technical features, identifying the specific emphases which arise in the course of enquiry in history, science, technology or the humanities, without being too formulaic. It is beyond the scope of this book to give a detailed account of genres, although an example of how they may be mapped across the curriculum is given in Table 6.1.

The teaching of genres within different subject areas has been one important strand of the follow-up training in schools, as teachers worked on the implications of the research project for classroom practice. At the secondary level, departments spent time drawing up action plans to reconsider the centrality of literacy within their subject teaching and to find more opportunities to cover process issues. Subject specialists were asked to articulate the specific reading and writing demands of their subject domains and to identify points where these might be taught, in the learning contexts which generate and exploit them. Follow-up training in the primary schools has begun to address what constitutes 'more advanced' reading skills, the kind of overlaps that exist between current primary practice and the subject specific requirements of the secondary school, and the initiation of a dialogue between primary and secondary teachers to coordinate work across the school phases.

STEP 9: MANAGING THE TRANSITION BETWEEN PRIMARY AND SECONDARY PHASES

One important issue addressed in this study, but which has received very little attention in research to date, has been the transition between primary and secondary phases of schooling, in terms of the demands made on pupils' literacy competence. We have argued that the functions of texts, in both written and read formats, change markedly between school systems, and that children need to be actively prepared for this shift.

Although the schools in our research study had a forum for exchanging views and met frequently as a cluster to plan and share in-service opportunities, aspects of teaching and learning at classroom level were often not considered. Questions can be asked about how well the primary school provides pupils with a foundation for the more subject-specialized demands of the secondary school. Similarly, how effectively does the secondary school build on what children have acquired at the primary phase? If there is a gap

Table 6.1 Literacy genres across the curriculum

Type of writing	Characteristics	Curriculum area
Personal account	First person account of direct experience. Writer organizes material by time to 'tell about' events. e.g. account of a family holiday	All subjects, particularly English, PSE, CDT
Report	Objective account of an incident or activity. Third person account of what took place, specifying actions or information in a time sequence. e.g. Experiment to find boiling point of different liquids	All subjects, particularly Science or Geography
Imaginative	First person account of an imagined experience involving writer in role of another. Creation of a context, characters and a time sequence. e.g. Letter home from the trenches during World War I	English, History, PSE
Instruction	Instructions which direct reader to a goal. Specification of steps and ordering of information in a chronological sequence. e.g. Operating procedure for a video-recorder	Science, CDT, Home Economics, Maths
Explanation	Objective interpretation of events or mechanisms. Causal relationships and technical vocabulary in a sequential chain of events. e.g. Effect of crop failure in Brazil on High Street coffee prices in United Kingdom	Geography, Science, CDT
Description	Selection of information which describes appearance and properties of an object or phenomenon. Third person factual, objective style. e.g. Description of an Iron Age hill fort	Science, Geography, History, CDT, Home Economics, Modern Languages
Opinion	Presenting a personal viewpoint supported by arguments or examples. Selection and organization of subjective information around a theme. e.g. Article on effects of violent videos on young people	All subjects
Narrative	Relating a story with plot, characters and sequence of events to entertain an audience. e.g. Science fiction story	English

Information	Formal, objective writing emphasizing factual information. Attempts to classify, using technical vocabulary or graphic devices. e.g. Information on pollution of British beaches	All subjects
Persuasion	Attempt to influence reader to a particular course of action or belief. e.g. Advertising leaflet	English, History PSE, RE
Compare and Contrast	Balanced and objective treatment setting out similarities and differences between two or more topics. e.g. Properties of metals/non-metals	All subjects
Reflection	Personal response to experience, organized thematically. e.g. Views on living through a bereavement	English, RE, PSE
Argument	Development of a logical argument supported by evidence. e.g. Case for legalizing euthanasia	All subjects
Analysis	Impartial and systematic exploration of a problem, evaluating conflicting evidence to draw objective conclusions. e.g. Patterns of poverty and health in different social groups	All subjects

between teacher expectations and the abilities of children to cope with curriculum demands, how can this be bridged?

The process of preparing children effectively for the challenge of the secondary curriculum hinges on communication. An ongoing exchange of views is required between teachers working in different phases, which focuses attention on progression in children's literacy experiences over time. Development of more advanced reading skills in the primary school, to use a term which primary teachers sometimes adopt, needs to be more explicitly defined, examples made tangible and teaching strategies shared. If secondary schools introduce pupils to more specific ways of using print, as an intrinsic part of subject-specific enquiries across the curriculum, what are they and when can they be introduced? Perhaps, more than anything, all teachers require a language for talking about literacy practice and process which moves beyond the limits of individual (or basic) skills.

STEP 10: CAPITALIZING ON THE MEDIA AND INFORMATION TECHNOLOGY

There is a commonly held view, expressed some twenty years ago in the 'Bullock Report' (DES, 1975), that watching television has displaced reading for many children. Certainly, children spend more time at home watching television, playing video and computer games, than any other leisure activity. Electronic media are not in themselves damaging: any harmful effects arise from the way in which the new media are used. Television is compulsive to many children because of its rapid pace and continually changing images. However, there is a danger that children become passive assimilators, unless steps are taken to turn television watching from a passive to an active process. Attention-holding though it is, the stimulus of television is not enough to ensure learning. Despite this, many schools now use video as a way of delivering some of the information content of the curriculum.

Our research data have thrown up a number of good examples of how teachers have used television as part of a topic focus, interacting with pupils around the content of a programme, so that the text of the video programme can be interrogated like any other evidence source. Rather than allowing television to pace the viewer, adults scaffold children's interactions around it, drawing up with children the questions to ask, locating and weighing evidence, selecting those things of value which reinforce or move children on in their thinking. The infant teacher in our primary school research who used a video-recording of Jill Murphy's story *Whatever Next!*, created a wealth of practical reading and writing activities around the conceptual centre, powerfully fixed by the television images.

New media forms are likely to escalate in profile. Schools have to find ways of harnessing these interests, and of utilizing their best features. Almost all teachers now recognize the importance of technologies such as the word processor and CD-ROM. One of the guaranteed experiences we feel all children should have, in both primary classrooms and all subject areas of the secondary school, is the frequent use of information technology for reference, research, composition and presentation.

STEP 11: INVOLVING PARENTS AS PARTNERS

Ten years ago, schools were only just beginning to acknowledge that parents had an important part to play in their children's literacy development, and that schools needed to build on children's early linguistic and cultural experiences, rather than trying to replace or compensate for them. There are many ways in which the schools in our research study involved parents: reading and writing workshops when parents came into school and used class resources; literacy events when book fairs, live readings and master classes were being held; home–school journals when comments travelled backwards and forwards along with each child's reading books. Several schools gave every parent of a new entrant to the school a copy of a 'Sharing Books' handbook. This gave hints about choosing books, enjoying rhymes, looking at photographs and remembering past events, helping the child to know where to look for information on the page, making up stories around picture books, how to form letters, and what to do when a child came across an unfamiliar word.

These examples confirm what a wide range of partnership initiatives have demonstrated: making positive suggestions about how parents can help, improves communication between home and school, boosts confidence and raises enthusiasm.

A real two-way partnership involves more than the school determining the nature of the initiative, and simply handing things over to parents which will be of use to the school. Many parents provide a richness of language and literacy experience, spanning different cultures, including a great deal of time sharing books with children. It would be more pertinent to ask of some families, how the school can complement what the parents are already achieving at home. In families where literacy has low status, a new idea is that by increasing family literacy and demonstrating its uses, for example, in finding employment, more positive attitudes towards print will transfer to the children. Regional family literacy projects have been set up by the Adult Basic Skills Unit, funded by the DfE, and are currently being evaluated. The implication of this work for schools, although still tentative, is the possibility of identifying and meeting adult needs for help in reading and writing, as a way of enhancing the whole family's interest and functional competence in literacy.

STEP 12: RESPONDING TO INDIVIDUAL NEEDS

One of the consequences of approaching reading as a set of taught skills which children bring to the curriculum, is that when learning difficulties arise these are often perceived in terms of the child's failure. Furthermore, if learning difficulties persist, teachers in primary or secondary schools may feel that it is no longer their responsibility, but the remit of a remedial specialist, to tackle a child's literacy problems. In Chapter 1 we discussed some of the pitfalls associated with what we have described as the 'individualization of failure'. Most questionable, perhaps, is the efficacy of emphasizing target skills without paying any attention to the classroom conditions in which children learn (Webster and Jones, 1990). In our view, an important component of any attempt to raise literacy competency in an individual or group of children is to enhance the classroom context. These issues go beyond the teaching of basic skills – the mechanics of reading or writing – to a consideration of how all teachers create opportunities for the functional use of literacy within a flexible and supportive teaching environment.

Under the new Code of Practice published by the DfE recently, all schools must take responsibility for identifying children with individual needs, for making initial assessments of the nature of the child's learning obstacles, and for drawing up teaching plans. In the early stages of the Code, it is the class or subject teacher, with help from support services or the school 'Special Needs Coordinator', who must take action to record concerns, draw up plans and intervene to accelerate learning. All schools must have in place policies and procedures for identifying children who are experiencing learning difficulties, for registering special needs, for liaising with parents and other professional bodies, and for planning interventions. (See Webster et al., 1994, for further details of the Code of Practice and its practical implementation.)

Some schools will prefer to support a child's learning through additional classroom help, or by offering intensive skill teaching for selected pupils, perhaps in part fulfilment of an Individual Education Programme or IEP. In some LEAs, advice and teaching help is still available from educational psychologists or special needs support services, though this is diminishing as responsibilities are devolved to schools themselves.

The evidence from our own research study informs a wider perspective on how individual learning needs may arise, and the conditions of teaching which may ameliorate or exacerbate children's progress. Whatever else schools do in relation to developing good practice under the new Code, we feel it is also highly important for teachers to consider factors within the teaching context. For example, we have identified the teacher's scaffolding of interactions as highly influential in children's learning, including aspects such as the teacher's visiting, contingency, pacing and pitching of challenges, the degree and nature of the child's print contacts, how teaching is organized so that pupils are assisted to construct their own writing and reading accounts, utilizing a wide range of formats and genres, fostering involvement in and control over their own learning. All of these factors suggest ways in which teaching conditions may be modified by all teachers, as part of a combined effort to overcome the learning obstacles which some children experience.

STEP 13: BECOMING A COMMUNITY OF READERS AND WRITERS

Not all schools operate in the same way and our society is much the richer for educational diversity and genuine choice. In this book we have tried to avoid global statements about how schools or teachers in general, go about their business. This has been an account of how a cluster of schools decided, with researchers' help, to find out about themselves. The data presented here informed a long-term programme of development in the schools concerned. We have no wish to present this as a recipe or prescription, but the data we have collated, the case studies we described, and the steps which we have outlined, should provide some valuable signposts to other people with an interest in supporting schools to become more effective communities for literacy.

One recurring theme in this work is the notion that schools, like other institutions, are characterized by social patterns which organize how people behave within them. Elsewhere we have described literacy as embedded within overlapping systems. At one level, written language reflects the primary code of communication between social actors, whilst at another level, literacy can be understood in terms of the transactions between participants. Finally, the scope and application of literacy as a tool for thinking and learning, changes radically as children move between family, classroom and school systems.

Understanding classrooms in terms of the social forces which organize them brings to the fore the important question of positive regard, which teachers unwittingly reveal to children and families in almost everything that they do: are the children valued for who and what they are, and is literacy for them, for real, for life?

Appendices

Appendix 1 Literacy questionnaire

Enter a cross in the corner of the box which best represents your view.
One cross only per line. Additional comments may be written in the last box.

PRINT SKILLS

Alphabet

1	The alphabet is discussed in relation to everyday experience of names, signs and labels and children's questions concerning print.	Best learnt by rote: e.g. chanting letter names.	Experience of books is emphasized before teaching about the alphabet	Gradually absorbed without direct teaching: e.g. by displaying letter friezes such as 'Letterland'.	Alternatively, you think:

Letter sounds

2	Rely on reading schemes based on phonic rules.	Basic phonic rules should be established as a first stage, even for older children.	Phonic rules can be highlighted and taught as children read.	Understanding of phonic rules will follow from regular experience of books.	Alternatively, you think:

Phonic blends

3	Avoid drawing attention to phonic blends so as not to disrupt enjoyment of reading.	Discuss as one of a number of strategies for identifying words (alongside picture clues, word shapes, reading on).	Use structured reading material to highlight phonic blends.	**Practise letter combinations in isolation.**	Alternatively, you think:

VOCABULARY

Sight vocabulary

4

Establish through frequent drill: e.g. flashcards.

Gradual exposure to sight words of increasing difficulty: e.g. through a graded reading scheme.

Relate reading and writing tasks to the language children use in conversation: e.g. 'Breakthrough' or language experience approaches.

Best acquired indirectly through reading.

Alternatively, you think:

Vocabulary development

5

Teachers negotiate the significant vocabulary embedded in a range of classroom texts or tasks.

Children encounter new words of any level of difficulty as they read or write.

Extend range of unfamiliar words gradually through a structured scheme: e.g. a 'key word' list.

Teacher selects new vocabulary which is taught through drills and frequently tested: e.g. sight-reading test.

Alternatively, you think:

READING

Assessment

6

By monitoring during class - non-invasive observation or listening - and assigning a level (NC AT2).

Through Schonell or word recognition quantification.

Assessment of child's performance reading out loud and assigning a reading age or level (NC AT2).

Through monitoring and discussion in a range of contexts, leading to a profile, which may be matched against levels (NC AT2).

Alternatively, you think:

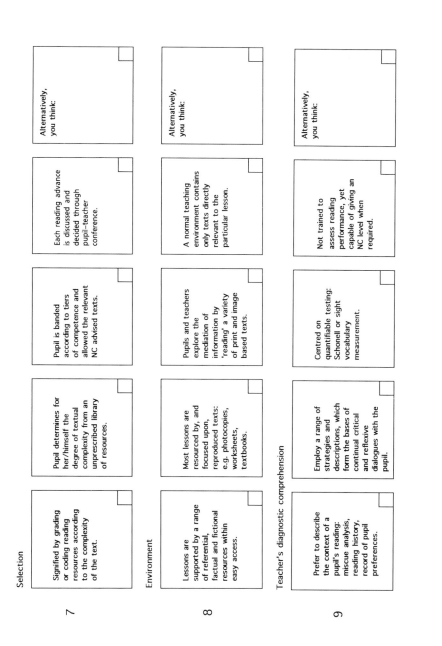

Selection

7

Signified by grading or coding reading resources according to the complexity of the text.

Pupil determines for her/himself the degree of textual complexity from an unprescribed library of resources.

Pupil is banded according to tiers of competence and allowed the relevant NC advised texts.

Each reading advance is discussed and decided through pupil–teacher conference.

Alternatively, you think:

Environment

8

Lessons are supported by a range of referential, factual and fictional resources within easy access.

Most lessons are resourced by, and focused upon, reproduced texts: e.g. photocopies, worksheets, textbooks.

Pupils and teachers explore the mediation of information by 'reading' a variety of print and image based texts.

A normal teaching environment contains only texts directly relevant to the particular lesson.

Alternatively, you think:

Teacher's diagnostic comprehension

9

Prefer to describe the context of a pupil's reading: miscue analysis, reading history, record of pupil preferences.

Employ a range of strategies and descriptions, which form the bases of continual critical and reflexive dialogues with the pupil.

Centred on quantifiable testing: Schonell or sight vocabulary measurement.

Not trained to assess reading performance, yet capable of giving an NC level when required.

Alternatively, you think:

WRITING

Spelling

10

Spelling strategies are discussed as an integral part of the composing, editing and publication process.

Rules are presented and rehearsed outside of other writing contexts.

The teacher's role is to correct faulty spelling as it occurs.

Teacher provides the resources for children to research their own spelling requirements: e.g. dictionary, thesaurus.

Alternatively, you think:

Presentation

11

Pupils express their ideas in a wide range of self-selected forms.

Teachers and pupils investigate the conventions which underlie different text forms and select the most appropriate.

Children write up rough work to produce a best copy.

Skills are practised as a specific exercise: e.g. cursive writing within tramlines.

Alternatively, you think:

Function

12

Teacher expects that children will discover different forms for expressing their ideas.

Teacher introduces different types of writing: e.g. poems, letters, diaries as an object lesson.

Teachers review with children the specific impacts certain formats have on audiences for specific purposes.

The teacher's task is to immerse children in a wide range of written forms and genres.

Alternatively, you think:

Letter formation

13

- Time should be given to children to practise letter shapes and handwriting.

- Strategies for letter formation can be considered as children write for a specific purpose and/or audience.

- The emphasis should be on writing meaningful messages not handwriting or presentation.

- Direct teaching and deliberate correction of hand movements.

- Alternatively, you think:

Letter patterns

14

- Letter features can be pinpointed in children's reading or writing to assist their reflection on word structures.

- Activities involving recognizing rhyming patterns or spelling families can be an enjoyable game.

- Rehearse common features as a listing or sorting exercise (e.g. common digraphs: 'th', 'qu', 'wh').

- Children will see spelling or rhyming patterns for themselves as reading experience grows.

- Alternatively, you think:

THE LITERACY CURRICULUM

Teacher constructs

15

- Literacy can be considered both as 'a garden of delights' and as 'a window upon knowledge'.

- Literacy is for understanding and producing correct English language.

- Literacy is a set of intellectual tools which enable children to become active problem solvers.

- Literacy is one of a number of forms of communication with greater relevance to some children than to others.

- Alternatively, you think:

Ownership

16

Responsibility for literacy development lies within English lessons.

The enthusiasm of children as readers and writers will determine whether they become literate.

Literacy is acquired indirectly as pupils work in different subject areas.

Literacy is reconstructed as a dialogue between adults, children and different forms of text and medium.

Alternatively, you think:

Architect

17

The literacy curriculum is dictated by the National Curriculum.

The literacy curriculum is determined entirely by the needs of the children.

Literacy can be considered as the curriculum: it is constructed by all those who take part in contexts in which reading and writing occur.

The literacy curriculum is drawn up by an English specialist.

Alternatively, you think:

Purpose

18

Literacy develops critical awareness of the power and purpose of written language across all curricular areas.

To acquire a prescribed set of skills to meet attainment targets.

Literacy is essentially the means for children to express and explore themselves in many rich and meaningful ways.

Literacy holds the potential for all individuals to enjoy and use it as a means of communication and learning.

Alternatively, you think:

Failure to read and write

19

Children who are poor at reading need to overlearn basics, such as phonic rules, through a highly structured remedial programme.

Teachers need to work with low achieving children, using a range of texts and strategies to develop specific skills and awareness.

Children who are poor at reading need much more experience of reading a wide range of books.

There will always be a proportion of individuals who will find literacy difficult to grasp.

Alternatively, you think:

Supporting learning

20

Lack of help or support at home accounts for poor literacy progress.

Opportunities should be taken across the curriculum to use literacy skills more effectively in different subject contexts.

Frequent encouragement and encounters with reading and writing formats (including IT) is the key to improving attitudes and self-confidence.

Extra help with literacy skills needs to be given through one-to-one, or small group, teaching outside main class lessons.

Alternatively, you think:

Appendix 2 Breakdown of questionnaire coding

Each of the twenty lines of the questionnaire contains five boxes.

The first four boxes on any line each represent one of the four quadrants (A,B,C or D) shown in Figure 2.1.

Each line is scrambled so that the boxes are in a random order.

The code for each line is as follows:

Line
1	D	A	C	B
2	B	A	D	C
3	C	D	B	A
4	A	B	D	C
5	D	C	B	A
6	C	A	B	D
7	A	C	B	D
8	C	B	D	A
9	C	D	A	B
10	D	A	B	C
11	C	D	B	A
12	B	A	D	C
13	B	D	C	A
14	D	B	A	C
15	C	A	D	B
16	A	C	B	D
17	B	C	D	A
18	D	A	C	B
19	A	D	C	B
20	B	D	C	A

Appendix 3 Lesson observation: observing critical literacy events

mins 0 2 4 6 8 10 12 14 16 18 20 22 24 26 28 30 32 34 36 38 40 42 44 46 48 50 52 54 56 58 60

- adult questioning — A
- teacher exposition/management
- reading to a group (passive audience)
- adult setting an exercise
- copying from board/teacher's notes
- recording from dictation
- drilling through repetition of an activity
- adult gets on with own work/monitors — B
- working through set scheme/prog
- reading or copying from textbook/worksheet
- listening/watch prepared resources
- unassisted work on set task
- pupils off task or hovering
- adult provides resources/advice on request — C
- pupils decide how to carry out task
- pupils pursue own interests/activities
- question raising
- shared discussion — D
- researching through reference
- generating/redrafting writing
- individually engaged with text
- purpose/objective/hypothesis raising
- reviewing process
- adult models ways of proceeding
- pupil/teacher on-task collaboration
- critical recording: making account
- critical reflection: rethinking account
- reflect ways of knowing/doing

Appendix 4 Lesson observation: field notes

mins 0   10   20   30   40   50   60

Teacher
M F
Faculty
School
Observer
Period
/ /9

Pupil 1
M F
Year

Pupil 2
M F
Year

Scan across the
following descriptors.
Number the appropiate
features as they occur
in the time box.
Amplify in field notes.
Add other descriptors,
as and when necessary.

A. TALK
B. READING
C. WRITING

Mother tongue
Second language
Foreign language

Process type:
1 whole class
2 small group
3 individual
4 resource-led
5 teacher-led
6 adult-assisted
7 child-led
8 peer-assisted
9 closed test

Text type:
10 worksheet
11 textbook
12 reference
13 reading scheme
14 fictional
15 manuscript
16 word-processed
17 diagrammatic
18 visual
19 aural

Functions:
20 personal narrating
21 familiarizing
22 reviewing
23 copying
24 transferring
25 practising
26 spelling/handwriting
27 layout
28 composing
29 editing

30 redrafting
31 discussing
32 listening
33 questioning
34 informing
35 imagining
36 describing
37 exploring
38 discovering
39 reporting
40 solving

41 explaining
42 retrieving
43 digesting
44 inquiring
45 summarizing
46 empathizing
47 exemplifying
48 generalizing
49 reiterating
50 researching
51 evaluating

52 analysing
53 arguing
54 speculating
55 surmising
56 reflecting
57 comparing
58 contrasting
59 persuading
60 proving
61 revising
62 translating

Appendix 5 Pro forma for recording teacher talk

event (see chart)	mins	**FIELD NOTES**	Date / /	Teacher M/F
			School	Observer
			Year	

event (see chart)	mins
1 2 3 4 5	0
1 2 3 4 5	2
1 2 3 4 5	4
1 2 3 4 5	6
1 2 3 4 5	8
1 2 3 4 5	10
1 2 3 4 5	12
1 2 3 4 5	14
1 2 3 4 5	16
1 2 3 4 5	18
1 2 3 4 5	20
1 2 3 4 5	22
1 2 3 4 5	24
1 2 3 4 5	26
1 2 3 4 5	28
1 2 3 4 5	30
1 2 3 4 5	32
1 2 3 4 5	34
1 2 3 4 5	36
1 2 3 4 5	38
1 2 3 4 5	40
1 2 3 4 5	42
1 2 3 4 5	44
1 2 3 4 5	46
1 2 3 4 5	48
1 2 3 4 5	50
1 2 3 4 5	52
1 2 3 4 5	54
1 2 3 4 5	56
1 2 3 4 5	58
	60

Appendix 6   Sample of Year 1 teacher talk

mins	SAMPLE OF YEAR 1 TEACHER'S TALK	EVENT
0	Need to fold it round...sellotape...then smaller circle/ This is Rebecca's.	1 2 3
	What's first letter I need to write?/ See a little word at end of 'rabbit'?	3 4
	...'reindeer': it's like 'rainbow'; got an 'e'/...'roundabout'? Not exactly.	3 4
	Do words first, then won't get glue all over/ What did other groups say?	1 3 4 5
	...sounds fireworks make?/ Didn't you see any?/ Look at those photos.	3 4
10	Can you think of a word to describe anything in those pictures?	3
	How do you spell 'bang'? / b,b,b,b – what's next? – a-n-g: bang.	2 3 4
	...when it's dry, else you lose the glitter/ Good boy/ Try to fold it over.	2
	I can guess what that one is/ Could you write the word for me?	3
	...not 'where to is', it's 'where is' the string?/ Oops, what's missing?	4
20	What do you think that one says?/...cr, cr, crackle.	3 4
	What's that letter and noise? (bang)/ When you come back, wash face...	1 5
	That's a scary film, I didn't like it/ Do you know what a rat is?	2 4
	Excuse me, please, I'm talking to.../ OK, can you read that to me?	1 2 4
	You don't say 'me' need the...'I' need the.../ Are you sure it said 'red'?	4
30	(hold hands) Just help you with the next one? Hayley/ Eddie Elephant.	3 4 5
	Let's look at your name!/...sellotape down length/ Could help each other?	3 4 5
	Let me help, Nicky/ If you bring the two edges together to meet, then...	3 4
	Then go and do your news/ I've got one you could do: Catherine wheel.	1 2 3 5
40	...r-a-t: t,t,t /Put it on the rack?/ What should we say instead of...	1 4 5
	You could use glue to put that on, it might be easier...	3
	Label for it?/ He helped, you made it/ Can you write: I made a robot?	3 5
	That's written upside down, but altogether it's very good.	2 3 4 5
	Lots of capital letters in that?/What does butterfly start with? Yes.	3 4
50	Let's look over here again at our 'r' things/ Name on it, or we'll never...	4 5
	...sure that rabbit hasn't got 'a' in? Think again. Lovely – that's rabbit.	4 5
	Beautiful/ We had that judged on Friday, but you never know this week.	5
	Clear up first...getting messy/ Can you write name again, down here?	1 4 5
	What do you think you should try not to do?/ If you're going to start...	4 5
	Don't forget to write down what you've made/ What've you forgotten?	3
60	I think you can do more...	4 5
	T: (reads) I made a rock [finger conceals -et)]/ P: [as finger lifts] et.	4 5
	I can't quite read that, shouldn't you write something lower?	1
	Could I see hands and could you close your lips so that you can hear me?	1 3 4
	We've got 5 minutes until playtime/ Listening and hands in the air...	3 5
70	Can you hurry?/ No, sweetheart, look, you need some string.	3 5
	We're going to put the other on the wall later/ Clear up before you...	1 2
	Put the lids on tight/ Where do you want to put it?	2 3 5
	You're tidying up usefully. Have you finished that?	2
80	Can you tidy, please? I'm going to have to go in a second.	2
	CLASS CONTINUES...	

mins	SAMPLE OF YEAR 1 TEACHER'S TALK	EVENT		
80	Did you ever find your rocket? Is it on the table?	1		5
	Could I see your hands?/ I asked you to stand still/Now. No, now. <u>Now</u>.	1		
	Could you line up at the door?/ Silly noise, N./ Because Mr K. said so...	1		
	AFTERNOON PLAYTIME (25 mins)			

mins		EVENT		
90	Could we just spend five minutes clearing up before our story?	1		5
	We must put that clock right, it's five minutes fast, otherwise...	1		5
	Those can go in there/...pencils that need putting away/...paper on floor	1	3	5
	...closer in, then we can tell the story?/ We've heard this story today...	1	3	5
100	I thought <u>we</u>'d do it together to see how much <u>we</u>'d remembered.		3	5
	Whatever next! There's something on the end of that word, I wonder...		4	
	...exclamation mark/ It tells you how to read the word: with expression.		4	
	Can I read...Can anyone read?/ That's a question mark.	1	4	
	Does anyone know what that is called, what it does? (sieve/colander)		3 4	
110	How come the rain's coming through?...the holes, it's not a real helmet.		3 4	
	Yes, that's him: nice and clean and ready for bed.	2	3	5
	I don't think I can sing this because it hasn't got any tune.		3 4	
	How many letters can you see?/Letters, not words/ Those four make?	1 2	3 4	
	Sand on the <u>shore</u> [pupils reading out: sand in a big pile]/ Let's read...		3 4	
120	Sand on my...begins with b, b-o- body, bod-y. Let's go back over that.		3	4 5
	Who can read this word? We write this word lots of times.		3 4	
	...just before we go home/ We'll have another look at it tomorrow.		3	5
	CLASS ENDS			

Appendix 7 Full script of Year 1 lesson

YEAR 1 TEACHER (F)

Code	Activity
T	demonstrates making a rocket
T	'r' sound: word-starts and ends
W	r-words written: ramp, rocket
T	task order/advises, suggests
T	soundscape for drawn image
T	collects together other group
T	working with individuals
R	predicting and shaping process
T	assessing/suggesting
T	standardizing spoken syntax
R	predicting/cuing/sounding
R	letter-word building/managing
T	empathizing/inquiring/defusing
T	ordering speech turns/feedback
T	standardizing syntax/checking
W	modelling/familiarizing
T	comparing/advising/grouping
T	intervening/demonstrating
T	redirecting/founding idea
W	spelling/organizing/comparing

mins: 0, 10, 20, 30

PUPIL 1 (F)

Code	Activity
L	sat in front of teacher, listening
T	rehearses, copying teacher
W	watching, finger-tracing writing
	collects stars made in morning
W	writes 'my star' on paper slip
R	sticks label on star, looks at list
	cuts out 'yellow' from list
W	writes name on label for star
	finds piece of cardboard tube
	constructing rocket
T	'Miss, can I cut my paper out?'
	cutting out wing shapes
	cutting out
W	helping neighbour with label
T	visited by teacher, needs glue
	resumes work on rocket
	sticking wings on
	sticking down tail fin
	colouring rocket in felt tip
	finishes quickly

mins: 0, 10, 20, 30

PUPIL 2 (M)

Code	Activity
T	at table, joining in talk
R	sounding out 'rabbit'
	draws roundabout on paper
W	copies 'roundabout'/leaves aside
	goes to find star
	finishes colouring it yellow
W	writes 'star' on label
	sticks label to star
	cuts out square for making tube
	won't stick/gets sellotape
	tapes tube... ends up with cone
	takes tape off, paper tears
	watches other activity in group
L	asks pupil 1 to help spell 'rocket'
T	writes label, cuts it out
W	looks at how partner built hers
	finds length of cardboard tube
	gets scissors/talks to partner
	draws wing shapes on tube
T	starts working alone

mins: 0, 10, 20, 30

	40
T	suggesting tactic
T	keeping/owning through words
R	contextualizing/affirming
W	querying convention/prompting
T	retracking/modelling/causality
	50
W	sound-spell check/reconsidering
T	praising/summative affirmation
	workplace process/name-keeps
T	reflective and conditional prompts
T	labelling/recalling process
	60
T	appraising, cajoling
R	breaking down word for reading
W	adjusting convention for labelling
T	gaining class attention
	looking ahead/managing time
	70
T	chivvying along/helping display
T	prioritizing/clearing up
T	checking/helping to decide
T	praising/appraising
T	cajoling/personalizing

	40
	moves to writing corner
R	reads prompt sheet with helper:
T	'today we made...' thinks/talks
T	through last activity/reflects
W	starts writing/helper moves
	50
W	continues prompt: a star and...
W	a r (looks to flipchart) ocket
W	reads through/continues
W	the star is/goes off
W	(copies) yellow/finishes/moves
	60
	starts drawing a guy, quickly
	drawing just in pencil
W	starts writing a caption
L	stops work to listen
L	listening
	70
	writing caption
W	writes name on picture
W	putting away equipment
	putting away picture
	moves to another table, clears

	40
	cuts tube to better length
	cuts notches in end of tube
	cuts out triangle, tries out as fin
	cuts a bigger triangle
	fixes tail-fin/colours rocket
	50
	uses base of can to draw circle
	cuts out circle
	colours circle red/gets glue
	sticks circle on end of rocket
T	shows teacher/finds label
	60
T	finishes rocket/pupil 1 returns
T	gets paper/goes to teacher
W	realizes label is too small
L	writes 'rocket' again/cuts out
	stops work to listen
	70
	attaches label lengthways
	takes rocket to display board
	waits for string, cuts a length
	goes back to table for tape
T	gives rocket to teacher

YEAR 1 TEACHER (F)

Code	Activity
T	checking away
T	gaining attention/silencing
T	teaching dismissal procedure
	AFTERNOON PLAYTIME
T	managing final clearing up
T	checking and indicating time left
T	clearing away routines
T	gathering together/recalling
T	planning ahead/reviewing
R	word-recognition/assessing
R	reading punctuation
R	explaining the question mark
T	reading together: talk on text
T	visual questions/narrative
T	narrative closure/empathy
R	performing poem
R	guiding reading/sounding out
R	reading and rehearsing
R	predictive strategies/attack
R	getting pupils to read ahead
T	final review/looking ahead
	END OF CLASS

PUPIL 1 (F)

(time markers: 80, 90, 100, 110, 120)

Activity	Code
clearing away	
moves to group round teacher	L
lines up at door	L
AFTERNOON PLAYTIME	
sitting in basegroup/listening	L
clearing group workspace	
picking up litter	
sitting on story mat	L
watching/listening	L
following reading out loud	R
listening, following text	L
listening, following text	L
'peas and things...'/suggesting	T
'he's getting wet...'/recounting	T
'he's going to bed'/explaining	T
listening	L
reading aloud, counting 'four'	R
reading, following	R
reading, following	R
reading, responding	T
listening	L
END OF CLASS	

PUPIL 2 (M)

(time markers: 80, 90, 100, 110, 120)

Activity	Code
clearing away	
'freezes', hand in air	L
lines up at the door	L
AFTERNOON PLAYTIME	
sitting in basegroup/listening	L
clearing group workspace	
taking back pencils	
sitting on story mat	L
watching/listening	L
following reading out loud	R
following text, talking	T
following text, recounting	T
'pan... kitchen'/suggesting	T
'holes, Miss... it's got holes'	T
'pyjamas on'/explaining	T
listening	L
calling out, 'sand... sand'	R
reading/suggesting	R
reading/suggesting	R
listening	L
listening	L
END OF CLASS	

Appendix 8 A model of adult–child proximation: literacy learning in classroom interaction

This examination of the way in which teachers and pupils interact during a lesson selects the degree of involvement (mediation) demonstrated by the teacher and sets it against the degree of initiative (initiation) demonstrated by the pupil. The orthogonal diagram represents four quadrants (A, B, C, D) of proximation, or learning through interaction. Each quadrant is described in terms of the qualities of learning allowed by the interaction. These descriptions are founded on classroom observation. No quadrant in itself proposes the best way to teach; each has its useful practices and worthwhile opportunities.

Most of the project's observational methods have been constructed on the basis of this model.

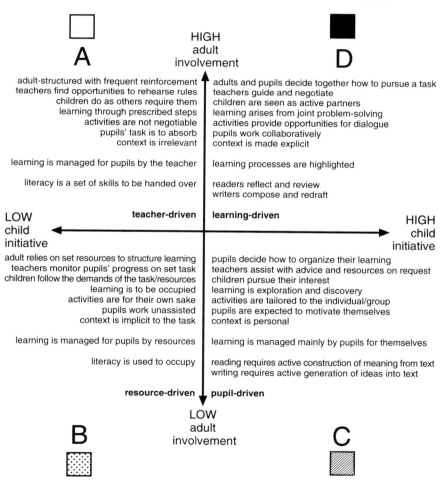

A

HIGH
adult
involvement

D

adult-structured with frequent reinforcement
teachers find opportunities to rehearse rules
children do as others require them
learning through prescribed steps
activities are not negotiable
pupils' task is to absorb
context is irrelevant

adults and pupils decide together how to pursue a task
teachers guide and negotiate
children are seen as active partners
learning arises from joint problem-solving
activities provide opportunities for dialogue
pupils work collaboratively
context is made explicit

learning is managed for pupils by the teacher

learning processes are highlighted

literacy is a set of skills to be handed over

readers reflect and review
writers compose and redraft

LOW
child
initiative

teacher-driven | **learning-driven**

HIGH
child
initiative

adult relies on set resources to structure learning
teachers monitor pupils' progress on set task
children follow the demands of the task/resources
learning is to be occupied
activities are for their own sake
pupils work unassisted
context is implicit to the task

pupils decide how to organize their learning
teachers assist with advice and resources on request
children pursue their interest
learning is exploration and discovery
activities are tailored to the individual/group
pupils are expected to motivate themselves
context is personal

learning is managed for pupils by resources

learning is managed mainly by pupils for themselves

literacy is used to occupy

reading requires active construction of meaning from text
writing requires active generation of ideas into text

resource-driven | **pupil-driven**

LOW
adult
involvement

B

C

Teachers' interactions through talk: scaffolded stages of learning

Consider these five stages of support for the teaching and learning process.

1   RECRUITMENT and MAINTENANCE
(to task)
  • Gaining attention
  • Directing to resources
  • Directing behaviour
  • Giving personal information
  • Monitoring and checking
  • Prioritizing progress through task

At the opening stage of a learning cycle, teachers proceed managerially, as learners are organized in line with an impending task. Pupils need recruiting; the use of resources and the environment needs formalizing; the investigation needs outlining and a point of entry; texts and writing formats need introduction: **prospects need definition**.

2   REPRESENTATION
and CLARIFICATION
(on task)
  • Adding information
  • Identifying problems
  • Exploratory questions
  • Procedural questions
  • Paraphrasing
  • Affirmations

Once pupils have been recruited, the immediate context of the task requires clarification. What conceptual demands are being made? How will pupils be helped to think strategically about the problems ahead? Much of what a teacher rehearses in talk helps pupils to **consolidate** their preparatory understanding. Key points should be noted down in writing.

3   ELABORATION
(in task)
  • Locating and weighing evidence
  • Routes: alternative ways of proceeding
  • Assessing need for additional support
  • Taking stock: revisiting nature of task
  • Bridging: finding analogies, parallels and links

Supporting pupils 'in-task' allows the teacher opportunities to listen in and add to pupils' accounts of how they are thinking. Pupils will express a variety of strategies, each more or less adequate to the task. Here, interaction needs to be carefully differentiated so as not to eclipse pupil initiative. **Think with; not for.**

4   MEDIATION THROUGH
PRINT/TEXT
(about task)
  • Selecting appropriate formats
  • Finding ways with words
  • Thinking dialogues
  • Strategic listening to learners' accounts
  • Meeting conventions

Most classroom learning involves reading and writing at points in the learning process. At this stage, attention is drawn to the generation of a written record of pupils' thought and activity. Texts offer conventions, or 'ground rules' for writing, which pupils need to be able to read and recognize, in order to **shape the account**.

5.   FINISHING
(after words)
  • Celebrating, displaying, storing
  • Sampling and selecting the valuable
  • Publishing
  • Convening (drawing together)
  • Reflecting on process and worth

A lesson might mean a space on a timetable, but it should also denote understanding gained. Finishing learning also requires support. Language, thought and memory keep learning alive. Each investigative outcome tells its history of a pupil's ideas trying to find words. **Remember how**?

In practice, there are no discrete boundaries between these stages. Teachers often switch between stages, mainly in response to individual needs across the duration of the investigation (or set of tasks).

Lesson scripts: connecting literacy learning to patterns of interaction

In order to begin to represent the complex situation of a lesson by attending to the types and qualities of interaction, we have developed the concept of a **lesson script**. Our unit of analysis is the teacher–pupil interaction, which occurs mainly through the medium of language and its textual and verbal codes. The lesson script is derived from data collected during a lesson observation. The teacher (T) and two pupils (P1 and P2) are tracked throughout the lesson, using the lesson observation formats you have considered already.

Through the **central column** of a person's script, we have given a brief *summary* (derived from field notes) of what each was observed doing over two-minute intervals. The code square to the **left** of the summary represents the *type of interaction* in which the person was involved; the square to the **right** represents the *type of literacy use* observed. Each square is given one of four shadings, representing the quadrants which describe adult–child interaction.

Quadrant

   Teacher-driven
  • characterized by didactic exposition, or in response to instruction

   Resource- or occupier-driven
  • characterized by unassisted work on a set task, or being kept occupied

   Pupil-driven
  • characterized by personal or group investigation, or discovery learning

   Learning-driven
  • characterized by process-specific dialogue, or reflection on context

Literacy is described in terms of the quality of interaction in which its practices are generated, by the same system of shading. Literacy is defined either through Listening, Talking, Reading or Writing, since both verbal and textual practices are found in the learning context.

Although these four modes of language use underlie the attainment targets of the National Curriculum for English, our *interactive* definition shows clearly that opportunities for learning through literacy arise in all classrooms and all subject areas.

Transcribing the data collected on the lesson observation charts into a lesson script is a productive way of analysing the pattern of interactive practices through a lesson, whilst describing those practices in terms of the literacy use sustained across two-minute intervals. A script can be further analysed through a brief written commentary.

When a number of lesson scripts have been constructed (ten would be an adequate start), representing a range of lessons across the school curriculum, or in relation to a specific class, or individual teacher or pupil, then a case study meeting may take place. In order to begin to make an informed statement concerning actual (*in vivo*) literacy learning, we need to take account of a variety of perspectives, dependent on the aspect of the curriculum under consideration. A faculty, or whole school, might target pupils according to categories of need and their groupings (sets, mixed-ability, in-class support,

LISTENING...	
to exposition or instruction	L
as audience to a reading, or viewing	L
as a respondent in a peer discussion	L
as a partner within a process dialogue	L
TALKING...	
to direct, order, manage, instruct	T
as an implicit task requirement	T
to discuss and explore	T
about reading and writing processes	T
READING...	
under direction or out loud	R
following another's reading	R
for personal or exploratory purposes	R
to learn about reading processes	R
WRITING...	
to copy or shift print	W
unassisted on a set task	W
to explore and generate ideas	W
to redraft text and review process	W

withdrawal); or by targeting specific environments (laboratory, studio, classroom, library); or by focusing on a particular mode (reading, writing, talking, listening), or genre (experiment, investigation, factual account, fictional account, practical, performance, etc.) of literacy in use.

References

Alexander, R., Rose, J. and Woodhead, C. (1992) *Curriculum Organisation and Classroom Practice in Primary Schools*. London: HMSO

Allington, R. (1984) Content coverage and contextual reading in reading groups. *Journal of Reading Behaviour*, no. 16, pp. 85–96

Barnes, D. (1976) *From Communication to Curriculum*. Harmondsworth: Penguin

Barton, D. (1994) *Literacy: An Introduction to the Ecology of Written Language*. Oxford: Blackwell

Bennett, N., Desforges, C., Cockburn, A. and Wilkinson, B. (1984) *The Quality of Pupil Learning Experiences*. London: Lawrence Erlbaum Associates

Beveridge, M. C. (1989) Staged assessments in literacy: implications for language problems in secondary schools. In K. Mogford and J. Sadler (eds) *Child Language Disability: Implications in an Educational Setting*. Clevedon: Multilingual Matters pp. 52–64

——— (1991) Literacy and learning in secondary school: problems of texts and teaching. In A. Webster (ed.) *Language and Language-related Difficulties. Educational and Child Psychology*, vol. 8, no. 3, pp. 60–71

Beveridge, M. C. and Edmondson, S. (1989) Microcomputer assessment of reading processes under word and phrase presentation. *Journal of Research in Reading*, vol. 12, no. 1, pp. 1–12

Beveridge, M. C. and Jerrams, A. (1981) Preschool children's language: an evaluation of a parental assistance plan. *British Journal of Educational Psychology*, no. 51, pp. 256–66

Beveridge, M. C., Jerrams, A. and Lo, P. (1987) The effects of a school based parental assistance plan on children's social sensitivity. *Journal of Applied Developmental Psychology*, vol. 8, no. 2, pp. 139–81

Beveridge, M. C. and Rymaszewski, R. (1991) Explanation in teaching and intelligent systems. In P. Goodyear (ed.) *Knowledge Acquisition in Intelligent Computer-assisted Instruction*. London: Ablex

Brown, B. B. (1968) *The Experimental Mind in Education*. New York: Harper and Row

Bruner, J. S. (1968) *Toward a Theory of Instruction*. New York: Norton

——— (1984) Language, mind and reading. In H. Goelman, A. Oberg and F. Smith (eds) *Awakening to Literacy*. London: Heinemann

——— (1986) *Actual Minds, Possible Worlds*. Cambridge, MA: Harvard University Press

Bryant, P. and Bradley, L. (1985) *Children's Reading Problems*. Oxford: Blackwell

Buckingham, D. (1992) *Television Literacy: Talk, Text and Context*. London: Falmer Press

———— (1994) Media education. In B. Stierer and J. Maybin (eds) *Language, Literacy and Learning in Educational Practice*. Clevedon: Multilingual Matters in association with The Open University

Burgess, R. (1985) (ed.) *Issues in Educational Research: Qualitative Methods*. London: Falmer Press

Burgess, T. (1993) Reading Vygotsky. In H. Daniels (ed.) *Charting the Agenda: Educational Activity after Vygotsky*. London: Routledge

Carnine, D. and Silbert, J. (1979) *Direct Instruction Reading*. Orlando, FL: Charles Merrill

Carr, T. and Levy, B. (1990) (eds) *Reading and its Development: Component Skills Approaches*. London: Academic Press

Christie, F. (1987) Young children's writing: from spoken to written genre. *Language in Education*, vol. 1, no. 1, pp. 3–13

Clay, M. and Cazden, C. (1990) A Vygotskian interpretation of Reading Recovery. In L. C. Moll (ed.) *Vygotsky and Education: Instructional Implications and Application of Socio-historic Psychology*. Cambridge: Cambridge University Press

Cope, B. and Kalantzis, M. (1993) The power of literacy and the literacy of power. In B. Cope and M. Kalantzis (eds) *The Powers of Literacy: A Genre Approach to Teaching Writing*. London: Falmer Press, pp. 63–89

Croll, P. (1986) *Systematic Classroom Observation*. London: Falmer Press

Department for Education (1992) *Curriculum Organisation and Classroom Practice in Primary Schools: A Discussion Paper*. London: HMSO

———— (1993) *English for ages 5 to 16: Proposals of the Secretary of State for Education and the Secretary of State for Wales*. London: HMSO

Department of Education and Science (1975) *A Language for Life* (The Bullock Report). London: HMSO

———— (1988) *Report of the Committee of Enquiry into the Teaching of English Language* (The Kingman Report). London: HMSO

———— (1992) *The Teaching and Learning of Reading in Primary Schools 1991*. London: HMSO

Desforges, C. (1988) Psychology and the management of classrooms. In N. Jones and J. Sayer (eds) *Management and the Psychology of Schooling*. London: Falmer Press

Desforges, C. and Cockburn, A. (1987) *Understanding the Mathematics Teacher. A Study of Practice in First Schools*. Lewes: Falmer Press

Donaldson, M. (1989) *Sense and Sensibility: Some Thoughts on the Teaching of Literacy*. Reading: Reading and Language Information Centre

Doyle, W. (1986) Classroom organisation and management. In M. Wittrock (ed.) *Handbook of Research on Teaching*. New York: Macmillan

Edwards, A. D. and Westgate, D. P. G. (1987) *Investigating Classroom Talk*. London: Falmer Press

Edwards, D. and Mercer, N. (1987) *Common Knowledge*. London: Methuen

Fleiss, J. L. (1971) Measuring nominal scale agreement among many raters. *Psychological Bulletin*, no. 76, pp. 378–82

Forman, E. A., Minick, N. and Addison Stone, C. (1993) *Contexts for Learning: Socio-cultural Dynamics in Children's Development*. Oxford: Oxford University Press

Frith, U. (1985) Beneath the surface of developmental dyslexia. In K. Patterson, M. Coltheart and J. Marshall (eds) *Surface Dyslexia*. London: Lawrence Erlbaum Associates

Gagné, R. M. (1965) *The Conditions of Learning*. New York: Holt, Rinehart and Winston

Galton, M., Simon, B. and Croll, P. (1980) *Inside the Primary Classroom*. London: Routledge and Kegan Paul

Goodman, K. (1967) Reading: a psycholinguistic guessing game. In H. Singer and R. Ruddell (eds) *Theoretical Models and Processes of Reading*. Newark, DE: International Reading Association

——— (1972) Reading: the key is in children's language. *The Reading Teacher*, March, pp. 505–8

Goswami, U. and Bryant, P. (1990) *Phonological Skills and Learning to Read*. Hove: Lawrence Erlbaum Associates

Greenfield, P. (1984) *Mind and Media: the Effects of Television, Computers and Video Games*. London: Fontana

Hammersley, M. (1993a) (ed.) *Controversies in Classroom Research*. 2nd edn. Buckingham: Open University Press

——— (1993b) (ed.) *Educational Research: Current Issues*. London: Paul Chapman

Harrison, C. (1992) The reading process and learning to read. In C. Harrison and M. Coles (eds) *The Reading for Real Handbook*. London: Routledge

Hickey, M. (1977) *Dyslexia: A Language Training Course for Teachers and Learners*. Bath: Better Books

Howe, M. J. (1990) (ed.) *Encouraging the Development of Exceptional Skills and Talents*. Leicester: British Psychological Society

John-Steiner, V., Panofsky, C. P. and Smith, L. W. (1994) *Sociocultural Approaches to Language and Literacy: An Interactionist Perspective*. Cambridge: Cambridge University Press

Jorgensen, G. W. (1977) Relationship of classroom behaviour to the accuracy of match between material difficulty and student ability. *Journal of Educational Psychology*, no. 69, pp. 24–32

Just, M. and Carpenter, P. (1985) *The Psychology of Reading and Language Comprehension*. Newton, MA: Allyn and Bacon

Kress, G. R. (1982) *Learning to Write*. London: Routledge and Kegan Paul

Lankshear, C. (1993) Curriculum as literacy: reading and writing in 'new times'. In B. Green (ed.) *The Insistence of the Letter: Literacy Studies and Curriculum Theorising*. London: Falmer Press

Lunzer, E. and Gardner, K. (1979) *The Effective Use of Reading*. London: Heinemann, for the Schools Council

McMahon, A. and Bolam, R. (1990) *Management Development and Educational Reform: a Handbook for LEAs*. London: Paul Chapman

Meek, M. (1991) *On Being Literate*. London: Bodley Head

Moll, L. (1990) (ed.) *Vygotsky and Education: Instructional Implications and Applications of Socio-historical Psychology*. Cambridge: Cambridge University Press

Norman, K. (1992) (ed.) *Thinking Voices: The Work of the National Oracy Project*. London: Hodder and Stoughton

OFSTED (1994) *Primary Matters: A Discussion on Teaching and Learning in Primary Schools*. London: OFSTED

Oldroyd, D. and Hall, V. (1991) *Managing Staff Development: A Handbook for Secondary Schools*. London: Paul Chapman

Palincsar, A. and Brown, A. (1984) Reciprocal teaching of comprehension-fostering and comprehension-monitoring activities. *Cognition and Instruction*. no. 1, pp. 117–75

Pollard, A. and Tann, S. (1987) *Reflective Teaching in the Primary School: A Handbook for the Classroom*. London: Cassell

Pollard, A., Broadfoot, P., Croll, P., Osborn, M. and Abbott, D. (1994) *Changing English Primary Schools: The Impact of the Education Reform Act at Key Stage 1*. London: Cassell

Pumfrey, P. (1990) Literacy and the National Curriculum: the challenge of the 1990s. In P. Pumfrey and C. Elliot (eds) *Children's Difficulties in Reading, Spelling and Writing*. Basingstoke: Falmer Press

Pumfrey, P. and Reason, R. (1991) *Specific Learning Difficulties (Dyslexia): Challenges and Responses*. Windsor: NFER/Nelson

Raban, B. (1991) The role of schooling in initial literacy. In A. Webster (ed.) *Language and Language-Related Difficulties. Educational and Child Psychology*, vol. 8, no. 3, pp. 41–59

Reason, P. and Rowan, J. (1981) (eds) *Human Inquiry: A Sourcebook of New Paradigm Research*. London: John Wiley

Reed, M. (1986) Sound and system. In S. N. Tchudi (ed.) *English Teachers at Work: Ideas and Strategies from Five Countries*. Upper Mouldlair, NJ: Boynton/Cook

Reed, M. and Beveridge, M. (1993) Knowing ourselves: practising a pluralist epistemology in teacher education. In G. K. Verma (ed.) *Inequality and Teacher Education: An International Perspective*. London: Falmer

Reed, M., Webster, A. and Beveridge, M. (1995) The conceptual basis for a literacy curriculum. In P. Owen and P. Pumfrey (eds) *Children Learning to Read: International Concerns. Volume 1: Emergent and Developing Reading: Messages for Teachers*. London: Falmer Press

SCAA (1993) *The National Curriculum and its Assessment: Final Report* (Dearing Review). London: School Curriculum and Assessment Authority

Schiller, J. (1979) You and that box in the corner. *Australian Journal of Early Childhood* vol. 4, no. 2, pp. 32–6

Schonell, F. J. (1945) *The Psychology and Teaching of Reading*. London: Oliver and Boyd

Sheeran, Y. and Barnes, D. (1991) *School Writing*. Milton Keynes: Open University Press

Shipman, M. (1985) *The Management of Learning in the Classroom*. London: Hodder and Stoughton

Sinclair, J. and Coulthard, R. (1975) *Towards an Analysis of Discourse: the English used by Teachers and Pupils*. London: Oxford University Press

Skinner, B. F. (1968) *The Technology of Teaching*. Englewood Cliffs, NJ: Prentice Hall

Smith, F. (1973) (ed.) *Psycholinguistics and Reading*. New York: Holt, Rinehart and Winston

——— (1978) *Reading*. Cambridge: Cambridge University Press

——— (1982) *Writing and the Writer*. London: Heinemann

——— (1992) *To Think in Language, Learning and Education*. London: Routledge

Solity, J. and Bull, S. (1987) *Special Needs: Bridging the Curriculum Gap*. Milton Keynes: Open University Press

Stanovich, K. (1980) Towards an interactive-compensatory model of individual differences in the development of reading fluency. *Reading Research Quarterly*, vol. 16, no. 1, pp. 32–71

Start, K. and Wells, B. (1972) *The Trend of Reading Standards*. Slough: NFER

Stierer, B. (1994) 'Simply doing their job?': the politics of reading standards and 'real books'. In B. Stierer and J. Maybin (eds) *Language, Literacy and Learning in Educational Practice*. Clevedon: Multilingual Matters Ltd in association with The Open University

Stubbs, M. and Robinson, B. (1979) Analysing classroom language. In *Language Development*, PE 232, Block 5, Milton Keynes: Open University Press

Swales, J. (1990) *Genre Analysis: English in Academic and Research Settings*. Cambridge: Cambridge University Press

Topping, K. and Lindsay, G. (1992) Paired reading: a review of the literature. *Research Papers in Education*, vol. 7, no. 3, pp. 199–246

Turner, M. (1990) *Sponsored Reading Failure*. Warlingham: IPSET Education Unit

Tyler, L. and Marslen-Wilson, W. (1982) Speech comprehension processes. In J. Mehler, E. Walker and M. Garrett (eds) *Perspectives on Mental Representation*. Hillsdale, NJ: Lawrence Erlbaum Associates

Vygotsky, L. (1978) *Mind in Society: The Development of Higher Psychological Processes*. Cambridge, MA: Harvard University Press

Waterland, L. (1988) *Read With Me: An Apprenticeship Approach to Reading*. 2nd edn. Stroud: The Thimble Press

Webster, A. (1986) *Deafness, Development and Literacy*. London: Methuen

Webster, A. and Jones, J. (1990) 'New paradigm' approaches to meeting individual needs in science. *British Journal of Special Education*, vol. 17, no. 1, Research Supplement pp. 23–6

Webster, A. and McConnell, C. (1987) *Children with Speech and Language Difficulties*. London: Cassell

Webster, A. and Wood, D. J. (1989) *Children with Hearing Difficulties*. London: Cassell

Webster, A., Beveridge, M. and Reed, M. (in press) Contrasting conceptions of literacy in primary and secondary schools. *Journal of Research in Reading*

Webster, A., Webster, V., Moon, C. and Warwick, A. (1994) *Supporting Learning in the Primary School: Meeting Individual Needs under the New Code of Practice*. Bristol: Avec Designs Ltd

Weinstein, C. S. (1991) The classroom as a social context for learning. *Annual Review of Psychology*, no. 42, pp. 493–525

Wertsch, J. V. and Bustamante Smolka, A. L. (1993) Continuing the dialogue: Vygotsky, Bakhtin and Lotman. In H. Daniels (ed.) *Charting the Agenda: Educational Activity after Vygotsky*. London: Routledge

Wilkinson, A. (1971) *The Foundations of Language: Talking and Reading in Young Children*. Oxford: Oxford University Press

Willinsky, J. (1994) Introducing the new literacy. In B. Stierer and J. Maybin (eds) *Language Literacy and Learning in Educational Practice*. Clevedon: Multilingual Matters Ltd in association with The Open University

Wood, D. J. (1986) Aspects of teaching and learning. In M. Richards and P. Light (eds) *Children of Social Worlds*. Cambridge: Polity Press

—— (1988) *How Children Think and Learn*, Oxford: Blackwell

—— (1992) Language, learning and education. In P. Gray (ed.) *New Concepts, New Solutions: Educational and Child Psychology*, vol. 9, no. 2 pp. 17–25

Wood, D. J., Bruner, J. S. and Ross, G. (1976) The role of tutoring in problem-solving. *Journal of Child Psychology and Psychiatry*, vol. 17, no. 2, pp. 89–100

Wragg, E. C. (1994) *An Introduction to Classroom Observation*. London: Routledge

Wray, D., Bloom, W. and Hall, N. (1989) *Literacy in Action*. London: Falmer Press

Index